'Fanon as educator? It's r
a powerful resource for e
Burman's detailed and scl
intellectual connections an

Her approach offers striking new thinking on race, coloniality, the psychology of child/adult relations, and the multiple meanings of childhood.'

Raewyn Connell, Professor Emerita, author
of *Schools & Social Justice* and *Southern Theory*

'Erica Burman's pathbreaking interpretation of 'child as method' builds on Frantz Fanon's understanding of racism and oppression and the transformative power of individual and social resistance. Burman's unique work constitutes a major contribution to the interpretation of Fanon's work and its radical implications for educational and childhood development.'

Irene L. Gendzier, Professor Emeritus, Department
of Political Science, Boston University, US,
author of *Frantz Fanon: a critical study*

'Education, globally, needs to be challenged. *Child as Method*, inspired by Frantz Fanon, is a timely intervention to imagine a different mode of thought for a more creative and better future of the world, earth, and planet.'

Kuan-Hsing Chen, Professor of Social Research &
Cultural Studies, NCTU, Taiwan, author of
Asia as Method: Towards De-imperialization

'"Child as method" is a unique and intriguing approach that contributes to postcolonial studies in education. The close involvement of this book with the re-reading of Fanon and the centrality of the child provide fascinating and substantial theoretical resources for ethically and politically committed educational research leading to a wider project of subjective and societal change.'

Yoonmi Lee, Professor, Department of Education,
Hongik University, Seoul, Korea

'*Fanon, Education, Action: Child as Method* is a unique conceptual intervention articulating a critical practice to mobilise "a pedagogy of and for decolonization and redistribution". It foregrounds how Fanon's theoretical, methodological and political activism coalesce with his conceptualisations of childhood to create a practice of child as method. In doing so, Burman offers a rare and distinctive way of reading educational and wider social pedagogical practices that offer some insightful relational and transformational possibilities.'

Sue Grieshaber, Professor of Education,
La Trobe University, Melbourne, Australia

'This book establishes the child as a recurring, pivotal figure in Fanon's corpus and conversely, presents Fanon as a major resource for those engaged in analysis of the child in cultural-political practices. In deft readings of cases and scenes which include but go beyond the famous racialising encounter with a white child in *Black Skin, White Masks*, Burman uncovers an intersectional Fanon attuned to instability and nuance, a Fanon whose psychiatric and political practices are inseparable. The close readings bring into relief four distinct modes of operationalizing the child, variously deployed, complicated, and subverted by Fanon. Burman offers these as the basis for 'child as method,' neither a child nor the child, but both and more: it is a way of thinking the social, cultural, and political through invocations of child and the models of temporality, capacity, vulnerability, and transformability they carry. This book will be an important tool for those working in Childhood Studies, Education, Decolonization, Globalism, Women's Studies and Cultural Studies.'

Jennifer Henderson, Associate Professor,
Department of English/School of Indigenous &
Canadian Studies, Carleton University

FANON, EDUCATION, ACTION

Bridging childhood studies, pedagogy and educational theory, critical psychology, and postcolonial studies, this unique book reads the role and functions of 'the child' and childhood as both cultural motif and as embodied life condition through the work of Frantz Fanon. Based on innovative readings of Fanon and postcolonial cultural studies, the book offers new insights for critical pedagogical and transformative practice in forging crucial links not only between the political and the psychological, but between distress, therapy, and (personal and political) learning and transformation.

Structured around four indicative and distinct forms of 'child' read from Fanon's texts (Idiotic, Traumatogenic, Therapeutic, Extemic), the author discusses both educational and therapeutic practices. The pedagogical links the political with the personal, and Fanon's revolutionary psychoaffective account offers vital resources to inform these. Finally, the book presents 'child as method' as a new analytical approach by which to read the geopolitical, which shows childhood, education, and critical psychological studies to be key to these at the level of theory, method, and practice.

By interrogating contemporary modalities of childhood as modern economic and political tropes, the author offers conceptual and methodological resources for practically engaging with and transforming these. This book will be vital, fascinating reading for students and scholars in psychology, psychoanalysis, education and childhood studies, gender studies, postcolonial studies, and mental health.

Erica Burman is Professor of Education at the Manchester Institute of Education, the University of Manchester, Honorary Fellow of the British Psychological Society, and a United Kingdom Council of Psychotherapists registered Group Analyst. She is author of *Deconstructing Developmental Psychology* (Routledge, 3rd edition, 2017), and *Developments: Child, Image, Nation* (Routledge, 2008).

Concepts for Critical Psychology: Disciplinary Boundaries Re-thought
Series editor: Ian Parker

Developments inside psychology that question the history of the discipline and the way it functions in society have led many psychologists to look outside the discipline for new ideas. This series draws on cutting edge critiques from just outside psychology in order to complement and question critical arguments emerging inside. The authors provide new perspectives on subjectivity from disciplinary debates and cultural phenomena adjacent to traditional studies of the individual.

The books in the series are useful for advanced level undergraduate and postgraduate students, researchers and lecturers in psychology and other related disciplines such as cultural studies, geography, literary theory, philosophy, psychotherapy, social work and sociology.

Most recently published titles:

Identical Twins
The Social Construction and Performance of Identity in Culture and Society
Mvikeli Ncube

No Body
Clinical Constructions of Gender and Transsexuality
Miguel Roselló-Peñaloza

The Psychopolitics of Food
Culinary Rites of Passage in the Neoliberal Age
Mihalis Mentinis

Queer Politics in India
Towards Sexual Subaltern Subjects
Hannah Botsis

FANON, EDUCATION, ACTION

Child as Method

Erica Burman

Routledge
Taylor & Francis Group

LONDON AND NEW YORK

First published 2019
by Routledge
2 Park Square, Milton Park, Abingdon, Oxon, OX14 4RN

and by Routledge
711 Third Avenue, New York, NY 10017

Routledge is an imprint of the Taylor & Francis Group, an informa business

© 2019 Erica Burman

British Library Cataloguing-in-Publication Data
A catalogue record for this book is available from the British Library

Library of Congress Cataloging-in-Publication Data
Names: Burman, Erica, author.
Title: Fanon, education, and action : child as method / Erica Burman.
Description: New York, NY : Routledge, 2018. | Series: Concepts
    for critical psychology: disciplinary boundaries re-thought
Identifiers: LCCN 2018006773| ISBN 9781138089945 (hardback) |
    ISBN 9781138089952 (pbk.)
Subjects: LCSH: Fanon, Frantz, 1925-1961. | Children. | Child
    development. | Education. | Critical psychology.
Classification: LCC H59.F28 B87 2018 | DDC 155.4—dc23
LC record available at https://lccn.loc.gov/2018006773

ISBN: 978-1-138-08994-5 (hbk)
ISBN: 978-1-138-08995-2 (pbk)
ISBN: 978-1-315-10889-6 (ebk)

Typeset in Bembo
by Swales & Willis Ltd, Exeter, Devon, UK

Printed in the United Kingdom
by Henry Ling Limited

CONTENTS

FOREWORD

Frantz Fanon was a revolutionary psychiatrist from Martinique who was radicalised by his experience of racism when serving in the French armed forces during the Second World War and then even more so during his work in Blida-Joinville Psychiatric Hospital in Algeria. He became active in the Front de Libération Nationale (National Liberation Front) working for independence from France, and wrote a number of what are regarded as classic texts about the interrelationship between colonialism and psychology, the most famous of which are the books *Black Skin, White Masks* (1952/1970) and *The Wretched of the Earth* (1961/1963) with a preface by Jean-Paul Sartre. That latter book was immediately banned in France. Fanon, as Erica Burman shows in this ground-breaking book, illuminates structures of subjectivity under conditions of colonialism and racism, conditions that persist to the present-day, but he does so not only as a theorist who has inspired radical educational interventions around the world but as a writer who demands to be put to work, to be turned into direct action against exploitation and oppression. And – here is the core of this book – Fanon illuminates how educational theory and practice revolves around the figure of 'the child', the child as a culturally configured position in which and from which we are able to understand better the manifold social relations in which we – all of us who have been children once upon a time – find ourselves and try to find a way out.

If there is a corner-stone of the discipline of psychology apart from its method – usually positivist laboratory-experimental research that aims mainly to confirm the world as it is – it lies in the figure of the child, a figure who, this book shows, has multiplied into kaleidoscopic fragments that we find at work in Fanon's writing as 'Idiotic child', 'Traumatogenic child', 'Therapeutic child', and 'Extemic child'. Each fragment operates in this book as a lens through which we can throw light on critique in psychology, on social relations, and on educational practice. Just as traditional psychology educates us to accept the way the world is, so the critical psychology worked through in this book is a form of pedagogy that opens up rather than closes down different ways of being human. We could, of course, multiply these figures of the child further. Why not, for example, analyse forms of 'commoditogenic child' as that which is the target of advertising and quintessential consumer of new commodities or 'lachrymogenic child' as that which exemplifies what is tragic about the human condition and when it suffers incites us to feel that suffering too? It is clear that the task in this book is to open up the figure of the child, to show that it is not what it seems and to find new ways of reading it, and so new ways of reading Fanon.

But, still remembering how important method always is as the cornerstone of psychology and much educational research, *Fanon, Education, Action: Child as Method* exemplifies not only the radical content of a new reading of Fanon but also the form of that reading that is marked in the subtitle as 'child as method'. Taking its cue from Chen's 'Asia as method' – a contested contradictory field of standpoints from a part of the world rendered 'other' to the often taken-for-granted conceptual frames developed in the historic colonial centres in the West – Burman's 'child as method' turns the figure of the child into a critical analytic tool. Psychologists and educational researchers do not really know what a child is, and when they attempt to pin it down within any one preferred theoretical framework something of it always escapes, breaks free. It is never completely liberated, but it can speak of the process of liberation, of what it is to be simultaneously inside a dominant ideological frame of reference and outside it, 'outwith' psychology and education, educating us, as Fanon did, to the role of resistance to the world instead of adaptation to it.

Ian Parker
University of Manchester

ACKNOWLEDGEMENTS

It takes a group to make an individual, and an individually authored book is no exception. I am fortunate to have been supported and inspired by many people and various important gatherings and networks – including the International Society for Theoretical Psychology (ISTP) (founded more than three decades ago by Hank Stam and Lorraine Radtke) and the 'Marxism & Psychology' conference in Morelia, Mexico in 2012, while my first efforts to write on Fanon had their earliest airings at Sarah Fielden public lectures hosted by the Manchester Institute of Education, University of Manchester, the first as my inaugural lecture as Professor there. I am especially grateful to Karin Lesnik-Oberstein for the invitation to present the 30th Tony Watkins Annual Guest Lecture, at the Department of English, University of Reading, where the staff and students on the MA Children's Literature offered really helpful comments. She, alongside Daniela Caselli and Jackie Stacey, have long helped me to connect educational, psychological, and psychoanalytic concerns with the gendered and queer politics of childhood, while Jane Callaghan, Rose Capdevila, Karen Ciclitira, Gill Craig, Marcia Worall, and Lindsay O'Dell, with other British Psychological Society Psychology of Women Section friends, have helped keep up the feminist vigilance.

My thanks go also to Marko Salonen whose invitation to speak at the 'Encountering otherness' conference of the 2016 Annual Finnish Social Psychological Society Conference at the University of Tampere prompted me to write the first version of what is Chapter 2 of this book, while the invitation to present the Keynote at the 30th ISTP conference incited me to write the earliest version of what is now Chapter 4, and I am especially grateful to Kareen Malone for her enthusiasm and support for its analysis.

Working with colleagues in and from India, South Korea, Taiwan, and the Philippines, and also especially South Africa (where I was also a visiting professor at the University of the Witwatersrand) sensitised me in particular ways to colonial legacies and current actualities, and has greatly shaped my thinking over the years, as well as with many South American comrades in Brazil, Chile, Colombia, Mexico, Puerto Rico, Venezuela, and also long-standing European colleagues especially in Greece, Italy, Malta, Portugal, Serbia, Slovenia, and Spain. As Tomas Ibañez said so many years ago, there are many norths and souths within the North and South, and such dynamics exist within Europe as well as between Europe and the so-called Rest.

Early versions of these chapters benefited from presentations and revisions undertaken while I was adjunct Professor (0.2) at Oslo and Akershus University College of Applied Sciences (now Oslo Metropolitan University), and I am especially grateful for the support and friendship of Oddbjørg Skjær Ulvik, Liv-Mette Gulbrandsen, Mike Seltzer, and Agnes Andeneas over what is now many decades, alongside old and newer Danish childhood studies colleagues. The Decolonising Early Childhood Education National Research Foundation (NRF) project network organised from Cape Town, South Africa, has been a useful virtual and imaginary reference point while preparing this work, while various psychologist, educator, and psychotherapist friends from Australia and New Zealand have, over the years, indicated the various ways colonial histories and legacies permeate everyday life alongside newer transnational dynamics, including what a decolonial commitment can mean.

All these people in various ways have helped to frame and confirm my sense of the relevance of Fanon's writings alongside the attention to modalities, political, and psychic economies of childhood. Reflecting the distillation of many years of exchange and dialogue, the list is long. So, thank you also to: Asha Achuthan, Husain Al-Hakami, Pam Alldred, Atsuko Aono, Fernando Alvarez Urio Rico, Sarada Balagopalan, Hannah Berry, Barbara Biglia, Jill Bradbury, Teresa Cabrujo, Hernan Camilo Pulido-Martinez, Narcisa Canilao, Khatidja Chantler, Lise Claiborne, Jude Clark, Eyal Clyne, Tom D'Arcy, Gail Davidge, Carla de Santis, Wendy Drewery, Keith Ferguson, Heidi Figueroa Sarriera, Flor Gamboa, Genie Georgaca, Charo González, Shaun Grech, Fernando González Rey, Angel Gordo López, Daniel Goulart, Anat Greenstein, Raquel Guzzo, Philomena Harrison, Lin Hsing, TungHung Ho, Yasuhiro Igarashi, Gregorio Iglesias, Rubina Jasani, Nick Jeffs, Bernardo Jiminez, Gordana Jovanovic, Manasi Kumar, Pushpam Kumar, Nadir Lara Junior, Ian Law, Ana-Cristina Lenz Dunker, Cristian Lenz Dunker, Manuel Llorenz, Ken Mclaughlin, Amana Mattos, Susie Miles, Zsuzsa Millei, China Mills, Marisela Montenegro, John Morss, Pauline Mottram, Ilana Mountian, Suryia Nayak, Maria Nichterlein, Conceição

Nogueira, Desmond Painter, Ingrid Palmary, David Pavón-Cuéllar, Monica Peña, Isabel Piper, Joan Pujal, Rachel Robbins, Annette Rimmer, Tania Rocha Sanchez, Miguel Roselló, Euclides Sanchez, Nuno Santos Carneiro, Susana Seidman, Sabah Siddiqui, Hans Skott-Myhre, Kathy Skott-Myhre, Sonia Soans, Helen Spandler, Jemma Tosh, Julia Varela, Sam Warner, Esther Wiesenfeld, Alexandra Zavos and Luting Zhou.

In addition, doctoral students and colleagues, including those taking Social Theories of Learning, and doing some rather unruly analysis in Discourse Unplugged, as well as colleagues in the Knowledge, Power and Identity subgroup of the Education and Psychologies research group and the Postcolonial Studies reading groups have often helped me see new angles and directed me to useful resources. Most especially I want to acknowledge Ian Parker, whose unwavering intellectual, emotional, and – not least – practical support for this book has kept me going over the many stages of its preparation. Final thanks go to Laura Booth for her attentive copy-editing, to Lewis Derrick for the meticulous indexing (once again!), to Eleanor Reed and Lucy Kennedy at Taylor & Francis for their continued enthusiasm and support for my work, and to Martina Street for the proofreading first aid. Thank you.

Erica Burman
January 2018

1

FANON, EDUCATION, ACTION

Towards child as method

This book elaborates the ideas and writing of Frantz Fanon to offer a renewed vision of the project of education. Its focus on action topicalises questions of subjectivity (self-awareness, understanding, and change) that include, but extend beyond, formal and informal spaces of learning to consider political engagement. Fanon's ideas are presented as central resources for an approach to analysing notions of childhood and development, here called 'child as method'. While Fanon's writings have attracted extensive discussion both inside and outside educational arenas, I suggest that we have not yet exhausted the relevance of his ideas, and indeed that this renewed attention may enable better interrogation – if not the resolution – of some persistent problems within educational theory and practice. The focus on action here also signals ethical-political commitments that are so clearly articulated in Fanon's writings towards challenging oppression and forging the subjective and societal conditions for political change and transformation. Child as method is put forward as a strategy of reading and envisaging what education is, and could be, that is aligned with the position of the marginalised and that builds from Fanon's ideas, but connects also with current feminist, postcolonial, and posthuman discussions. Questions of resistance and both personal and political transformation are central preoccupations guiding this book. Fanon's passionate descriptions of the alienation produced by oppressive colonial conditions also include discussion of the conditions for what (he calls) 'disalienation'. These ideas are taken up in the discussion of child as method as an anti-, de-, or postcolonial educational project.

The contribution of this book

This is an interdisciplinary or cross-disciplinary intervention. It brings educational studies into dialogue and debate with childhood studies, feminist and queer theory, postcolonial studies, psychoanalysis, and political theory. In one sense, the mobilisation of these resources reflects my own trajectory from critical developmental psychology into education, alongside a therapeutic sensibility from my training as a group analyst and current work in training counselling psychologists. From this background, however, I aim to indicate how reading Fanon alongside, through, and in relation to these resources helps pose new questions and invites further research agendas. As a contribution to education and psychology, this book extends the theoretical and methodological appreciation of Fanon's relevance as engaging with core questions around subjectivity and change. As a contribution to the wider (and extensive) field of Fanonian studies, it also offers a critical and systematic reading of Fanon's representations of childhood. This focus has not previously been explored, and so the originality of this book's intervention works in (at least) two disciplinary directions: first, by reasserting Fanon's relevance to education through an evaluation of his repertoires of childhood, and, second, to take his text, and associated commentaries, as an exemplary field for the interrogation of the performative pedagogical politics mobilised by child. Thus, child as method extends, updates, and then evaluates this Fanonian engagement, also identifying corresponding conceptual and methodological implications.

Specifically, the readings of Fanon's writings presented here underscore the importance of three key points. First, they emphasise the inextricable links between emotions and learning. Second, they emphasise how the political inscribes the personal, albeit in specific and idiosyncratic ways (as Fanon's case histories in *The Wretched of the Earth* (1961/1963), hereafter *Wretched*, indicate). While many other models in current discussion (such as sociocultural theory) also subscribe to these commitments, I will suggest that reading them from and with a Fanonian perspective offers some further insights. Added to this is a third argument or point, concerning how rhetorics or mobilisations of appeals to notions of child (including abstract concepts of 'childhood' as well as discussion of specific children) perform particular and significant ideological work that connects educational with political arenas, and individual psychology with social policy. The substantive chapters comprising this book identify and evaluate the political significance of complex, multiple, and shifting conceptions of child at play within Fanon's texts, connecting them with other more current debates and arenas. Each chapter explores a distinct problematic (or conceptual framework) and pedagogy of (or approach to thinking about and engaging with) childhood, as read from and through Fanon's (and related) texts. These analyses indicate that even if we cannot entirely escape ideology we can nevertheless notice what and where it is at work.

Child as method, as a Fanonian-informed approach, offers an analytic methodology for reading the practice of child within social and political theory; that is, it interrogates representations of, or attributes associated with, childhood, and also correspondingly of children, as an analytic tool to better understand those socio-political coordinates. As a contribution to educational theory, it wards off some of the problems attending the agency–structure binary. It also offers an approach that is normative (in the sense of being politically aligned) without being normalising. As method, rather than theory (or even meta-theory), its focus on process avoids the limits (or what Fanon would call the 'reactional' problems) of utopian commitments. This utopian position of mastery that Foucauldian arguments (Ferguson, 1991) have shown limit future possibilities is also reflected in its process. I suggest that Fanon's subscription to what he called a method of 'failure' (Fanon, 1952/1970: 17) brings a psychoanalytically informed critique of the limits of certainty and knowledge to the project of educational pedagogy, or theories of teaching and learning. This project performs its democratising pretensions by refusing to offer authoritative prescriptions, as well as anticipating the ethic of humility and reflexivity indicative of current postcolonial educational approaches (Andreotti, 2011; Connell, 2014). That is, there is a repudiation of the paternalist (colonial) position of knowing better, or even of advanced foresight. As Gordon (2011) notes, Fanon's commitment to 'failure' offers a 'sociodiagnosis': 'The social diagnostics of failure in an antiblack and colonial world relies on the human capacity to construct a symbolic world that transcends, at least at the construction of meaning, reductive biological and other natural forces' (18). In this sense, while it may appear foolhardy and presumptuous to mobilise and engage Fanon for this apparently minor purpose of exploring his relevance as a resource for childhood and education debates (albeit that 'minor' theory is perhaps an especially relevant description of some current childhood theory (c.f. Deleuze, & Guattari, 2004; Hickey-Moody, 2012)), I do so with a Fanonian commitment to productive 'failure' and reflexive critique that is open-ended and generative of other (and others') possibilities. Indeed Gordon (2015) posits Fanon's approach to 'failure' as profoundly indicative of an ethical-political commitment that ironises his own position as both subject and analyst of his text:

> The motif of failure raises, still more, the question of the *type* of text Fanon has composed and how he is situated in relation to it. What we find is that each failure is not necessarily Fanon's, for he is both the voice of the text (the black) and the voice about the text

(the theorist and guide). Fanon, the critic of Western discourses of Man, Fanon the revolutionary theorist who demands systemic and systematic change, succeeds (by identification of each failure). Paradoxically, if the hero of the text wins (that is, achieves his [*sic*] aims), the hero of thought (the theorist) fails, and vice versa.

(Gordon, 2015: 25, emphasis in the original)

This approach to 'failure' is thus both methodology and even pedagogy, which, as we will see, informs Fanon's clinical practice as well as his theoretical-political orientations. It informs his trenchant repudiation of essentialisms of all kinds (especially those attending racialised positions) evident throughout his writings, and his passionate arguments against historical determinisms – both political and personal – are taken up here as resources to inform recently emerging discussions of pedagogies of solidarity (Gaztambide-Fernández, 2012). Such Fanonian-informed pedagogies of solidarity are not based on past histories or identities but are rather forged through currently negotiated and renegotiated relationships of mutual engagement. Crucially, and this is where the interrogation of work done through the mobilisation of child is so important, such perspectives both rely upon and promote critical analysis of the goals and purposes of development, whether child or individual, or social and national. In philosophical terms, reflecting Fanon's analyses, then, teleology is problematised and its symbolisation, even personification (Steedman, 1995), via child becomes a matter for exploration or better diagnosis of our current conditions, rather than naturalisation of them.

Wider significance for educational theory

This book is devoted to thinking with, rather than an exegesis of the thinking of, Fanon through a feminist, childhood studies reading. Fanon's texts are taken here as both analytical resources and resources for analysis via child as method. That is, they are inspirational intellectual tools and exemplary arenas for critical interrogation. This is significant in two directions. First, in relation to Anglophone contexts, it returns Fanon to the centre of educational thinking in a way that is largely new for mainstream British educational debate (unlike in North America where Fanon's writings have long figured on the curriculum). Second, this book supplements the longstanding North American attention to Fanon that has largely been concerned with questions of alienation and disaffection among minority students. Third, as explicated in Chapter 6 (and through a different lens, in Burman, 2018a), through engagement also with wider critical theory and arguments informed by contemporary decolonial and postcolonial studies, it adds to the international educational studies arena such that child as method is an educational and psychological resource paralleling recent analysis of *Asia as Method* (Chen, 2010) and *Border as Method* (Mezzadra, & Neilson, 2013).

The Fanonian reading undertaken here (whose status is discussed further below), while grounded in the larger debates surrounding Fanon's contribution, is of course partial and orientated to a very particular focus on subjectivity and change as relevant for social pedagogues and educationalists. Fanon emerges as an educational theorist to be situated alongside Pierre Bourdieu, Michel Foucault, and Paulo Freire as analysts of educational practices. Education, then, is understood to function as a mode of social regulation, stratification, and pacification but is also understood as central to the restoration of the capacities for creativity and correspondingly for emancipatory struggle. Clearly, this is not the only way of reading and drawing upon Fanon's writing. Rather, its treatment here makes a specific contribution by connecting current educational concerns with those in critical theory and postcolonial debates in mutually informative ways. Further, to my knowledge, no previous study has systematically read Fanon with a specific attention to the significance of his conceptualisations of childhood.

Situating and evaluating the arguments

In situating my claims here, I should outline four considerations. First, as reviewed below, while other commentators identify various periodisations and thematisations within Fanon's writings, that also reflect particular times and places of reception and interpretation, so also my reading here cannot but be as a 'history of the present', to use the Foucauldian formulation, which as Roth (1981: 32) puts it, is 'a self-conscious field of power relations and political struggle'. That is, it is necessarily both framed from and oriented to the preoccupations of my own geographical, disciplinary, and political positions. Specifically, it is concerned with exploring what a reading of Fanon's conceptualisations of children and representations of childhood offers, both to childhood and educational studies but also to the evaluation of the status of Fanon's own work and contribution.

Hence, second, this project both inspires and is analytically grounded in a more systematic elaboration of the analytic and methodological presuppositions mobilised through the approach discussed here (both as outlined in this chapter, and in Chapter 6) as child as method (see also Burman, 2018a,b; 2016a). This project arises from a more longstanding engagement with exploring the work done in socio-political practices by the appeal to notions of childhood, or what may be called the trope or figure of the child (Castañeda, 2002), which I have previously traced within aid and development discourse (Burman, 1994; 2008a), psychological models (Burman, 2017a), popular culture (Burman, 2012a) but also within the writings of other key social theorists such as Walter Benjamin and Jean-François Lyotard (Burman, 1998). This last anticipates the further discussion of childhood, modernism, and modernity undertaken by Caselli (2016), and is also informed by wider critical discussions of development (Nandy, 1984; Escobar, 2000; Sachs, 1992). Child as method is a research analytic, or a set of conceptual propositions, that offers a perspective on and invites ways of working with particular research questions, rather than prescribing particular procedures or topics. Like Fanon's work, though (and hence its alignment with this), it is framed from a set of commitments aiming to transcend disciplinary and methodological particularities, including those arising from methodological nationalisms (Chernilo, 2008), whose limits are attracting increasing critical commentary within transnational education debates (Dale, & Robertson, 2009; Shahjahan, & Kezar, 2013). Each chapter in this book is the outcome of a specific analysis oriented to particular research questions, and I include more details of the rationale for these questions and how the analysis was undertaken there.

Having acknowledged this positioning, third, I should, however, clarify that the analyses presented in this book arise from a sustained and deep engagement across the corpus of Fanon's writings (albeit not all equally, but nevertheless not merely focusing on just a single text), and also with the extensive commentaries on and discussion of them. Perhaps fortuitously, my own historical engagement has followed Fanon's chronological order of writing, such that continuities and developments of key themes across his texts have seemed very apparent. (In this I concur with Gendzier's, 1973, reading.) I hope this has at least to some extent limited the kind of effect Lazarus (1993) identified in Bhabha's readings – as working from *Wretched* backwards and so overlooking not only how *Black Skin, White Masks* (hereafter *Black Skin*) constitutively paved the way for this but also misreading Fanon's political commitments. Moreover, the logic of the ordering of the chapters reflects how I read the development of Fanon's own arguments, first by the simultaneous mobilisation but critique of psychoanalysis in Chapter 2 (Idiotic child), to consider his account conveying the 'misery of the black man. Physically and affectively' (*Black Skin*, 61) in Chapter 3 (Traumatogenic child). Chapter 4 (Therapeutic child), however, shifts to consider how Fanon addresses the 'stain' of political and existential trauma and dehumanisation, by considering his clinical work. Chapter 5 (Extemic child) considers child as part of, rather than excised from, the social order, including how this also corresponds with Fanon's later, explicitly political, engagements.

Earlier versions of these chapters have also benefited from critical and engaged feedback on presentations and previous publications on which this book is based, but for which they are substantially revised, reworked and extended. While it would be impossible to claim exhaustive command of the vast literature on Fanon, nor to review all of this here, it is important at least to note that I have aimed to engage with what, given my own linguistic, intellectual, and time limitations, I have been able to access of the serious scholarship on Fanon. Perhaps this should be an unnecessary point to make but I would claim that my treatment here contrasts with many works (including some educational texts) that merely include passing reference to or citation of Fanon with little deeper or critical engagement with his ideas. As Robinson (1993: 79) notes, in an otherwise critical evaluation of Fanon's treatment of class alongside/as race, 'it is an ungracious conceit to employ him merely as a background device' – and one can frequently see what Alessandrini (1997: 241) describes as 'simply invoking his name as a way of avoiding further analysis'.

This sustained engagement is also important given the sometimes inaccurate and even potentially irresponsible claims made for and from Fanon's writing, perhaps informed by his biography. Batchelor's (2017b) discussion of Homi Bhabha's claim, in his Preface to the (2004) edition of *Wretched*, that Fanon directly influenced the Irish Republican movement, whose 'incendiary spirit' (Bhabha, 1996: xxix, quoted in Batchelor, 2017b: 55) 'set alight IRA passions' (ibid.) is merely one (perhaps extreme) example. (Indeed, she proposes that Che Guevara would be a more credible candidate for this role.) That such meticulous work has been done to evaluate (and in this case prove as substantially unfounded) such claims is a testament to the value of critical scholarship, even if Batchelor (2017a) eschews the kind of activist position attributed to other Fanonian scholars, such as Gibson. Such scholarship also highlights how the reception of a key theorist such as Fanon as much evaluates his readers and their times as his writing.

Nevertheless, fourth, I should clarify from the outset that the analysis here, corresponding also with my reading, is not uncritical of Fanon. Like many other readers, I find his writing as frustrating as it is also provocative and inspirational. It is often uneven in analytical depth, and variations and reformulations across and within single texts allow for inconsistent and sometimes contradictory interpretations. This is what leads Gates (1991: 458) to describe his writings as 'highly porous' such that 'Frantz Fanon, not to put too fine a point on it, is a Rorschach blot with legs' (ibid.). Such selective engagements and appropriations are not necessarily a problem if they are appropriately acknowledged. Hence, I will outline below which (version of) Fanon I am reading here and why.

Yet before doing so, there is a wider point to make about such criticisms. It is worth recalling that Fanon was not a professional academic, but rather a medical student and, later, qualified psychiatrist writing to make sense of his place in the world and what he could do with it (indeed, as further discussed below, Gendzier, 1966: 535, sees him as engaged in a 'program of self-education'). Seen in this light, it is perhaps more understandable that Fanon moves across disciplines and issues, sometimes engaging with the philosophical canon of Europe (Freud, Nietzsche, Hegel, Sartre) and at other times repudiating this. In this sense we could interpret commentators' frustrations with his lack of formal academic 'rigour' as itself a reflection of our own particular institutional investments and disciplinary boundary-ma(r)king. It should, however, be acknowledged that, notwithstanding their fruitfulness, there are some clear limits to some aspects of Fanon's political understandings, framed as they are from a particular historical moment without foresight of what was to come. The portrayal of women and of (hetero)sex stands out here as a key example, even though feminist and queer theorists have found ways of re-interpreting his ideas to sustain a deeper engagement (Khanna, 2004; Pellegrini, 2008; Wane, 2010; Wright, 2004).

Rationale: why Fanon?

Frantz Fanon (1925–1961) has long been recognised as a key theorist of colonialism and decolonisation whose biography traced the links between subjectivity and action, a commitment to individual and collective transformation, and a shift from treating the casualties of colonial oppression and brutalisation to joining the revolutionary struggle for liberation. Although his history is probably well known to readers, it is probably worth recapping some main points here. Born into an upper-middle-class family in Martinique, a French colonial territory, Fanon earned military honours by fighting for the French in the anti-fascist struggle in the Second World War. He trained first as a medical doctor in Paris, then specialising in psychiatry in Lyon where, under the mentorship of François Tosquelles, he was trained in the latter's approach of institutional psychotherapy. Tosquelles was from Catalonia, arriving in southern France as a refugee from the Spanish civil war where he had worked directly with the POUM (Workers' Party of Marxist Unification), running clinics providing psychological support to resistance fighters. His model of social therapy was particularly innovative in Francophone contexts (although equivalent approaches were developed in Britain during the Second World War, see Harrison, 2000) because it treated the person's problems through supportive milieu interventions designed to restore social bonds, that is, through reconnecting with other people and with everyday life activities rather than working only symptomatically or biomedically (Giordani, 2011; Khalfa, 2015; Keller, 2007). It is likely that it was through Tosquelles that Fanon learnt not merely how mental health and politics were linked, but how practically to work with these links (Gendzier, 1973; Tosquelles 2017a, 2017b).

Fanon applied and developed these methods when he took up the post of clinical director of the psychiatric hospital at Blida-Joinville outside Algiers in 1953. At first, he applied himself to psychiatric reforms in a national context where 'for a population of 10 million, including 8.5 million Muslims and 1.5 million Europeans, there were 8 psychiatrists and 2,500 beds. Under such conditions psychiatric care was necessarily limited' (Gendzier, 1973: 73). As was not untypical for that time, Fanon found patients chained to beds, and given no therapeutic support beyond medication to maintain control. Fanon set to work with enthusiasm, and by all accounts was tireless and inspiring in applying Tosquelles' methods of work groups, activity groups, and cultural activities. As Abane (2011: 30) puts it: 'Despite the hostility of his European colleagues, he used group therapy to free native patients who had been put in shackles, in the guise of treatment, and put an end to the carceral regime in the asylum.' The innovative and enduring character of these reforms, sustained alongside his increasing political engagements, deserve particular recognition alongside the attention, and corresponding adaptations, to the cultural and linguistic context that he and his colleagues found necessary to implement to create successful social therapy for the Muslim as well as European population. Also here, doubtless sensitised also by his own experiences of growing up in a country that had suffered a particularly brutal history of colonisation (Macey, 2012), he encountered firsthand the psychic suffering and depersonalisation accompanying both colonisation and the ongoing and increasingly brutal suppression of independence movements. Fanon's arrival at Blida coincided with the violent escalation of the struggle and he soon became directly politically involved, as well as challenging the physical as well as symbolic violence of colonial psychiatry meted upon the native population. Whatever his pre-existing political sympathies, it was primarily through his commitment to supporting his patients' mental health that he became politicised. As Gendzier notes:

> As Fanon watched French troops coming in and out of the Blida-Joinville hospital to remove suspected nationalists, as he watched others carry in men who had been tortured and lay dying under the hand of doctors who preferred not to risk themselves by doing anything, Fanon began to turn towards Algeria.
>
> *(1973: 90)*

While both the tortured and the torturers sought treatment at the hospital, in some cases encountering each other there (as Fanon discusses in *Wretched*), Fanon offered shelter to activists for the Algerian anti-colonial struggle as well as treatment for its psychic effects (Razanajao, et al., 1996; Khanna, 2013). Gendzier, drawing on Simone de Beauvoir's memoirs, claims he went further in providing support to the resistance, even helping prepare guerrillas for action:

> He protected members of the resistance, the National Liberation Front (FLN), he gave them medicine, he treated their sick and he instructed them in the elementary care of the wounded. But the near futility of such action was clear. With the agreement of superiors in Algeria, Fanon helped to train guerrillas; he taught them how to control themselves while throwing bombs and grenades, he taught them what psychological position to adopt the better to carry out their illicit activities; and in fulfilment of his professional obligations he went to treat patients who were sometimes French activists fighting the FLN.
>
> *(1966: 536–7)*

In evaluating this intervention, we may recall that Fanon had himself already served twice in armed resistance against fascism, as also had many British psychiatric reformers and innovators of group therapies and psychoanalysis. Eventually finding his position untenable (since he was at risk of assassination), in 1956 Fanon resigned his clinical post (which, it should be recalled, was a state government position) in a remarkable letter of indictment against the French state (Menozzi, 2015) and spent the last years of his (short) life mainly based in Tunis, travelling and working for the FLN (Algerian National Liberation Front), dying of leukaemia at the age of 35 while undergoing treatment in the United States. There remains considerable discussion of the relative weight of his political and clinical preoccupations (Keller, 2007; Murard, 2008; see Gendzier, 1973 for an early and authoritative discussion). Nevertheless, what is undisputed is that Fanon retained an engagement with mental health practice, and reform, continuing to practise and offer clinical leadership when in exile from Algeria, in Tunis (Cherki, 2011).

During his short life, Fanon published three books, with a further volume of his (largely anonymous but traced to him and so collected) political writings for FLN associated outlets that were assembled for publication after his death (see Batchelor, 2017a, for a discussion of the disparities in order of publication of his texts across different languages as reflecting the particular cultural political situations of those countries). Further collections of his academic, clinical, and even creative writings (including plays) are now emerging (for example, Fanon, 2018). Fanon's books trace a geographical as well as political trajectory, albeit maintaining continuity of themes. These include a concern with the psychic impacts of colonial oppression and racialisation, which are largely recognised by commentators to be applicable to wider forms of oppression, and a forceful critique of colonial psychiatry and its role in both intellectually legitimating and practically abetting this oppression (including participating in torture) (see, for example, Turner, 2011; Gilroy, 2010). This is alongside an enthusiastic analysis of the positive possibilities of political liberation for personal and subjective change. Indeed, it is said that what Fanon offered was a 'psycho-socio-political diagnosis of the effects of colonial alienation, its logical developments, notably the rude awakening of the colonized, their awareness and taking in hand of their national destiny' (Abane, 2011: 37).

Peau Noire, Masques Blancs/Black Skin, White Masks was written originally as Fanon's medical thesis (which was rejected as unsuitable, so that he subsequently wrote another – more conventional – research thesis) (Macey, 2012). (Gendzier, 1973: 272, notes that his accepted thesis was entitled 'Troubles mentaux et syndromes psychiatriques dans l'Hérédo-Dégéneration-Spino-Cérébelleuse: Un cas de maladie de Friedreich avec délire de possession' ('Mental Illness and Psychiatric Syndromes in Hereditary Cerebral Spinal Degeneration: A Case Study of Friedreich Disease with Possession Delirium'); for a recent analysis see Gordon, 2015; and Khalfa, 2015.) Of all his texts, this was the most explicitly philosophically engaged with phenomenology and psychoanalysis. Fanon here claims that it is a 'clinical study' (*Black Skin*: 11). Indeed, after topicalising the 'dual narcissism' (*Black Skin*: 9) that structures black–white relations, Fanon's introductory remarks in *Black Skin* outline this as his key framework:

> I believe only a psychoanalytical interpretation of the black problem can lay bare the anomalies of affect that are responsible for the structure of the complex. I shall attempt a complete lysis of this morbid body. I believe that the individual should tend to take on the universality inherent in the human condition . . . But in order to arrive at this judgment, it is imperative to eliminate a whole set of defects left over from childhood.
>
> *(Black Skin: 9)*

This book includes discussion of his experiences growing up in Martinique, the psychosexual dynamics of racialisation as they enter into heterosexual structures of eroticisation and, most famously, in a chapter entitled in the original English version 'The fact of blackness' – although Gordon (2011: 19) prefers to translate 'L'expérience vécue du Noir' as 'The lived experience of the Black'. This is the iconic scene (presumably set in Paris) of the constitution of racialisation and subsequent alienation from self and body via the hailing by a (white) child of him as 'a Negro' (which will be discussed in detail in Chapter 3). (As various commentators point out, the French term *négre* is even more offensive.) It is relevant to note here Fanon's later chapter in the same text repudiating (even in its title) the 'so-called dependency complex of colonised peoples'. This direct critique of Octave Mannoni's framework (which Fanon describes as 'dangerous', *Black Skin*: 12), published by Mannoni (in its second edition) in 1950 under the title *Prospero and Caliban,* will be discussed further in Chapter 2, and foreshadowed his later treatments of this question in *A Dying Colonialism* (hereafter *Dying Colonialism*) and *Wretched* specifically in relation to the Algerian context.

Dying Colonialism and *Wretched* directly address the colonial context of Algeria, the former heralding the transformative effects of the revolutionary struggle for independence (fought through a bloody war from 1954 to 1962) and its impacts on and for every aspect of Algerian life – including for gender relations among the native population, as well as for the European colonial minority. *Wretched,* hurriedly finished just before Fanon died (Gordon, 2011: 23, suggests it was written in just ten weeks), addresses challenges for decolonial democratisation, including strong critiques of both the ways the national bourgeoisie are likely to resist genuine empowerment of the poor, and of claims to found black unity on past heritage or culture. The final long chapter of *Wretched*, comprising a third of the book, catalogues the psychic casualties of the 'colonial war', including on torture survivors, mobilising a discourse of medical expertise to report a typology of case histories indicting these political conditions.

It is noteworthy that Fanon was a socialist (if not a Marxist) (Hudis, 2015; Rabaka, 2011). Fanon was critical of Marxist analyses and their (insufficient) engagement with colonialism. He saw the Algerian peasantry as the true revolutionary force, rather than – as with orthodox Marxism – the industrialised proletariat. His criticisms can be read as enriching rather than undermining Marxist analyses (Rabaka, 2011), and were certainly not as politically naïve as they have sometimes been portrayed. Gendzier (1973) reports that alongside his psychiatric training in Lyon he was reading Marx and was particularly interested in Trotsky's writing and the Fourth International. She notes the reciprocal interest of Trotskyists in Fanon's writing (as also in the Algerian revolution), as indicated by Pablo's detailed and favourable review of *Wretched* (Pablo, 1962), if also a more critical engagement with *Dying Colonialism* (Pablo, 1959). Fanon was critically engaged with nationalism as a form of anticolonial struggle, and, if not a direct political protagonist throughout the Algerian liberation struggle, he was certainly a spokesperson for it in various high-level arenas, both cultural and political. (Macey, 2012, for example, cautions against overstating his actual political impact within and for the FLN, while Gendzier discusses reasons why the Algerian leadership subsequently may have downplayed his intellectual influence and even direct role in training of the military.)

This both explicit and implicit involvement is reflected in his fourth book, *Towards an African Revolution* (hereafter *African Revolution*), which is composed of speeches and articles directly supporting this that were either originally published without authorship or under a pseudonym (since one role that Fanon assumed was as political editor of the FLN organ *el Moujahid*, Gendzier, 1973).

Fanon was clearly a secular modernist (such that successive Arabic receptions of his writing have criticised his underestimation of the importance of Islam, Harding, 2017), albeit subscribing to an 'alternative modernism' to that underlying European domination. He was also an internationalist who saw the project of national consciousness, rather than nationalism, as a necessary route to broader international engagement (*Wretched*: 199). While not actually qualified as a psychoanalyst, he drew on psychoanalytic ideas and practised psychoanalytically oriented psychotherapy (as well as some more orthodox kinds of medical psychiatry, including drug therapies and even electro-convulsive therapy) (see also Cherki, 2006; Macey, 2012). He was also profoundly influenced by the phenomenological philosophy of Jean-Paul Sartre, which frames his humanist commitments (Gendzier, 1973; Hallward, 2011; Desai, 2014), as is most evident in *Black Skin* but reflected continuously across his writings in his resolute anti-essentialism and commitment to the human capacity for transformation and recreation. Interpretation of Fanon's position on violence and armed struggle has largely been framed through Sartre's Preface to *Wretched*, which both helped publicise the book but also significantly misrepresented Fanon's position (as Gendzier, 1973, Gibson, 2011b, Macey, 2012, and Kuby, 2015, among many others argue) – and also thereby contributed to it being banned in France on its publication in 1961 (unsurprisingly, considering that at that time France was precisely militarily opposing Algerian independence), even as it was also eagerly – if informally – read by the Left.

Which Fanon?

My reading of Fanon, reflecting my own time and place, is necessarily more aligned with the history of the UK presentation and reception of Fanon's ideas that have emphasised links with contemporary global applications. It contrasts with that of the US, for example, as identified by Batchelor (2017a), where Fanon's writings continue to be mobilised to inform the contemporary cultural politics of race, including ongoing direct and institutionalised racism towards African Americans (Yancy, 2012, 2017), albeit that such readings are relevant to the dynamics of racialisation and minoritisation in the UK too (for example, Phoenix, 2009; Bhopal, & Preston, 2012). Clearly, I read Fanon from a First World or minority world context, from an imperial centre that has at least as significant complicities with colonial oppression and brutality as the French colonial state that Fanon critiqued, which continue to deeply structure its dynamics of racialisation and minoritisation, both 'at home' and 'abroad' (Birmingham Centre for Contemporary Cultural Studies, 1982). Moreover, my reading is inevitably shaped by my class privilege and whiteness, albeit as also shaped by various forms of cultural and political minoritisation and feminist commitments that afford specific nuances and resonances with his analyses.

The chapters in this book therefore engage Fanon as offering an analysis of the continuing significance of racialisation as addressed to both proximal (nationalist) dynamics of minoritation and majoritisation (specifically in Chapter 2 as impacting on anti-immigrant discourse) and also the wider transnational historical cultural–political dynamics that gave rise to and sustain these. Its feminist, intersectional reading explores the specific constitution and functioning of racialisation alongside its imbrication with other relevant axes and positionings (including gender, class, and sexuality), not to diminish but rather to enrich the analysis of its impacts (Crenshaw, 1991; Collins, & Bilge, 2016; Phoenix, & Pattynama, 2006). As Preston and Bhopal (2012: 215) put it: 'We are wary that for some "race" always calls out for the kind of intersectional analysis which obscures it. Intersectional analysis does not mean that we cannot "speak" to "race" alone, and we should address its primacy when necessary.' I engage intersectional analyses throughout this book and evaluate the role of intersectionality in relation to other resources informing the analysis here, and child as method as an approach, in Chapter 6. For now, it should be noted that, irrespective of the continuing debates over the status of intersectionality (as method, theory, or metatheory), like child as method, and southern theory, intersectionality approaches are resources to be put to work, to inform the posing of better questions and guiding analysis, rather than doing the work of analysis.

As discussed later, as an educationalist, psychologist, and psychotherapist, I also share with Kuby (2015) (among others), a reading of Fanon that focuses on the negative psychic impacts of violence documented in the final third of *Wretched*, rather than according violence a cathartic or curative role, as the first essay 'On violence' in that book is often interpreted. This last reading is influenced also by the juxtaposition with Sartre's Preface, which

Kuby highlights not only misrepresented the text but also was addressing a different audience – the French white Left, with a particular agenda about 'whether that Left could be reenergized through overt, violent alignment with Algerian independence fights' (61). Mobilising a logic that she describes as 'frankly homeopathic' (73) rather than dialectical, Kuby argues that 'Sartre was not simply interested in "supporting" Fanon rhetorically. From the start of the Preface, he signalled that he was interested in the use of violence to heal metropolitan France' (73). This is not to discount the key role that violence plays in Fanon's writing, but rather (as Gordon, 2015, also notes) how his claims of the subject's emancipation through violence have to be read as a response to the already existing violence comprising the colonial context. Lou Turner (2011: 124) similarly interprets the relationship between 'Concerning violence' and the final chapter ('Colonial wars and mental disorders') as 'his way of strategically undermining the liberal-left pitfall of assuming a moral equivalence between anticolonial and colonial violence'.

In adopting this position, I do not wish to discount the problematic status of the catharsis with which Fanon endowed violence, to which he did undoubtedly subscribe. Gendzier's account, reflecting on Fanon's impact soon after the struggles he sought to contribute to, cautions against an ahistorical reading that abstracts Fanon's comments not only from their political context but also from later events:

> The objective, in Fanon's terms, of the cathartic effect of violence was not only to transform men, it was to make them capable of creating a better society. In retrospect, it is hardly possible to claim it is the absence of adequate illumination by violence that is responsible for the political tragedies of post-independence nations. It is the prohibition of politics and the inadequacy of political organization that have robbed yesterday's partisans of their rewards. That Fanon knew this himself is clear from *Wretched of the Earth*.
>
> *(Gendzier 1973: 202)*

In Gendzier's (1973) careful assessment

> his forte was not a programmatic approach to the problems of underdevelopment, or the persistence of economic imperialism. Yet his ability to diagnose the universal characteristics of colonizer and colonized, his unique talent for translating these characteristics into meaningful human terms allowed him to write from the vantage point few others have approached.
>
> *(269)*

Without underestimating the complexity of the political conditions he was addressing, Gendzier situates Fanon's formulations philosophically as arising from his engagement with Sartre and especially Hegel on the master–slave dialectic. Just as Fanon was propelled into revolutionary action through his psychiatric work, he remained both practically and philosophically engaged with the question of subjectivity and transformation. As she concludes: 'It is tempting to conclude that Fanon's concept of cathartic effect of violence does not belong to the realm of politics. On an individual level, it appears to synthesise the wish for retribution and the hope of redemption' (Gendzier 1973: 202).

Indeed, in *Black Skin* Fanon describes how contact with the white world orients the Negro (as a 'sensitising action'). Situating the (capacity for) 'action' outside the Black subject has devastating effects:

> If his psychic structure is weak, one observes a collapse of the ego. The black man stops behaving as an *actional* person. The goal of his behaviour will be The Other (in the guise of the white man), for The Other alone can give him worth.
>
> *(Black Skin: 109, emphasis in the original)*

I take up later Fanon's contrast between being actional and reactive. Here we may note that for Fanon the impact of this orientation to 'The Other (in the guise of the white man)' gives rise to a challenge 'on the ethical level of self-esteem. But there is something else' (*Black Skin*: 109). That 'something else' is what takes Fanon's ideas beyond compensatory or therapeutic discourse into political action. Butler (2015: 191) also draws continuities between *Black Skin* and *Wretched* in her analysis of the status of violence in both Sartre's Preface and Fanon's account in that book, suggesting: 'Violence here is not defended as a way of life, and certainly not as a way of imagining the normative goal of a social movement. It is an instrumentality in the service of invention.'

As the above summaries indicate, the engagement with Fanon's ideas here is oriented to five key concerns. These will be elaborated further throughout this book. In brief, however, they include: first, a commitment to a psycho-affective (Fanon's term) understanding of subjectivity that sees emotions, the body, and thought as inextricably connected. This is what may now be called a psychosocial model (see Frosh, & Baraitser, 2008) of individual experience (including suffering), so reversing conventional models prioritising the individual over the social. Indeed, he qualified his claims to be offering a 'psychological' analysis at the outset of *Black Skin* with the rider:

In spite of this it is apparent to me that the effective disalienation of the black man entails an immediate recognition of social and economic realities. If there is an inferiority complex, it is the outcome of a double process: primarily, economic; subsequently, the internalization – or, better, the epidermalization of this inferiority.

(Black Skin: 10)

Second, Fanon (like other liberation theorists) addressed how individual and social change, including barriers to these changes, must be linked. This converges both with understandings of critical pedagogy and radical mental health movements. Third, like other psychoanalysts and psychotherapists of his time, Fanon engaged a materialist analysis that understands class, gender, sexed, and racialised relations as constitutive of subjectivity, and not mere supplements to it – even as he also analysed them as indications of assimilation and acculturation to colonial norms. This understanding of the sexualised component of racism is both fruitful and widely discussed (and will feature especially in Chapters 2 and 3) (see also Kovel, 1970; Young, 2005; Mercer, 1996). Fourth, he offered a socialist and anti-colonial critique of the politics of the project of development, seen as both economically and psychically exploitative. Here we may note how in *Dying Colonialism* he writes of the challenge for the Algerian to 'bring his life up to the revolution' (77). He even extends this to offer some psychodynamic insights into the colonial struggle: 'The Algerian's reaction was no longer one of pained and desperate refusal. *Because it avowed its own uneasiness, the occupier's lie became a positive aspect of the nation's new truth*' (ibid., emphasis in the original). Fifth, he elaborated a therapeutic practice that was both politically principled and interpersonally and relationally engaged. Together, these five commitments combine to make a distinctive contribution to understanding how and why education and action are linked, and must engage the project of both personal and political transformation. As Dei (2010b: xiv) puts it: 'We need to understand education therefore as a process involving embodied knowledge. Knowledge is not void of the social, nor is it some absolute linear procedure or universal certainty.'

While Fanon's life and writings have attracted considerable attention, and some mythologisation, engagement with his work has not been continuous – as both Macey (2012, 2010) and Cherki (2011) both point out. *Wretched* may have circulated as a key text in the 1960s as a text for decolonisation processes in Africa and Asia, as well as a key resource for civil rights struggles in the US, but his writing has been rediscovered and interpreted anew in every generation. Cherki (2011) claims that the period from 1980 to the late 1990s was noteworthy for its silence on Fanon. Moreover, the resurgence of interest in his ideas from 1996 onwards corresponds also to different reading practices, alongside changed conditions. Some accounts privilege Fanon as a man of action, while others treat him as a theorist (see Renault, 2011). Some commentators (including Macey, 2012) criticise the overlooking of Fanon's Antillean origins in favour of his Algerian involvements. Others highlight the lack of attention to his revolutionary clinical practice and work in psychiatric reform (Keller, 2007).

Tracing the reception of his writings, as indicated by publication of translations, Batchelor (2017a) identifies a revolutionary Fanon (of the 1960s), a postcolonial Fanon (from the 1990s) that marked serious engagement from and with such key figures as Edward Said, Gayatri Spivak, and extensive commentary from Homi Bhabha. Corresponding with ongoing anticapitalist and revolutionary movements starting from the 2010s following both the 'war on terror' and the 'Arab spring' movements, she also identifies a contemporary activist reading of Fanon. As both Hook's (2012) and Gibson's (2013) engagements indicate, Fanon was a key resource for the Black Consciousness movement in South Africa (alongside and perhaps through Steve Biko), and now continues to be mobilised in popular social movements across Africa (see also Sekyi-Otu, 2011). Batchelor attributes the 'postcolonial Fanon' as arising largely through Edward Said's pivotal role in reviving interest in his writing. However, as Gates (1991) and Gibson (2011) note, this also marks his incorporation within a cultural studies or literary theory reading, which has tended to downplay direct political engagement, while Lazarus (1993) and, in particular, Parry (1994) blame Bhabha for this. Batchelor also distinguishes a fourth, minor, reading, of Fanon as (spokesperson for) the other(ed). This last is relevant also for my reading here, since child is a key (perhaps prototypical) example of an othered position.

A different typology is put forward by Kipfer (2011), who distinguishes a historical, spatial and dialectical, and revolutionary Fanon across his writings. This attends to the ways Fanon engages with the role of the past, of specific current conditions, and how these combine. Commentators highlight his attention to the ways colonialism was organised as a geographical practice of segregation and appropriation, but also as a subjective and political ossification and petrification under conditions of colonial oppression, a spatial stuckness (Ficek, 2011). But this was not at the expense of either overestimating the role of past colonial legacies, nor under-estimating how internal colonisation could continue psychologically even after political decolonisation (as Lazali, 2011, claims is the case now in Algeria). In this sense, the dialectical tensions between individual and social, as well as between space and time, are sustained and discussed across his writings.

Fanon underscored the contradictions of colonial rule (including that revealed by colonial violence) because he searched for opportunities to transform the colonial social relation. He not only suggested that colonialism and racism must be understood in spatial as well as historical terms; as Kipfer suggests, he also indicated that

> the transformation of (weakly hegemonic) colonial space must be understood as a historico-geographical process, a strategy of appropriating space and breaking with linear-repetitive time (Weate 2001:178). Space and geography in Fanon's work thus existed in an integral relationship to time and history. They were part of an overarching project of liberation.
>
> *(Kipfer, 2011: 97)*

These questions of time and space, of history and geography are important to the arguments of this book since discourses of child and childhood so typically – as we shall see, also within Fanon's own writing – represent both individual and national past and future, whether (to take a couple of indicative examples) in his description of the national bourgeoisie as 'spoilt children of yesterday's colonialism' (*Wretched*: 37), or the fact that the biographical and political problematic of commitment, responsibility, and change is posed by Fanon through reference to Nietzsche's trope about childhood. Indeed, he cites this twice, first at the beginning and then on the final page of *Black Skin*, with a slightly different gloss each time: 'Man's tragedy, Nietzsche said, is that he was once a child' (9), 'the tragedy of man is that he was once a child' (165). It is worth also noting that Fanon mobilises this trope in order to pose his own claim about human capacities, since the first citation is immediately followed by: 'None the less [*sic*], we cannot afford to forget that, as Charles Odier has shown us, the neurotic's fate remains in his own hands' (9). (Charles Odier (1888–1954) was a Swiss psychoanalyst who published more than 60 papers. Fanon does not provide a specific citation here.) This mobilisation of the child (as well as 'the neurotic' – which Fanon, as a psychoanalytic practitioner – would understand as including us all) as humanist subject is taken up in this book as both an object of critique, and – reading Fanon closely – is also understood as representing a subject under construction. Indeed, it can be read as indicating the constructionist possibilities of and for the subject, alongside the struggle to ward off merely repeating the effects of past constructions. This tension and set of alternations will form a substantive focus in subsequent chapters, including what is lost as well as gained through such elisions between the individual and the social as performed through the trope of child.

Notwithstanding such problems, Fanon's resolute commitment to an anti-essentialist position marks his position out as noteworthy and useful. While part of a counter-colonialist movement, as discussed further in Chapter 6, Fanon was explicit and different in his repudiation of culturalist aspects, favouring (as previously indicated) current alliance and engagement over claims to common heritage or history.

Fanon's efforts to galvanise action and dialogue extend to the style of his writing, the narrative form of which performs the passion of which it speaks. This performative aspect of Fanon's pedagogy often engages beyond even his programmatic claims and arguments. (Gendzier, 1973, claims that Fanon's 'sensitivity to language and terrifying love for the Word' (xiii) was an 'open secret' (ibid.), such that it 'sometimes seemed to eclipse the action these words were designed to provoke', ibid.) Fanon's writing is often mobilised to give voice to the marginalised, to the agonised experience of the abjected and vilified racialised other. For Fanon, the question of identity arises only through oppression, through alienation, but this negation dialectically can, he insists, produce new possibilities. This, alongside his humanist assertion of subjectivity as necessary to both personal and political liberation, leads to claims of the relevance of Fanon's writings as extending even beyond the dynamics of colonialism: 'Anticolonialism is not the end; it must be filled out and developed into a practice and awareness of political and social inclusion of the most marginal, and only then will it have developed into a true humanism' (Gibson, 2011b: 9). Commentators have also highlighted the importance of Fanon's contribution in navigating a way between culturalism and universalism (Cherki, 2011), as also between nationalism and internationalism (Gibson, 2011b), and between humanism and its critics. That is, he elaborates a radical, rather than bourgeois liberal, humanism (Hallward, 2011). Butler (2015) offers a reminder that the exclusions of liberal humanism arose not only on the basis of racialisation but also presumed the masculine as norm. While Fanon's writing certainly includes such presumptions, I share Butler's reading that, unlike Sartre, they also offer more ambiguity – in relation to the analysis of their status as reactive compensatory formations, rather than idealised or normalised positions. Fanon, then, claimed the benefits of European enlightenment values, reformulating them into a revolutionary modernism. His ideas preceded more recent debates about alternative, global, or connected modernities (see Bhambra, 2007) and indeed can be read as anticipating these.

As indicated, Fanon's writing covers a range of philosophical and political positions (see, for example Gibson, 2011a; Alessandrini, 2005). Indeed, alongside his passion and empathic evocation of the suffering wrought through oppression, and his programmatic declarations, there is a further reading of

Fanon that I draw on here. This is the Fanon discussed by Farred (2011) as offering nuance and subtlety, in particular as warding off the unthinking rush to action. In political terms, this rush gives rise to the problem of spontaneity that Fanon discusses in *Wretched*. This Fanon emphasises ambiguity and multiple perspectives. Farred suggests that his

> subtle moments reveal not only an intellectual nuance but articulate as a provocative uncertainty. In its more powerful enunciations, subtlety in Fanon is nothing if not a precondition for thought, especially in the moment of decolonization, where thought alone stands as the political and philosophical guarantor of the decolonized nation. Subtlety is a bulwark against 'ecstasy'.
>
> *(Farred, 2011: 168)*

It is this reading of Fanon as eschewing certainty, or mastery, and uncritical emotionality that I identify especially via the reading of Fanon as a psychotherapist in Chapter 4, and that is later taken up as part of child as method's pedagogy (see also Gordon, 2015).

Why Fanon and the child

As already indicated, while various kinds of children populate Fanon's writings this fact has attracted little attention. Such discussion as there is has largely focused on the child who utters the famous 'Look, a Negro!' exclamation presented by Fanon in *Black Skin* as an iconic act of racialisation, and one that precipitates irreparable anguish and both psychic and bodily alienation for the thereby racialised other. This is taken up in this book as Traumatogenic child, discussed in Chapter 3. Some, especially more recent, commentators have addressed the various damaged children described by Fanon, especially in *Wretched*, including consideration of both the distress and the murderous rage produced through brutal colonial repression and violence (see, for example, Khanna, 2013). Other treatments can be read through discussions of Fanon's representation of gender and cultural issues, notably in his treatment of 'the veil', and the role he advocated for girls and women in the Algerian resistance struggle (both in *Dying Colonialism*) (see, for example, Haddour, 2010). While elsewhere I have identified the figure of child and children in Fanon's writing in terms of their metaphorical, gendered, generational, and empirical status (Burman, 2017b), I develop this further in Chapter 5 as indicative of Extemic child – that is, an understanding of childhood as constituted as much outside as also within social relations. Inbetween these, in Chapter 4 I identify Therapeutic child, that is, the child constituted as object of discourse within a therapeutic narrative, based on a reading of the most (and perhaps only) complete account of a psychothera-peutic intervention, that Fanon offers in *Wretched*, of a distressed FLN fighter struggling to deal with his wife's rape by French soldiers. We will begin in Chapter 2 with the child separated from the social, on whose segregation the weight of ideology relies, that I call (following the classical definition of this term, but also mobilising some of its other resonances) the 'idiotic' child to reflect this singular, isolated status.

The unusual or disfluent adjectival forms by which I designate these ver-sions of child ('idiotic', 'traumatogenic', 'therapeutic', and 'extemic') are intended to focus analysis precisely through this textual estrangement. The 'difficulty' and, perhaps, inelegance as well as counter-intuitive character of such formulations is not mere obscurantism. Indeed, it could be read as an exemplification of Dei and Simmons' (2010b) approach that they term a 'critical Fanonian discursive framework' (xvi). These forms of child work and are *worked with* across the pages of this book as a provocative strategy to resist the too easy recruitment of child to other political agendas. The suffix 'ic' works here not merely to indicate these as characteristic or properties of child/hood (arising from the Greek ικός) but, further, to highlight the work this mode of child instigates. Hence, I mobilise an emphatic form ('trauma-togenic', rather than 'traumatic') to indicate active processes at work that are generated through particular constellations of social dynamics and rela-tions, that are (consistent with Fanon's philosophy of language, discussed in Chapter 3) performed anew within spoken interaction. That is, these forms of child are not simply conceptual categorisations whose attributes may be exemplified by specific historical, embodied children. Rather, they are modes of address towards, or engagement with, child/children. Indeed, they are pedagogies of childhood, constituted by others' relationships with and orientations to them. Such children may therefore not even exist as embodied entities, but rather as figures of other discourses and others' imaginations (although, as with all understandings of childhood, their influ-ence may be such as to also constitute the subjectivities of children in their image). As Plastow argues: '*childhood* has always been something different to the period itself in which one is a child. Rather, it is a fabrication of the adult based upon selective memory, amnesia, and a post hoc account that is determined by the desire of the subject' (2014: 13, emphasis in the original). In terms of modes of practical, therapeutic engagement, he continues: 'In this sense there is no structural difference between the analysis of an adult and that of the child: each has a *childhood* or a previous time' (15, emphasis in the original). What such formulations also deliberately leave open, then, is the question of whether and how such versions of child qualify or even include (those we may describe as) empirical children, that is, those currently occupying the social status and subjectivity of children; and, if so, to what extent such 'real', empirical children may recognise or identify with those orientations or positions. On this question we see a key contribution that debates in childhood studies bring to educational theory, as also all the other social and critical theories engaged with in this volume.

Having clarified the status of these various forms of child who each form the focus for subsequent chapters of this book, what needs to be acknowledged from the outset is how these various forms of child are all ideological (that is, they work in the service of promoting particular organisations of social relations). They are juxtaposed in this book without presuming that any one is better than another, but rather to suggest the wider affective and symbolic repertoires comprising the politics of childhood. Further, reflecting such ideological processes, they may share overlapping features. Nevertheless, these different forms can be identified as performing particular roles within wider narratives or discourses. While not an exhaustive typology (as the additional versions of 'child' identified in Ian Parker's opening Foreword indicate), these versions of child are presented here as indicative of what a close attention to evaluating these different models *in relation to one another* can achieve. I argue that this analytic project enables a systematic interrogation of the cultural meanings and affective investments performed through the narrative recourse to child. The wider implications of this project are explicated further in Chapter 6 on child as method, where I also consider how these cultural imaginaries or symbolisations may impact on actual, embodied children who (as Fanon's ideas also illuminate) are both subject to such representations and also subjectified – made into conscious subjects – by them.

It will be noted that I have already moved between such formulations as 'trope', 'rhetoric', 'figure', and 'imaginary' of childhood, as well as discourse and narrative. These terms, while also signalling some specific conceptual frameworks, are mobilised here to signal a broad alignment with constructionist understandings of models of childhood, in particular those engaging with the emotional, relational, and fantasy as well as socio-political features they set in play. As childhood theorists have long noted, children have always, and probably always will, fulfil broader cultural-political agendas that include evoking understandings of both pastness and futurity (the latter particularly associated with modernist narratives of progress and development). Whether as malleable fodder for the labour market or indexing longing for a biographical or historical past, children continue to preoccupy individual and cultural-national narratives. While not exclusive to modernity, this cultural-political modality – with its emphasis on (the presumed positive) directional change combining the physical-ecological with the economic via the notion of 'growth' – has intensified the proliferation of symbolic associations with children and childhood.

Taken together, the substantive chapters of this book address a number of key questions that (as various theorists have noted) are recapitulated through these images or models of child. First, there is the problematic of development. As a fierce critic, as well as both beneficiary and victim, of the project of European modernity – with its necessary reliance on the dehumanisation and exploitation of non-Europeans and their lands – Fanon was engaged with the wider political project of development, spanning individual subjectivity and the socio-political. Fanon's status as critic of colonisation and attempted architect of decolonisation meant that, as various commentators discuss (Renault, 2011; Kipfer, 2011), like other politically engaged theorists, he was centrally concerned with questions of history, of change. This included identifying both obstacles to change (both personal and political) and considerations of whether such change could be arrested or even accelerated; whether it is continuous or discontinuous; and whether there is inevitable rupture, or some new revolutionary synthesis can emerge. These philosophical and political concerns are inscribed also within models of child development, with resonances that, albeit not merely coincidental remain striking (since children figure importantly within political discourses of national and international development).

Second, at issue therefore is the question of subjectivity as well as, and in relation to, political conditions. Fanon was centrally concerned with 'subjective development', with what enabled the psychological subject to engage in (interpersonally and politically) fruitful activity, or (as will be discussed further below) what he called 'actionality'. While he also vividly described the barriers to such 'actionality', in the form of alienation and disaffection, his is far from being a socially determinist account. He accorded individual subjects specific agencies, alongside highlighting the role of cultural-political conditions in producing particular forms of subjectivity. Thus, unlike liberal humanist accounts, Fanon's revolutionary humanism (Hallward, 2011) initiates an agentic voluntarism that is forged through the social, rather than abstracted from it.

Third, Fanon's engagement with subjectivity, and the conditions framing and constraining this, clearly foregrounds the necessary engagement with emotions or affect. Alienation is an emotional as well as political condition, as also is its dismantling or transformation (what he calls 'disalienation'). As a psychoanalytically engaged psychiatrist and mental health practitioner, as well as phenomenological theorist, Fanon recognised that the conscious psychological subject is affectively driven, is conflicted, and is produced through relations with others, such that particular experiences and relationships (as well as historically sedimented cultural-political practices of the form that comprise racism and colonialism) matter; that is, they are materially and psychically significant.

Fanon's children, that is, the children inhabiting his writings (as also any other writers'), reflect and express his cultural-political projects. Hence, fourth, this analytic attention – as a particular exemplification of child as method – is an intervention aiming to ward off the abstraction from socio-political conditions that typically attend representations of child(ren) – that is, as abstracted from family, community, specific cultural and historical context. Rather than signifying some universal, historically transcendental life stage or even affective quality (of spontaneity, creativity, nostalgia), attending to the work done by Fanon's various references to and mobilisations of children/childhood in their narrative context of anti-colonial and revolutionary struggle, works to ward off such abstraction. In this sense my own commitment to a socio-political and psycho-affective account of childhood echoes that of Fanon, alongside a concern with the project of enabling agentic action. Which brings me to the role of education.

Fanon and education

As is discussed further in Chapter 5, Fanon discusses aspects of schooling and education across his books, ranging from (for example) the distorting and de-subjectifying effects of racist folk tales and comic books in *Black Skin* to assertions of the importance of education within the political project of decolonisation and the building of a national consciousness (in *Wretched*). For Fanon, education is profoundly linked to politics even as it is also a practice of the restoration of subjective capacities. Indeed, it is worth noting that in translating *Wretched* into English, Constance Farrington chose the formulation 'educate . . . politically' to render the French *'politiciser'*, which Batchelor (2017b: 49) interprets in terms of her efforts to use everyday language rather than (what would then perhaps have been interpreted as) Marxist jargon. Such moves, Batchelor suggests, while motivated by the 'desire to convey Fanon's call to action' (111), also inadvertently oversimplified his philosophical position.

Fanon's work is attracting increasing interest from educationalists, in particular in relation to his account of alienation, addressing the conditions limiting learning and subjective development (Dei, 2010a, 2010b; Dei, & Simmons, 2010a, 2010b; Leonardo, 2011; Richardson, 2012) as well as interpreting the ways the curriculum (Pinar, 2011) and other formal processes of evaluation contribute to continuing modes of colonisation and regulation

(Shahjahan, 2011; Marginson, & Rhoades, 2002). Dei (2010a: 8) identifies three key implications of Fanon's analyses for schooling and education, as first, understanding the positions of the 'contemporary victims of education', that is, to create decolonised spaces in classrooms that reward rather than punish resistance, and promote a process of healing and restoration of dignity. Doing this also involves legitimating experiences and enabling a sense of ownership and responsibility. Second, this project concerns decolonisation at the level of discourse, which includes warding off the impetus towards hegemonic pedagogies and instead building bridges and solidarities across oppressed groups. Third, it involves exploring what a decolonised education may be – as both transformative and engaging multiple knowledges – and as breaking up power hierarchies, including renegotiating with learners about what counts as success. As Dei and Simmons argue:

> Education must consider the geohistorical local of all learners in relation to the attending pedagogies and curricula. . . . In fact even more now given the currency of neoliberal discourse do we need to engage with anticolonial and decolonizing methodologies. Anticolonial and decolonizing knowledge allows for the transformation of one's lived social existence.
>
> *(2010: xv)*

Whether in discussions of the identities of minority students (Phoenix, 2009; Watts, & Erevelles, 2004) or the structuring of bilingual education for linguistic minorities (Grinberg, & Saavedra, 2000), or even citizenship education (De Oliveira, 2011), Fanon's work has been cited as a source. Fanon's ideas also constitute a significant resource within emerging discussions of 'southern theory' (Connell, 2014). In this he joins Bourdieu, Foucault, and Freire as key theorists mobilised to understand the role of education as both a potentially enabling but often disabling process that links the individual pedagogical and developmental project with wider socio-political dynamics. In particular, educational treatments of Fanon engage with the traumatic insults generated through racialised marginalisation (Dutro, & Bien, 2014; Leonardo, & Porter, 2010).

While it lies beyond the scope of this first chapter to comprehensively review this educational engagement, some key points about Fanon's role within the education canon should be noted. The links with Bourdieu are characteristic. First, Fanon and Bourdieu both lived and worked in Algeria contemporaneously (since Bourdieu was posted there initially for his military service and then worked as a sociologist at the University of Algiers) and there is considerable discussion (including from Bourdieu, 2004, himself) both of the ways the Algerian colonial context dramatically shaped Bourdieu's theoretical and methodological approach (including his shift from philosophy to sociology, and his move into ethnography) (Yacine, 2004), as well as the links between their approaches. Go (2013) and Calhoun (2006) claim that Bourdieu knew and drew upon Fanon's writing quite extensively, although he disagreed in the end with his revolutionary politics. These commentators highlight not only commonalities but also the ways that these two authors' ideas complement each other. As von Holdt (2013) also proposes, both Bourdieu and Fanon can be considered to offer resources for postcolonial and decolonial analysis. In particular, the role accorded subjectivity and the domain of the psychological provided by Fanon can be understood as further grounded sociologically through Bourdieu's reflexive and relational sociology.

There is also considerable overlap in analytic framework and political project between Freire and Fanon. Both address questions of (lack of) recognition as well as the role of formal education as a mode of subjugation alongside its emancipatory potential. They share a similar humanist discourse (in part forged through the common influence of Hegelian Marxist ideas) and indeed Freire (1972) cites Fanon in *Pedagogy of the Oppressed*. As will be discussed below, Fanon's notion of 'actionality' shares commonalities with Freire's 'conscientisation'. Allen argues,

> Freire, as well as other early critical pedagogists, chose to selectively hear what race-radical scholars, such as W. E. B. Du Bois and Frantz Fanon, were saying, as if racial politics were not a significant story. In the process, many moments of possible racial solidarity have been lost.
>
> *(2005: 66)*

Moreover, Tuck and Yang (2012) suggest that Fanon offers a better, more materially grounded, account of subjective psychological process than Freire. They argue that Freire's version of humanism risks the abstraction of internal psychological states from socio-political processes and so paradoxically renders 'the oppressed' vulnerable to a deficit and depoliticised model. Their critique aligns with other discussions of the problems of psychologisation, or the reduction of subjectivity to the self-enclosed individual (Gordo López, & De Vos, 2010; De Vos, 2013). By contrast Dei proposes:

> Like Fanon, we must be concerned with the quality of humanism being formed through our day to day social interactions. We need to be alert not to be seduced by the ethical and moral register of colonialism. Ultimately, education as praxis ought to foster a climate of communal care.
>
> *(2010: xvi)*

Notwithstanding also a common engagement with Marxism, considerable tensions as well as complementarities follow from setting Fanon's ideas alongside those of Michel Foucault (that I have addressed more extensively in Burman, 2016b, and take up further in Chapter 4 here). The frictions of (self-)regulation and surveillance are highlighted by both authors, with a common focus on questions of subjectivation (see also Hook, 2005, 2012; Oliver, 2004, 2005). While Foucault has sometimes been criticised (arguably unjustly, see Stoler, 2002) for insufficiently addressing colonialism (he had planned a volume of *History of Sexuality* on racism and racialisation but did not live long enough to write it), his critique of therapy as a confessional mode of regulation is clearly situated in a line of continuity with Fanon's critique of colonial psychiatry even if, as Butler (2005) notes, his later work converges with a focus on the creativity as well as regulation at play in the staging or performance of narrative encounters. Both, moreover, share a central preoccupation with subjectivity, although, as a psychiatrist, Fanon was of course directly involved in treating distress and so also subscribes to a more positive view of therapeutic change that complements Foucault's genealogical concerns with the conditions of possibility for particular subjective forms. Fanon, as already noted, was practically and professionally engaged with psychoanalytic ideas unlike Foucault, although the latter also did not reject this. Notwithstanding his programmatic commitments and direct political engagement and subscription towards a specific political goal (of decolonisation), at times Fanon comes close to Foucault in his model of temporality and change, specifically the need not to foreclose future subjective and political possibilities. He frames the future through a resolute acknowledgement of his own positioning. As he puts it: 'In no fashion should I undertake to prepare the world that will come later. I belong irreducibly to my time' (*Black Skin*: 12). As a final point of comparison, Macherey (2012) argues that Fanon's analysis of interpellation (or hailing) as indicated by the child's instigation of Fanon's racialisation through 'Look, a Negro!' (in *Black Skin*), offers a more situated analysis than that provided by either Althusser or Foucault, and so offering a grounding of the formation of subjectivity within a specific historical and geographical (colonial) field.

Fanon and action

Fanon, of course, was a man of action, in his political and professional work. His writing was a form of action, an intervention that challenged prevailing professional and political concepts and approaches, and he used his positions to advocate for and legitimate marginalised perspectives. He was thus unapologetically aligned, albeit not uncritically or unreflexively so. Indeed, tracing

through the deliberative character of his arguments across his texts is suggestive of precisely the kind of 'effort' and 'struggle' to arrive at understanding
that he topicalises in *Black Skin*. Action centrally involves transformations of
subjectivity. Indeed, Gibson (2013) opens his paper addressing the relevance
of Fanon in contemporary South African housing struggles with this quotation from one of Fanon's letters: '[I]f action does not transform individual
consciousness then it is nothing more than incoherence and agitation' (1).

In this book I topicalise action, rather than agency, as this is more situated/
specific (and therefore relational). Indeed, agency is never as complete or
enclosed as the term is usually read to mean, and this is most important in
relation to conceptualising children and childhoods – whose subjects are
perhaps prototypically dependent and relationally constituted. Fanon's primary project is one of enabling the subject to 'act'. He distinguishes action
from reaction – highlighting how reaction is limited by its relationship with
history: 'there is always resentment in a *reaction*' (*Black Skin*: 158, emphasis in
the original). As Gibson (2011b: 7) notes: 'Fanon demanded action; action –
not reaction but commitment – and then also reflection on commitment. At
his most ethical, Fanon demanded a stand against any injustice.'

Action, therefore, is forward and future-facing. It involves the liberation
of the subject from the determinations shaped by their past (an understanding shared by both existentialism and psychoanalysis). While action may be
behavioural, the notion of act presupposes intention and therefore human consciousness. This is where we encounter both the strengths and limitations of
Fanon's humanism. Moreover, 'action' should be distinguished from the psychoanalytic notion of 'acting out', which implies substituting action for thought.
Rather, as discussed above, for Fanon thought and reflection are central.

Fanon contrasts being 'actional' with 'reactional'. ('Man's behaviour is
not only reactional. And there is always resentment in a *reaction*', *Black Skin*:
158, emphasis in the original.) A reaction implies a relationship with the
past that defines and limits it to that relationship. As indicated above, Fanon
highlights the limits of this position many times at the end of *Black Skin* (for
example, 'The Negro, however sincere, is a slave of the past'). He links this
call to action with the educational project of disalienation: 'To educate man
to be actional, preserving in all his relations his respect for the basic values
that constitute a human world, is the prime task of him who, having taken
thought, prepares to act' (*Black Skin*: 158). To be 'actional' goes beyond
reacting, then, but rather is to be ready to 'act'. In other words: 'To educate
is the prime task of, having taken thought, prepar[ing] to act' (ibid.).

'Actionality' is, however, a curious term that is not much discussed in
Fanon studies. In a rare mobilisation of the term (although without significant comment), Gibson (2011: 9) asserts that subjectivity is central to this:

'Fanon discussed the problematic of subjectivity that is essential to actionality in terms of alienation and insisted that liberation will be the result not of mechanical forces but of human subjectivity.' The focus, therefore, is on preparation for action, as a considered practice formulated in 'respect for the basic values that constitute a human world' (*Black Skin*: 158). That is, there is deliberation, ethical reflection, and readiness. What is specified is a sense of potential, of capacity and readiness, rather than foreclosure of goal or outcome. Leonardo (2011: 686) notes, citing Fanon, that 'a post-race project is not only an intellectual project but equally political, conceptual on one hand but actional on the other'.

What remains clear, then, is that action is linked to activism, realised by Fanon in a practical living out of his political commitments. Also, action necessarily involves being active – being engaged in particular material and relational contexts, and so cannot only be individual. Fanon emphasises the links between the individual and social: 'And, through a private problem, we see the outline of the problem of Action' (*Black Skin*: 163). An act transforms symbolic coordinates; it does not simply effect changed conditions, but also how we understand the limits to those conditions. This is how action is linked to transformation, resistance, and change. As applied to education, as Dei and Simmons (2010b) put it: transformative education works 'as consciousness raising action, thus illuminating the decolonizing nature of resistance, [whereby] educators must seek to transform themselves in order to transform education' (xxii).

Pedagogical links

Across his writing, Fanon expresses both the problems and the possibilities posed by education; that is as central to oppression as also a prerequisite for liberation. His first book *Black Skin* has been described as structured around two issues: 'the fact of blackness and the education to whiteness' (Gendzier, 1973: 46), in which he details how language, cultural, and pedagogical practices work in the service of colonialism to cut the colonised off from their indigenous forms of knowledge and to instil in them instead an orientation to the cultures, practices, and – crucially – standards of the coloniser. Alongside this, throughout his writing strong arguments are made about self-awareness and correspondingly education as politicisation and as emancipation, that are practiced in his texts as a pedagogy that combines poetry and polemic. Indeed, in an early review of his corpus, Gendzier (1966) described his writing as a project of 'self-education': 'Transposing the concept of life as struggle from its philosophical moorings to the political arena, Fanon began to evolve a program of self-education that he later applied to the Negro question and the colonial situation' (535). Philosophical theory both inspired and was also subject to rigorous critique by Fanon. By his final writings he depicted education as a normative (but not normalising) project of transformation.

In brief, three educational contributions are taken forward in this book, through its particular reading of the work of Fanon and its development as child as method. These comprise, first, an interrogation of the significance of connecting the personal and the political, alongside correspondingly, second, the psychic and the social, and, third, the redress of distress to enable political, agentic engagement. This perspective is not new in educational research, although these specific points are not always clearly differentiated. In their critique of the limits of so-called 'safe spaces' in teaching race literacy, Leonardo and Porter (2010) offer a detailed overview that takes seriously Fanon's conceptualisation of the role of violence as a 'productive force that can be life affirming through its ability to promote mutual recognition' (149), taking on board the idea that 'Fanon leaves us with a dialectical definition of violence, one that accounts for its potential for brutality, but also its power to destroy, create, and unify' (144).

Fanon's direct engagement as both psychiatrist as well as revolutionary is critical here. Alongside consideration of some implications for antiracist educational strategies, in each chapter I develop the pedagogical implications of Fanon's ideas. As will be seen, these take forward some of the guiding preoccupations of and for this book, as also reflected in Fanon's commitments, of the necessary and vital relations between emotions and learning (whether as barriers or facilitation). This aspect is well recognised in educational applications of Fanon's work, in terms of formulating the project 'to nurture the "pedagogy of rage" to serve the broader cause of a "pedagogy of subversion"' (Dei, 2010a, 3–4). Yet as well as 'rage' there is 'anger, humility of knowing, and politics in different ways to ensure social transformation' (4). Leonardo (2011), considering a 'post-race' perspective, is more circumspect about rage and indignation, but nevertheless addresses discomfort and challenging the silence over whiteness as very much on the agenda (Applebaum, 2012; Yancy, 2012, 2015).

Some specific modes of pedagogical address and application can be read from Fanon's writing, in particular from the last sections of *Black Skin*, both in relation to its content and its form. Indicating these here, at the beginning of this book, may also indicate a flavour of Fanon's writing style that communicates something of why and how his work has been so inspirational to generations of readers across the world. By pedagogical address, I mean the way in which Fanon constructed his text to address his readers to lead them towards a particular conclusion or understanding. A well-known feature of

Fanon's narrative style, in particular in *Black Skin,* is its shifts of narrative voice between philosophical analysis and explication, searing critical argument, and seeming self-disclosure or analysis, although, as Gordon (2015) comments, this is never only autobiography but rather functions as an exemplary mode of subjective action. Thus, Fanon moves from analysis of his own position (as a Black man) to general account. Hence, in an explicit reference to 'solidarity' he affirms his as a joint project: 'every time a man has contributed to the victory of the dignity of the spirit, every time a man has said no to an attempt to subjugate his fellows, I have felt solidarity with his act' (*Black Skin*: 161). We may note that such acts of solidarity are not only refusals but also positive affirmations. Such claims to 'dignity of the spirit' also align with current movements against dehumanisation of the poor and dispossessed.

In particular, contrary to perceptions of being committed to specific programmatic endpoints, Fanon's account in *Black Skin* of enabling subjectivity focuses on being 'prepared' or 'ready', rather than specifying particular (pre-defined) actions. This explicit repudiation of teleology is important for my analysis below, and it is what enables Fanon to be mobilised as a (postcolonial) critic of development as well as also sometimes its advocate. To show how he does this, it is necessary to consider his text closely. Instead of presuming the goal to be attained, Fanon topicalises effort, scrutiny, and questioning, posing the project of freedom within a narrative voice of the performative conditional. He writes: 'It is by going beyond the historical, instrumental hypothesis that I will initiate the cycle of my freedom' (*Black Skin*: 164). That is, he topicalises both lexically and grammatically what is needed to make this emancipation happen rather than prescribing what should happen: While most commentators emphasise the preceding sentence 'I am my own foundation' (ibid.), here I want to attend to the practical elaboration of performative strategy within Fanon's formulations: 'by going . . . I will initiate' as marking a beginning (an 'initiat[ion]'), not a foreclosed endpoint.

Further, starting points as well as endpoints are put in question. Acknowledging that too often history (both individual and cultural or national) traps and constrains, Fanon insists on the need to avoid being defined and limited by that past. This relates to his analysis of 'action' and 'actionality' discussed in the next section. Fanon ends *Black Skin* by arguing:

> I do not have the right to allow myself to bog down . . . I do not have the right to allow myself to be mired in what the past has determined. I am not the slave of the Slavery that dehumanized my ancestors.
>
> *(164)*

This is closely followed by a demand not to be caught in the dynamic of resentment/recrimination: 'I as a man of colour, to the extent that it becomes possible for me to exist absolutely, do not have the right to lock myself into a world of retroactive reparations' (165). That is, he marks as a political imperative the need not to be stuck in the past, nor to uphold fixed positions between black and white. As he puts it in a famous passage: 'The Negro is not. Any more than the white man. Both must turn their backs on the inhuman voices which were those of their respective ancestors in order that authentic communication is possible' (ibid.).

In this sense, as Renault (2011) notes, notwithstanding (or perhaps because of) his practical-political engagement in decolonial struggle, Fanon's account diverges from subsequent postcolonial analyses by being centrally engaged in a project that seeks to envisage the possibility of future reconciliation. He asserts the reciprocity of the liberatory project that is general rather than individual: 'Was my freedom not given to me then in order to build the world of the *You*?' (165, emphasis in the original), outlining an emancipatory project that requires collective action and communication across axes of power. Butler (2015) in fact topicalises this second-person address (to 'you') as specifically allowing for, mandating even, a relationality that not only envisages changed and changing (racialised) subject formations, but that also offers scope for a reconfiguration of gendered positions. Fanon therefore elaborates a vision of a pedagogical process that wards off fixed positions: 'Superiority? Inferiority? Why not the quite simple attempt to touch the other, to feel the other, to explain the other to myself?' (*Black Skin*: 165).

While at the very end of *Black Skin* Fanon celebrates the 'open door of every consciousness' (ibid.), he envisages this as happening through 'effort' (a term mentioned twice in the final page of *Black Skin*). That is, the 'effort at disalienation' (ibid.) is a prerequisite and condition for the emergence of a 'positive voice' (ibid.). It is a project requiring agentic action, rather than something that can be guaranteed. Moreover, it is agentic action that is not only individual: 'There are in every part of the world men who search' (163). The project is thus one of searching out, and allying with others who 'search', alongside the effort of subjective restoration and self-analysis: 'It is through the effort to recapture the self and to scrutinize the self, it is through the lasting tension of their freedom that men will be able to create the ideal conditions of existence for a human world' (165). Indeed, the final sentence of *Black Skin* underscores the project of learning, of not taking answers for granted, with *Black Skin* ending with the 'final prayer' (ibid.): 'make of me a man who questions!' (ibid.).

In sum, Fanon's writing gives rise to (at least) eight lessons for educational theory and practice. These include, first, the project of 'disalienation', which involves identifying specific geo-historical positions, as in how Fanon explicitly topicalises the question of time as central (Renault, 2011):

> The problem considered here is one of time. Those Negroes and white men will be disalienated who refuse to let themselves be sealed away in the materialized Tower of the Past. For many other Negroes, in other ways, disalienation will come into being through their refusal to accept the present as definitive.
>
> (Black Skin: 161)

Similar formulations follow: 'I am not the slave of the Slavery that dehumanized my ancestors' (164). 'The body of history does not determine a single one of my actions. I am my own foundation. And it is by going beyond the historical, instrumental hypothesis that I will initiate my own freedom' (ibid.).

Second, he advocated making a critical claim on the discourse of development. This involved taking a stance on developmental discourse that does not presume the need to divorce child from this, but rather invites the possibility of attending to the consequences of differently oriented and nuanced positions in this (which includes how denying children access to the discourse of development may also be exclusionary as well as resistive, as we shall see).

Third, there is an exploration of the conditions for being open to change, or learning – through relationships, and relational approaches. Dei (2010a) suggests this is:

> a process of affirming multiple knowledge (based on experience and affective relations) and having learners coming to claim a sense of ownership and responsibility for their own knowledges. It is about bringing to the fore subjugated voices, histories, and experiences. It is about legitimizing practice and experience as the contextual basis of knowledge. The process of creating a decolonized classroom space also entails learners and educators being able to acknowledge the link of identity, schooling and knowledge production. It is about negotiating around power and the asymmetrical power relations that structure schooling processes. It is about placing questions of responsibility and complicity on the table for discussion to see how we are each implicated in the process of creating conducive learning space for all.
>
> (9)

There is, fourth and correspondingly, a commitment to focusing on process rather than outcome.

Alongside this, fifth, there are psychoanalytic contributions, which include acknowledging and working with experiences that lie beyond the rational, attending to the role of emotions but situating them within social and material practices. This is the 'psycho-affective' approach Fanon is said to have enabled, which now would perhaps be called psychosocial. This also includes understanding experience as embodied and material. As Butler notes:

> What is remarkable about Fanon's view, perhaps put more strongly than Sartre is willing to replicate, is that the body becomes historical precisely through an embodiment of social life. The wrecked and muted body is not merely an example of the condition of colonial rule; it is its instrument and effect.
>
> *(2015: 189)*

A sixth aspect concerns how subjective development figures as a necessary educational and cultural-political project (which also involves risking the annihilation of the past to transcend its determinations, c.f. Leonardo, & Porter, 2010, as well as avoiding teleological prescriptions). Related to this, seventh, is the link between the specific and the general: since each individual carries their own history and its meanings within them, as the ontogenetic analogue also of, eighth, negotiating a route between culturalism and universalism (Cherki, 2011).

Fanon now: towards 'child as method'

In Chapter 6 I outline the broader frame of child as method that was both inspired by and now informs this reading of Fanon. Specifically, child as method is informed by twenty-first century debates that extend the explorations of the exclusions of humanism through feminist, ecological, and postcolonial and decolonial arguments. While Fanon's humanism may read strangely to readers now, we should recall that the recent posthumanist turn does not claim a temporal succession to humanism but rather to go beyond its exclusionary binaries (Braidotti, 2013). While I cannot attempt to grapple with all the political and philosophical issues Fanon sets in play and indeed speaks to in his writing, nevertheless some recent convergences can be noted.

In the service of developing his theory of anticolonial consciousness and practice, Fanon mobilises Hegel, Nietzsche, and Marx, as well as Freud and other psychoanalysts. Others have already assessed his re-reading of humanism (Hallward, 2011; Gilroy, 2010; Butler, 2015; Alessandrini, 2000, 2009), of Marxism (Rabaka, 2011; Hudis, 2015) and even countered Hannah Arendt's critique of Fanon to offer a Fanonian reading of her work (Farred, 2011). Clearly questions of pedagogy, action, the relation to the other, the constitution of the subject, and its agentic status, all engage major questions in moral philosophy as well as social and political theory. These are, of course, also all at play in the question of education: what it is, who it is for, how it happens, if it happens, and why. Posing such questions from Fanon's anticolonial starting point focuses these questions materially and socio-politically, situating them within structural axes of inequality and inviting, indeed agitating for, better understandings of the ways that particular individuals and groups can transform these.

Fanon also graphically depicts how such relations of inclusion, exclusion, and marginalisation are reproduced, with his depictions of how these are played out in interpersonal as well as intergroup and communal conflict. My reading of his writing concerns how it performatively prefigures transformation, rather than re-iterates those determinations and so condemns us to them, and so recalls the concerns informing Butler's (1997) discussion of subjectivity and subjection, and her later engagement with accountability (Butler, 2005). Recent educational commentators (for example, Schostak, 2016; Galloway, 2015) are drawing on Rancière's analysis of the reception and impact of Bourdieu in sociology (Rancière, 1991) as well as his searing critique of Althusser's delegitimation of the radical movements and moment of Paris 1968 in the service of both the French Communist Party and maintaining the status of philosophy and the position of the university (Rancière, 2011). Neither Rancière nor Butler reference Fanon, although their arguments echo many of his. (Butler has, however, addressed the relationship between Sartre and Fanon in a more recent text, Butler, 2015, while Rancière does discuss the significance of the Algerian War of Independence in relation to how this polarised the French Left.) Rancière, in particular, appears aligned to Fanon's ideas in highlighting the role of politics as pedagogy, as either reproducing or challenging prevailing power relations.

Similarly, Butler's (2005) engagement in moral philosophical debate around narrative address and recognition highlights how cultural-political and historically and biographically structured intrapsychic dynamics enter into any and every interpersonal encounter (including those constituted as institutional and disciplinary). These include questions of judgement, the ethical relation with and responsibility to the other, whether this is a specific, singular other, or a generalised Other (society, the law, and so forth), and what normativities are reproduced or alternatively open to renegotiation (by the narrator, in their address to the other).

While generated independently of both these authors, my reading of Fanon here, through child as method, resonates with these wider debates, elaborating them specifically through attending to Fanon's work as both psychoanalytically engaged mental health practitioner and revolutionary theorist and activist. I link these two domains not only because, empirically,

Fanon was both, but because his writing offers resources for understanding how these are linked. That is, I highlight how this dual commitment brought a sensitivity to process and helps towards rethinking and renewing a radical politics of pedagogy, as well as the pedagogy of politics. The first is surely needed amid these regimes of instrumentalised education, in the name of standards (whether national or international), which, as post-colonial and Fanonian educational scholars have noted, maintain and (at the level of cultural imperialism) deepen earlier colonial dynamics (Shahjahan, 2011), and foster pedagogical practices of educational engagement that overlook or diminish the subjectivities of those deemed marginal by those standards (Shahjahan, & Kezar, 2013; Shahjahan, et al., 2017; Parker, 2012). What Fanon brings to such understandings is not only a critique but also a methodology that is forged from his unique blending of psychoanalysis with existentialist and anticolonial ideas. This methodology is, in my view, a pedagogy as well as an ethical approach (see also Gordon, 2015), with implications for models of political organisation (Gibson, 2013).

This performative pedagogy of openness and uncertainty, of refusal of closure and mastery is what Butler (2005) reads from psychoanalytic process, and in this we can see just how true to a Freudian psychoanalysis Fanon was. Butler, like Fanon, sees the position of (psycho)analyst as prototypical ethical actor, as one requiring humility that, alongside the acknowledgement of one's own situatedness and limits, involves a commitment to working with these to take forward the encounter, the relationship. In a later formulation, Butler (2015) describes the ethical not as conduct or disposition but rather says that it 'characterises a way of understanding the relational framework within which sense, action, and speech become possible' (12). Notwithstanding his mobilisation of other psychoanalysts (Alfred Adler, even Carl Jung), I suggest that Fanon is a Freudian in his deep acknowledgement of the conflicted character of the subject's relation to itself. This is not only an effect of the biographical, of lived history, but also because embodied and psychic biography is both inscribed by and, in turn, inscribes sociohistorical (or what we now seem to call geopolitical) conditions. Butler (2015) sums up Fanon's contribution to the understanding of the psychic impacts of racialised alienation as an embodied, lived process as engaging the core question of 'how what is "external" becomes not only "internal", but the driving force of psychic life' (10). Fanon can also be read as almost Lacanian (in a feminist reading, see Chapter 3) in asserting the necessary but alienating relationship with the social order, exemplified by language – 'the retaining wall to the group', as he puts it (*Black Skin*: 29). Alongside the Lacanian re-reading of Freud, informed by structural linguistics, where that retaining wall is seen to compose the subject even as it also separates the subject from its earlier pre-symbolic experiences, Fanon imports a racialised reading of the Freudian/Lacanian account of the layering and (re-)activations of trauma, via *Nachträglichkeit*, as activated anew in each ethically charged encounter. In this he not only, as Macherey (2012) suggests, contributes a more social, and sociologically grounded, theory of subject formation, but he also gives us some practical examples of how to work, therapeutically and educationally.

Via this focus on Fanon's pedagogies of child, as a practice of child as method, I hope to indicate how Fanon is owed a place in contemporary social and educational theory, as well as also in discussions of strategy for the compensation of social and educational disadvantage. What Fanon's revolutionary humanism brings is both an interrogation, and also critical reworking, of the bourgeois psychic investments in child that are now instrumentalised by capitalism as economic investment. His contribution and challenge is not only theoretical, methodological, and political, but in showing how these work together in the service of subjective and societal change.

2

IDIOTIC CHILD

I am speaking here, on the one hand, of alienated (duped) blacks, and, on the other, of no less alienated (duping and duped) whites . . . the subject of our study is the dupes, and those who dupe them, the alienated.

(Fanon, Black Skin: *22–3)*

This chapter reflects on the specific workings of one predominant position of child within socio-political practices of oppression, which within Fanon's account is exemplified by colonial racism. This is the position of the child who does not know, or (yet) know better. This position is one that, of course, founds many educational practices (notably of the kind Freire, 1972, described as the 'banking system' of knowledge transfer that sustains adult–child and other – especially classed – paternalistic relations), as well as widely circulating socio-legal, cultural, and media practices. Many childhood and feminist theorists have highlighted the double-edged character of the innocence, or claimed lack of knowledge, accorded childhood as not only characterising few (if any) actual, embodied children but also rendering those who in fact do show indications of 'knowledge' (whether of sexuality, or of work, to take two key examples) as deviant, even disqualifying them from accessing membership of the category of child. (It may also be noted how violent children are particularly likely to be excised from such membership, which perhaps is indicative in a number of ways, as we shall see.) Not only does this highlight the gendered, cultural, classed, and racialised selectivities governing access to mainstream models of childhood (Meiners, 2016), with major consequences for children of the majority world, but the vigour and affective investment with which such boundaries are regulated through the trope of innocence and (lack of) knowledge (such that to question them typically evokes outrage or suspicion) also demands some further interrogation.

Idiotic child

Hence, this chapter takes up this problematic of knowledge, belief, and adult–child relations in a different direction. The provocative designation, Idiotic child, is not mobilised here in its current idiomatic everyday understanding as an attribution of stupidity or ignorance except in an indirect way, as an effect of particular social dynamics. It arises from the Greek term '*Idios*' (ΙΔΙΟΣ), meaning the self, or 'private person' elaborated at a time when notions of privacy or solitude were not culturally valued. While Parker, et al. (1995) take this up to discuss the culturally specific character of popular representations of distress, whereby the moral treatment of the 'mad' was deemed to require solitude and segregation, here I consider how it designated those 'selves' or parties who did not demonstrate social responsibility and political awareness. The term acquired meanings of inexperience and, from thence, associations of ignorance and lack of education, and remedial treatment requiring deliberation and reflection on the subject's experience. But where Parker, et al. (1995), following Padel (1981), mobilise this to discuss the position of those designated 'mad', and so rendered unaware or unknowing and correspondingly exonerated from social responsibilities via this marginal status, here I apply it to describe a positioning of child as excluded or separated from societal understandings and conventions.

To clarify, I am here neither advocating (nor celebrating) a positioning of Idiotic child, nor presuming that this is an accurate or necessary positioning. As we shall see, this is *a rendering of the position of* child, rather than one that is claimed or assumed, that fulfils particular (individual and societal) purposes for those elaborating that position. Hence this chapter addresses what is at stake in this process of making or constructing child as Idiotic. Taking up the original Greek meaning of the term 'idiot', as unengaged with or as not contributing to political life, this chapter correspondingly highlights a conventional pedagogy of childhood, or socially sanctioned positioning that renders the child/children as separated from and outside the principal social body. This separation works to exclude children from – what within contemporary discourses of children's rights would be termed – social and political 'participation', so potentially or actually denying children's protagonism.

Developing the arguments made by the psychoanalyst Octave Mannoni in his influential essay 'I know well, but all the same' (originally published as *'Je sais bien, mais quand-même'*) (Mannoni, 1969/2003) on the structure of ideology, this exclusion will also be seen to function productively to secure particular sets of assumptions. In this sense, then, anticipating the arguments made by Mezzadra and Neilson (2013) in their text *Border as Method* (which is a parallel political resource to child as method), we can see how a practice of exclusion, in this case the exclusion of child from social participation or from accessing the knowledge allowed to full social participants, *thereby constitutes that very social practice*. Not only is inclusion provisional and discretionary, it also relies upon and is constituted by exclusion. Here we see how discourses of inclusion and exclusion of child carry consequences not only for children, but also how that exclusion structurally warrants that of others.

As will be seen below, structuring such an 'unknowing'/excluded position for children institutes a socio-psychic order that enables other, at least as pernicious, forms of unknowing (such as the wilful adherence to racist ideas) to subsist undetected. The psychic mechanisms that this process relies upon are individual and idiosyncratic but also social and cultural, in part through transhistorical and universalised understandings of the meanings accorded childhood. Explicating these mechanisms takes us into psychoanalytic theory, notably discussions of fetishism or a particular psychic configuration of defending against lack, which Fanon and others recognise as underlying the dynamic of racism. This is because, as Hook (2012) indicates:

> the fetish is not simply 'socially constructed', the result that is, merely of trans-subjective factors. It is instead the imaginary outcome of a negotiation between a given subject group and the trans-subjective, the result thus of a to-and-fro tension between the intersubjective and the trans-subjective.
>
> *(201, Note 10)*

In this chapter, I show how fetishism, as a combined dynamic of avoidance and fascination that racism relies upon, is built from a contingent positioning constructed for children: Idiotic child.

Idiotic child as deception

Mannoni's (1969/2003) essay explores the dynamics of (self and other) delusion and misrecognition, with corresponding exclusionary effects. He proposes that cultural pedagogies involving the deception of children are pivotal to forms of socially shared, wilful adherence to convictions that are recognised to be untrue. Central to this nexus of deniability and persistence are a set of practices around children that, I suggest, have far-reaching effects for understandings of childhood, pedagogy, and education. Put simply, adults deceive children to produce children who sustain their own adulthood. A critical reading of Mannoni's essay extends his social psychoanalytic reading, highlighting how this motif not only underlies racist discourse but also accounts for its intractable characteristics and so enables it to persist. Specifically, by reading Mannoni's essay intersectionally, alongside Fanon's critique, the mutual implications of class and gender – as well as generational alongside racialised relations – can be identified.

So, alongside psychoanalysis, two other analytical frameworks inform this chapter: intersectionality theory, as primarily formulated from feminist theory (Cho, et al., 2013; Crenshaw, 1991; Collins, & Bilge, 2016) but also extensively discussed in psychology and education (for example, Bhopal, & Preston, 2012). This imports a particular sensitivity to the mutually constitutive character of gendered, racialized, classed, and sexuality positionings and is widely applied to social research (Winker, & Degele, 2011); and, from childhood studies, the attention to adult–child relations as articulating a generational order (Alanen, 2005). From these analytical frameworks, Mannoni emerges as subject to the very dynamics (including, but not only, racialized othering) that he discusses. While this is perhaps unsurprising given his sociocultural positionings, Mannoni can be interpreted as exemplifying what Fanon (also mobilising psychoanalysis) called his method of 'failure'.

By elaborating how racist discourse relies on unanalysed assumptions about the position of the child, this chapter addresses and engages wider educational debates in four ways.

First, it offers routes into understanding how racism's irrational basis resists conventional pedagogical strategies of provision of (more accurate) information, including attending to the affective and relational role accorded children in sustaining such pedagogies. Crucial questions arise about the social structuring of knowledge and belief – as well as memory – that relate closely to but deepen discussions of current socio-political conditions. As we shall see, this invites political pedagogies that are transformative for both children and adults, that go beyond Idiotic child.

Second, in the service of this exploration of incomplete knowledge, rather than presuming the possibility of full knowledge, Fanon's 'pedagogy of failure' – in part also exemplified by Mannoni – is seen as offering fruitful strategies for working with partial knowledge, including partially conscious knowledge.

Third, this analysis also highlights an important differentiation identified by Mannoni between the wilful ignorance warranted *for adults* by the figure of the child, and that of children themselves. This distinction invites some complex, if as yet unresolved, questions about children's agency, responsibility, and complicity that engage with specific pedagogical strategies.

Finally, in discussing a recent media text, as informed by a critical reading of Mannoni, this chapter indicates both the continuing and renewed relevance of Fanon's ideas specifically as read through his claims about children and childhood, which engages the wider field of Fanonian studies.

Conceptual and methodological orientation

The methodological and analytical frameworks mobilised in this chapter include discursive analysis of social texts alongside discussion of and conceptual interrogation of psychoanalytic theory, while also reading that theory critically. Feminist and postcolonial sensibilities are brought into play to reconsider the status of psychoanalysis as a resource for antiracist pedagogies, situating that theory through reading Mannoni alongside as well as against Fanon. It should be noted that this use of psychoanalysis is consistent with Fanon's own theorisations, which (as discussed in Chapter 1) were a social psychoanalysis or social diagnostic as Gates (1991: 469) puts it '[at]t the intersection of colonial and psychoanalytic discourse', showing how emotional states are both built from and so maintain societal dynamics. As well as supplementing Fanon's account with and through that of Mannoni, other psychoanalytic readings of racism will be mobilised, reading both through an intersectional lens, which – as Dei and Simmons (2010b) also noted – poses both a challenge and resource for Fanonian engagements.

As already indicated, a brief excursion will be undertaken into the psychoanalytic theory of fetishism and how this arises as a way of managing anxiety, both the anxiety generated by (racialised) differences and the defensive need to avoid awareness of the source of that anxiety, which is what precisely makes racism difficult to challenge. In a significant reworking, taking material from the South African Apartheid Narratives Archive, Derek Hook (2012) revisits Bhabha's (1994) well-known treatment identifying dynamics at play within the formulation of racialised stereotyping that are both 'epistemic' (concerned with the status of knowing and knowledge) and 'libidinal' (pertaining to the structuring of individual emotions and desires). What we will see is how both such dynamics can be seen to be socially articulated through the culturally widespread rituals surrounding Idiotic child. That is, the constitution of generational difference as a key axis through the sociocultural trope of (withholding) access to knowledge makes Idiotic child central to the production of other oppressive social dynamics including, crucially, those that sustain racism.

Idiotic child, the fetish, and psychoanalysis of the stereotype

Contrary to accounts provided by experimental social psychology, the process of stereotyping supposedly underlying racism is not merely a question of inaccurate cognitive processing, but rather relies on highly invested affective dynamics warding off an awareness of lack and denial of difference. This difference then becomes projected into, and specifically reified or essentialised as, the black or minoritised figure. Hook (2012) emphasises that 'the racist stereotype requires no "realist" basis . . . Stereotypes can function quite adequately outside this domain of reference; not all instances of racism need to be linked to the conscious or rational precepts of the racist's own personal experience' (191).

The dynamic of dehumanisation as well as essentialisation that Fanon identified as central to racism is built from the effort to avoid encountering this difference that, in the examples I will discuss below, become transposed into protecting children from encountering such knowledge. As discussed further in the next chapter, in relation to Fanon's graphic depiction in *Black Skin* of its traumatic effects, racism is not always an issue of (malign) inter-subjectivity but rather of the excision from inter-subjective relationship. This is why a model that includes, but also exceeds, the social is needed to situate unconscious psychic processes within the constitutive political and cultural fields of their elaboration.

Psychoanalytically speaking, then, the fetish substitutes or stands in for the object of anxiety or lack. Put simply, this lack (or 'castration') is understood as psychically constituted as a pre-condition for societal membership, albeit that recognition of this constitutive lack is strenuously avoided, such that anything that approaches bringing it into awareness becomes a source of anxiety. This is what underlies complex self–other dynamics of fascination and repudiation. Hook (2012) reworks Bhabha's (1994) analysis of the role of narcissism in the structuring of racism (as driving the defensive avoidance of difference or lack). He wards off the potential for psychological reductionism in Bhabha's account to offer instead a socially contingent but idiosyncratically produced account that is situated within specific socio-political conditions. As he argues:

> [T]he fetish, like the stereotype, must always be a *constructed* object, both in the sense that there is no underlying realist basis for its presence (it is precisely *fantasmatic*), and in the sense that it is idiosyncratically determined relative to a contingent set of social and historical circumstances . . . This overlapping of inter-subjectivity and transsubjectivity,

the fact that fantasy emerges from an engagement with what is meant, needed, desired, by prevailing societal structures thus permits for the role of the discursive in the psychical operations of racism.

(Hook, 2012: 189, emphasis in the original)

Importantly, this means that the fetish does not dispense with difference, but rather domesticates it, that is 'difference may thus be domesticated firstly by producing a stand-in object that might take the place of the actual different other, and secondly, by stabilizing this other, by reducing him or her to a given set of attributes' (Hook, 2012: 189). I suggest that the prototype 'stand-in object' is structured through the elaboration of Idiotic child. Hook goes on to elaborate how the psychoanalytic processes of condensation and displacement identify two

crucial elements of ideological construction then: *essentialization* (reduction to minimal caricatured elements) and *reification* (a constant reaffirmation within given empirical circumstances of what one wants to be the case), [these are] two means of protecting against the castration of difference.

(2012, 193, emphasis in the original)

Having outlined some of the wider psychoanalytic (and Fanonian-informed) framings of the problematic of racism, I now engage Mannoni's analysis in terms of the structure of racist discourse, specifically by addressing forms of racialised stereotyping enacted within recent UK media coverage of Brexit, where immigrants are racialised as other and so not seen as belonging to the national polity. This is not only to take forward a Fanonian preoccupation with challenging and transcending racialised dynamics, although it will also claim to offer this. To do this, this chapter revisits the considerable engagement between these two authors, suggesting that a revised assessment of Mannoni's ideas may supplement, rather than challenge, Fanon's. Mannoni's writings are (at least to an English-speaking audience) now largely known principally through Fanon's trenchant critique in *Black Skin* of Mannoni's mobilisation of colonial psychiatry and apology for colonial psychological dynamics. A critical reading of Mannoni follows Fanon's critique in highlighting Mannoni's complicity in the very features of mistaken belief that he topicalises. Nevertheless, I suggest that reading Fanon with, as well as against, Mannoni can enable a renewed engagement with aspects of Fanon's thinking, specifically by clarifying aspects of his model of child and childhood that would otherwise remain ambiguous.

Racism's tolerance: 'Brexit' problems

Now we turn to a practical arena to see how the psychoanalytic understanding of fetishism can help address the paradoxical characteristics of
racism – its rigidity (in maintaining a fixed negativity) but corresponding
flexibility (in apparently tolerating contradictions by simply shifting to a
new instance). This flexibility and rigidity are the corollary of the dynamics of condensation and displacement that have been seen to characterise
essentialisation and reification.

The 'surprise' referendum result of June 2016 indicating that (by a very
small majority) Britons wanted to leave the European Union was followed
by increased racist incidents, including physical and verbal attacks, against
European and non-European migrants. These attacks were also against black
and minority ethnic British people presumed to be 'foreign' (Weaver, 2016).
While the unexpected character of this result was widely discussed in post-
Referendum press coverage as an expression of the rift between metropolitan
elites (presumed 'Bremainers', that is, the opposite of Brexiteers, those who
voted to remain in the EU) and the peripheral working class (presumed to be
for Brexit), such attributions of racist ideas to poor white marginalised communities fail to account for the significant numbers of British middle (and upper)
classes who voted to leave Europe. Presumed alignments between class and
political orientation require critical scrutiny, since they risk reiterating pathologising representations of the working class as reactionary and uneducated. As
will be seen below, class presumptions emerge as being as much at play, and as
constitutive of and with, those around gender, generation, and racialisation, so
highlighting the need for an intersectional reading of Idiotic child.

While in early 2016 Donald Trump presciently promised 'Brexit plus plus
plus' for the US, during his Presidential election campaign, the complexity
of the (ir)rational (economic and nostalgic) status of xenophobic and anti-
European sentiments has emerged as a key concern *within* European states.
In a long article connecting contemporary modes of racism with economic
policies (of privatisation and globalisation) through tracing individual labour
histories across the UK and Poland (and their significant relations), the inves-
tigative journalist and author James Meek commented:

> The rise of [the Polish] Law and Justice and the Brexit referen-
> dum victory only make sense if economics and culture are seen
> as two aspects of a single field, whose fundamental substance is
> the collective psyche of voters: a field in which apparently uncon-
> nected economic and cultural abstractions (GDP, a lost empire) and
> apparently unconnected economic and cultural particularities (how

much you get paid, the history of the building where you work) have links and relative weights that economics, and globalised consumer capitalism, struggle to measure.

(2017: 3)

Idiotic child addresses this attachment to such 'cultural abstractions', alongside a seemingly puzzling capacity to overlook direct economic interests in relation to the question of immigration. 'I'm not a racist, but . . .' works as a well-known way of claiming to deny the import of what follows (Rojas-Sosa, 2016; Singh, 2016), but other claims about (self)knowledge, its limits, and – perhaps – the desire not to know, invite discussion through the frame of Octave Mannoni's (1969/2003) essay entitled 'I know well, but all the same'. Mannoni's essay highlights how although questions of self-delusion or wilful unknowing may figure as core material for the psychoanalytic consulting room, they clearly do not only occur there.

'Brexit Street'

The months following the UK Referendum instituted a period of public reflection and exploration. On 20 July 2016, a five-part mini-series 'Brexit Street' was first broadcast on BBC Radio Four (the 'middle-class' UK radio station) and subsequently excerpted with follow-up commentary on the Radio Four news show 'PM' (on 10 September 2016, and throughout that week (BBC Radio 4, 2016a, 2016b)). 'Brexit Street' interviewed people from an area of high social deprivation (in the de-industrialised north east of England, identified in online commentary as Thornaby in Teeside) that had predominantly voted to leave the EU. In fact, subsequent online commentary has disputed its status as *representative* of the deprived North East, since the area was identified as having unusually high numbers of migrants dispersed there, somehow presumed to warrant the concerns expressed. Commentators put forward socio-political considerations as 'justifications' of such resentments – including lack of housing and high unemployment. Yet such 'real' reasons did not appear to be sufficient, nor sufficiently rationally grounded to uphold such arguments.

Apparent contradictions expressed in interviewees' 'reasons' for voting for Brexit suggested a striking capacity to overlook or even to tolerate inconsistencies. It should be noted that the 'problem' of immigration featured strongly in the 'leave' campaign, and was brought into mainstream political discussion by UKIP (United Kingdom Independence Party), a small Right Wing party that emerged during the 2015 electoral campaign that had disproportionate impact on the political scene generally, in part due to the media coverage they received. Although since the Brexit vote, UKIP is on longer a significant political actor (its rationale of leaving Europe now having been fulfilled), Widfeldt and Brandenberg (2017: 1) note 'with increasing success, UKIP has established itself as the only viable electoral option for British extreme right voters while also making serious inroads into more traditional conservative circles, who are Eurosceptic but not extreme'. In this context, the interviewer pointed out that most of the immigrants in the area were not EU economic migrants and so would be unaffected by Brexit. Fifty-two-year-old Mark, who was described as an unemployed carpet layer who had lived in the area for 40 years, said: 'I know I know I know this (pause) but obviously they still take up housing.' (This and the following quotations are all my transcriptions from the online record of the radio programme.) Similarly, Carol, described as caring for her children and a volunteer at the food bank in a local church, claimed that 'as long as they are willing to pay into our country and support and work in our country then I don't see great a great problem but they if they're just coming over for our money and our income . . .'. When the interviewer challenged such claims about competing for jobs and income, pointing out 'but as asylum seekers they aren't allowed to work at the moment' (since under current UK law people in the process of seeking asylum status are unable to engage in paid work), Carol responded: 'Yeah I understand yes yes (pause) they should be made to pay back a little each week for the resources they're getting to prove that they're not here just to take take take but also to give.'

This emphatic claim to know ('I know I know I know') followed by a 'but' from Mark demands interrogation, especially as it occurs alongside significant spatial markers of here/there and us/them (such as 'They get everything paid for. None of us get it round here', with 'here' coding for the white 'us'). Similarly significant is how the 'Yeah I understand yes yes' is succeeded by a demand that completely disregards the import of what it was Carol claimed to 'understand'. This is what seems to allow Carol precisely to *mis*understand, ignore, or exclude the new arrivals in the polity of families and communities lacking resources that she describes.

This form of discourse recalls the structure that Octave Mannoni described as 'I know well, but all the same'. Although little discussed in educational theory, some links have been made. For example, Chris Higgins (2009), discussing pedagogies for 'open-mindedness', refers to Mannoni's trope to highlight that '[w]hat is disavowed is not the piece of reality that challenges my belief, but its challenge' (48), so highlighting the structure of avoidance that protects particularly invested beliefs. It is this wilful ignorance – produced by disavowal – that is the symptom of Idiotic child, albeit that children have not yet been encountered in this trope. For this we need to retrace Mannoni's argument, before evaluating and applying it further.

'I know well, but all the same'

Octave Mannoni was a teacher and philosopher, who later trained and practised as a Lacanian psychoanalyst. His 1969 paper 'I know well, but all the same' (*'Je sais bien, mais quand-même'*) (which was first published in English translation in 2003) discusses forms of claims to self-knowledge that seem to work precisely to permit the disavowal of that same knowledge. Analysing these, he suggests that something more active is at play than the psychoanalytic mechanism of repression: repudiation. He analyses how the question of belief becomes connected with fetishism, in the sense that the 'but all the same' stands in for the fetish, or disavowed belief (in the same way that the fetish itself stands in for the object of anxiety, or lack). While this paper has been very influential in political theory, taken up in discussions of the functioning of ideology, a key feature of Mannoni's argument that has not (yet) been topicalised is that children are accorded a key role in this process. Or, rather than the child or children, it is the *position in relation to (lack of) knowledge* that children are accorded that comes to be significant, such that 'children are a kind of prop for the adults' belief . . . in all societies beliefs are based on the credulity of children' (Mannoni, 2003: 76).

As well as explicating Mannoni's own claims, I discuss below how this psychic thesis is premised on complex and culturally potent intersections between axes of gender, class, generation, and racialisation that demand that such analyses extend beyond the consulting room to socio-political, and educational, relations. It should be noted that Mannoni critiqued the developmental narrative that subordinates the child to a narrative of progress:

> We have more or less implicitly accepted a rather dubious notion of development: the idea, for example, that people once believed in magic, that ontogenesis repeats phylogenesis, and therefore that children . . . and so on. But nothing warrants regarding magical thinking as infantile; as children, in their 'ignorance', can serve as a support for the disavowed beliefs of adults.
>
> *(Mannoni, 2003: 87, ellipsis in original)*

Nevertheless, I indicate how his account re-inscribes the child–woman–'primitive' linkage, so configuring that combined 'other' in relation to which the European (white, male, middle class, adult) constitutes 'his' fragile self.

I will argue that although Mannoni was subject to precisely the kind of dynamic he discusses, this should not lead us to disregard his analysis. Conversely, this complicity can be read as a precise exemplification of the wider sociocultural analysis he propounds since, even he, as its analyst, is subject to its effects. Rather than undermining his claims, I suggest this can be read as indicative of a pedagogical approach that acknowledges the partiality of self-knowledge and its inevitable societal complicities, rather than claiming mastery or omnipotence. Indeed, it is through this pedagogy that Mannoni's thinking in this 1969 essay (unlike his earlier work, Mannoni, 1950/1964) could be said to come closest to Fanon's. (Indeed Mannoni, 1966, does reflect critically on his earlier assumptions.) Alongside Fanon, this enables Mannoni's account to be mobilised as an antiracist and anticolonial resource to help understand phenomena such as the Brexiteer contradictions noted above, alongside their class, generational, and gendered presuppositions.

On method and 'failure' (or the failure of 'method'?)

Despite being a fierce critic of Mannoni's theories (in particular on the psychology of colonisation in *Black Skin*), Fanon also mobilised a social psychoanalytic, or psychosocial, approach to offer a pedagogy of 'failure' that paradoxically empowers and promotes psychosocial change (Burman, 2016b). As discussed further below, mistakes form a key topic in Mannoni's essay, including his own. Mannoni is particularly concerned with a kind of error that arises from how the contradiction in the 'but all the same' that follows 'I know' simultaneously indicates a glimmer of knowledge and disavows (or denies) it. While Mannoni's account mainly discusses socioculturally sanctioned mistakes and deceptions (including some recapitulating a colonialist imaginary, as will be seen), he includes a clinical example. Mannoni presents an incident in which a client (or, in psychoanalytic terminology, 'analysand') appears to overlook, and even enjoy, an invitation to have 'pre-dinner drinks' that was mistakenly issued by his analyst. (Here the mistake is both the analysand's interpretation and also how this 'invitation' reached him.) Mannoni uses this example to illustrate the way false beliefs and knowledge can coexist within the same statement (since the analysand must have realised that this invitation was not meant for him). Or, beyond this, how the claim to knowledge precisely permits or enables its repudiation: 'I know well, but all the same.'

It is important to recognise that, as a psychoanalyst, Mannoni does not subscribe to claims of full knowledge. Rather, what is of interest is the form and significance of the selective understandings arrived at. Indeed, towards the end of this essay, Mannoni refuses to claim intention or 'deliberate choice' (1969/2003: 91) guiding his approach, citing Lacan's 'two axioms: that there is no unconscious belief, and that belief presupposes the Other as its support' (ibid.). I take up later debates on how the consulting room connects with the politics outside it, in relation both to attributions of knowledge to children and wider pedagogical practices. Of significance here is how Mannoni's account of the analysand's mistaken belief, including Mannoni's own 'mistake' in issuing it, brings into focus the methodological significance of fallability, and even error.

The theory and practice of psychoanalysis is founded on the analysis of seeming mistakes that are taken seriously, as significant indications of psychic processes. These mistakes take the form of parapraxes – slips of the tongue and slips of action – as well as dreams and fantasies. Such slips disclose the unconscious at work, highlighting how we do not have full access to what we know, and correspondingly that we know more than we think we know (Freud, 1901/2003). While the unconscious is individual and idiosyncratic in its formation and functioning, it is also profoundly social. This is indicated, for example, by the affective dynamics and interpersonal relations elaborated by joke-telling (Freud, 1916/2003). Indeed, Freud's work on jokes offers a particularly clear example of the social character of unconscious processes, but – arguably – the same logic applies to all psychoanalysis. Additional literature from group analysis also takes this further with the notion of the social unconscious (Hopper, 2003), some of which has been specifically applied to the analysis of processes of racialisation (for example, Dalal, 2002).

From his position as a psychoanalyst, then, Mannoni cannot assume a position of mastery, for this would involve claims to full knowledge that are precisely what such an approach undermines. Such a position both resonates with and can inform current critical educational theory and practice (Britzman, 2003, 2010), which engage feminist and postcolonial theory to formulate social and educational research approaches embracing partiality, mobilising the latter's dual meanings as both necessarily incomplete and situated (or perspectival) (Haraway, 1988; Lather, 2007), and so demanding reflexivity (Andreotti, 2011). Correspondingly, I must acknowledge that my analysis here is incomplete and subject to its own dynamic distortions. Further, my account below departs from most readings and applications of Mannoni's essay to focus specifically on the role that children play within his analysis of social phenomena. Hence, this reading of Mannoni's text could be understood as minor (Katz, 1996), or awry from its original focus and indeed reception, which is more concerned with questions of the links between sexual perversion and ideology (see, for example, Žižek, 1991).

Fanon against or alongside Mannoni, and the status of 'failure'

The elaboration of this discussion demands situating Mannoni's work along-side that of Fanon. However, doing so requires acknowledgement of the complexities of their geopolitical relations. Mannoni worked in Madagascar for more than 20 years, where he taught Philosophy at the Liceo Gallieni de Tananarive but also previously served there as Chief of Information within the colonial service and editor of a (French) propaganda magazine. He is principally known for his text *Prospero and Caliban* (1950/1964), in which he analysed settler–colonised dynamics in terms of the so-called 'depend-ency complex' of the natives and its fit with the 'inferiority complex' of the settler-colonists. As is well-known, this account was severely critiqued by Fanon (1952/1970) in his first book *Black Skin, White Masks*. Moreover, Fanon's critical engagement with Mannoni also should be situated in rela-tion to other proximities. In the 1920s Mannoni taught in Martinique at the same school, the Lycée Schoelcher, that Fanon's teacher and mentor Aimée Césaire attended (see also Larrier, 2010).

Although Fanon rejected most of Mannoni's arguments on the dynamics of colonialism (while also acknowledging that the project to analyse such dynamics was well founded) Fanon, too, was influenced by phenomenol-ogy and psychoanalysis. As both philosopher and psychoanalytic practitioner, Fanon also upheld a methodology of 'failure' as a curb to omnipotence and narcissism (the narcissism that he indicated underlay black–white dynamics). He wrote:

> I grasp my narcissism with both hands and I turn my back on the deg-radation of those who would make man a mere mechanism . . . I am willing to work on the psychoanalytic level – in other words, the level of the 'failures'.
>
> *(1952/1970: 17)*

Gordon (2015) notes that for 'failure' Fanon uses the French word '*raté*' rather than '*echec*', which would more closely resemble the ordinary English 'failure', as in notions of defeat or setback. He comments:

> *Raté* more properly refers to a misfire, missing the mark, or something backfiring, as in an old combustion engine, which explains Fanon's reference to engine failures. The word is also used, however, to refer to not measuring up, of failing to meet a standard, as in the expres-sion *raté de pére,* a man failing to meet the expectations or standards of fatherhood, a concept rich with psychoanalytic content. Fanon is

thus referring to the frustration not only of missing the mark but of the repercussions which, inevitably, lead to therapy. That is why he says he is willing to work on the 'psychoanalytical level'. Fanon further raises the question of whether such a psychoanalytical approach is exemplified or transcended because of not measuring up or failing to meet its own standard. There is thus a paradox of failure: to fail at it is to succeed; to miss the mark is to demonstrate the validity of rejecting it, and therefore affirming or achieving it.

(2015: 24–5)

Alongside Gordon's consideration of its ethical and philosophical features, this methodological focus on 'failure' can also be attended to as having pedagogical implications. Indeed, Fanon explicitly countered moves towards systematization and methodological elaboration characteristic of psychology and psychiatry, at first declaring himself at the outset 'derelict' (*Black Skin*: 11) in this regard, but then commenting: 'I leave methods to the botanists and the mathematicians. There is a point at which methods devour themselves' (ibid.). He also refused the lure of scientific 'objectivity': 'I have no wishes to be objective. Besides, that would be dishonest: it is not possible for me to be objective' (*Black Skin*: 61). This acknowledgement of his own situatedness can be contrasted with Mannoni, who in his earlier (1950/1964) text *Prospero and Caliban,* celebrated as central to Western subjectivity 'the experimental spirit' (the title of the penultimate chapter), albeit that, in his analysis, this 'spirit' also ushers in the Western condition of having an inferiority complex.

In this elaboration of a methodology of failure, Fanon was thereby not only critiquing psychology and psychiatry, but he was also highlighting how the latter's grandiose methodological commitments constructed those disciplines. It should be noted that Fanon's claims have inspired some specifically pedagogical applications for decolonial analyses (Pinar, 2011), while Mannoni's essay attracted educational and philosophical appreciation from Higgins (2010: 192) as indicating a discursive logic conveyed by the truism or cliché such that 'if you embalm a claim in a cliché, its truth can be acknowledged as an empty gesture, one that calls for no action on our part'. Since Mannoni's discussion engages sociopolitical distributions and dynamics of (lack of) knowledge that lie beyond (as well as within) the intrapsychic domain, it been taken up in discussions of ideology (see Žižek, 1991). Alongside this, it is this capacity to tolerate and so enable socio-political exploration of failure that links Fanon's (psychoeducational) theory with both his political and therapeutic practice (Burman, 2016b; Hook, 2012; Oliver 2004). Thus, methodologically and conceptually equipped, we can return to the incomplete but invested project of constituting Idiotic child.

Children, gulls, and gullibility

I now outline the trajectory of Mannoni's argument to clarify the position and role accorded children and childhood. Mannoni begins the essay by discussing ethnographic examples of adherence to seemingly strange ideas. He then reviews how many modern, Western cultural practices (from enjoying 'magic' tricks to going to the theatre or other cultural events) rely on the pretence of belief, and a corresponding belief in, or attachment to, pretence. Crucially, he argues that the question of belief has to be connected with a psychoanalytic understanding of fetishism. The fetish literally attempts to cover over, and so – by association – comes to substitute for 'lack' (that is, symbolic castration). A key point here is that such fetishes are both individual and societal, of which key indications (noted by Mannoni, following Freud) are totems, flags, and national symbols. Mannoni discusses Freud's 1927 paper on 'Splitting of the ego in the process of defence', to point out that this disavowal of belief *both changes the reality while it also represses the memory of the disavowal*. Mannoni argues that this complex process of disavowal produces an anomalous subjective experience: 'one finds oneself torn between an impression of extreme banality and a powerful feeling of strangeness' (1969/2003: 70). In support of his argument for the prevalence, and indeed the banality, of this phenomenon he cites examples outside the clinic, in daily life. Examples he discusses include superstitious behaviour and horoscopes, where, as he notes, we may not believe them but are nevertheless pleased if they are positive. 'I know well' therefore both narratively and psychically precedes 'but all the same', while what drives the latter – the belief in something known to be untrue – is not completely unconscious but rather is somehow distanced, or put away: that is, disavowed.

As an exemplar of this dynamic, Mannoni discusses a text, Talayesva's (1942) *Sun Chief: The autobiography of a Hopi Indian*, which he claims will be known to the 'French reading public' (73), the first US edition of which was published in 1942 but was published in French in 1959 as *Soleil Hopi*. Presumably this warrants his selection of this as an iconic text for analysis, albeit one whose colonial features may reflect not only French imperial involvements in Africa as in the Antilles but also aligns it with the settler colonialism that gave rise to the United States, since the Hopi are the indigenous people of what is now Arizona State. That Talayesva's text can be interpreted rather differently is a matter I return to at the end of this chapter. At any rate, in Mannoni's account of *Sun Chief*, the author is said to narrate his traumatic experience of almost discovering that the Katcinas (the masked dancers supposed to be demon-gods) were people (and recognisable ones at that) during the ritual of offering food to appease them. The memory of this near-knowledge, the narrator claimed, would be reactivated later at initiation, when children are told that the Katcinas were indeed the known elders. Interpreting this, Mannoni links this traumatic moment to Freud's analysis of castration anxiety as 'the model for the kinds of panic that erupt later in life, when people are suddenly overwhelmed by the feeling that "Throne and Altar are in danger"' (74). Developing Freud's (1921) analysis of group psychology alongside a Lacanian model of castration, this anxiety is portrayed as a social condition for membership of a society and the basis of inter-subjective relations (Lacan, 2006a), whereby the relation with the symbolic order is understood as a social bond structured around lack (Parker, 2010; Burman, 2011, 2012b). The resolution of this traumatic anxiety is what drives the establishment of the superego (as is deliberately structured in initiation rites) 'but it also and all but indiscernibly recalls the moment when belief, shedding its imaginary form, is symbolized sufficiently to lead on to faith, that is, to a commitment' (Mannoni, 1969/2003: 75).

Idiotic child or the need to deceive children

Mannoni moves on to explore particular roles played by children within the social scenario. Of particular significance are the younger, 'non-initiated children' who 'continue to be taken in by the imposture' (76) or strange belief. He emphasises that these children fulfil a central role in maintaining that very 'imposture': 'one might say that the children are a kind of prop for the adults' belief' (ibid.). While he comments that 'some societies' (ibid.) also require women to be 'credulous' (ibid.), he continues: 'in all societies, beliefs are based, first and foremost on the credulity of the children' (ibid.). Indeed, perceptively, Mannoni comments:

> I do not think we have paid enough attention to the question of what transpires when, in our societies, an adult feels the need to deceive a child – about Santa Claus, the stork, and so on – to the point that she sometimes fears that Throne and Altar, to use Freud's expression, will be endangered if someone suggests disabusing the victim.
>
> *(1969/2003: 76–77)*

(The significance of Mannoni's use of the female pronoun qualifying the adult position will be taken up later.) It is here that Mannoni identifies what underlies the strength of the investment in maintaining an illusion. Such investments, he suggests, are what underlie culturally widespread ritu-als that amount to a social pedagogy premised on the deception of children.

Further, Mannoni suggests why it is that children fulfil this role: 'in synchronic perspective, the child can, as someone who is both present and an outsider play a non-negligible role by assuming, as he does among the Hopis, the burden of our beliefs after disavowal' (77).

This positions the child as a witness, but not as privy, to insider (societal) secrets. (This is a matter of significance for performances of racialisation and even racism, as discussed later in this chapter and the next.) By this analysis Mannoni de-naturalises entire pedagogies and philosophies of childhood, and he extends this also to critique his own professional discipline by arguing: 'if psychoanalysis has delivered us of the myth of children's purity and innocence, it has not gone very far in analyzing the function of this myth . . . infant credulity helps us disavow our own beliefs' (ibid.). (It is worth noting that Mannoni's wife, Maud Mannoni, initiated a psychoanalytic practice that created radically new ways of working with and services around children and families, see Mannoni, 1970/1987, 1963/1973.

Mannoni claims that the need to make children 'innocent' arises in order to protect adults' beliefs from challenge that in this process thereby secures them. That is, adult uncertain beliefs are rendered warrantable through an attributed need to indulge the beliefs of the gullible child. Hence the 'myth' of 'children's purity and innocence' (1969/2003: 77) becomes 'only a way of talking about their credulity' (ibid.). Yet this credulity is in fact an elaborate manufacture or construction on the part of adults. Mannoni further points out that this dynamic process (for adults) to sustain the fictions secured by the attributed gullibility of children does not even rely on direct contact with children, arguing that 'mental representation of them [children] suffices' (ibid.). Such needs, he suggests, drive concerns over (for example) children's spiritual education (and I will consider further applications below). Crucially, it is what creates the cultural psychodynamic terrain of affective (re)distribution that enables beliefs to be retained without the subject's apparent knowledge.

Mannoni's argument can be summarised as follows: the elaboration and maintenance of an adult position relies upon the deception of children. This social conspiracy to deceive and delude children evokes a dim social memory of a knowing overlooking. Hence, the indulgence typically socioculturally accorded children works to preserve certain core (social) fantasies and protect them from challenge. That is, the deception of children is institutionalised, and functions to secure the beliefs of the adult. What Mannoni identifies as a position of prescribed gullibility, is what I am here calling Idiotic child.

Idiotic child arises from societal/cultural needs to deceive children, not only to constitute children's 'ostensible innocence' (ibid.) but also to render more intractable the position of the child 'as someone who is both present and an outsider' (ibid.) – that is, as disclosing some of the cultural-social resistance to according children greater socio-political participation. But what must now be addressed is how this position accorded the child/children also works within, and is produced through and alongside, wider networks of power relations.

The mistake as disclosing the exclusions of psychoanalysis

I have so far shown how Mannoni proposes that the structure of false beliefs relies on the deception of children, Idiotic child, with examples from history, across cultures, including modern Western contexts, that extend (in Freud's terms) to 'Throne and Altar', or such widespread core beliefs as patriotism and religion. But some further critical evaluation of his account is needed. Mannoni's 'clinical example' is based on his account of a 'mistake' (79), mentioned earlier, of the patient who thought he was invited for a pre-dinner drink. Since I will discuss this in some detail, I quote Mannoni's account of this in full:

> Someone who had taken a call for me had distorted the caller's name, making it sound like that of a black poet from whom I had been expecting a friendly visit. I was busy so I asked that the poet be given the message to come see me as soon as he could; we would have the time, I added, for a pre-dinner drink. The person who was to open the door was informed of all this. The doorbell rang, and, a bit surprised despite himself, he came to tell me, 'Monsieur, it's not a Negro, it's a client of yours.'
>
> *(79)*

Mannoni next describes how he led the patient (as he calls him, not 'client', significantly) to the couch whereupon the latter's first words were:

> 'Yes, I knew that you were joking about that pre-dinner drink. But all the same, I'm terribly pleased'. Almost in the same breath, he added, 'especially because my wife thinks you meant it.'
>
> *(80)*

Here is the 'I know well, but even so', which Mannoni characterises as expressing his patient's wish that, in turn, is disclosed in displaced form, by being presented as *his wife's* (childish) false belief. Yet some significant assumptions, or rather (within a psychoanalytic frame), repudiated but known unbeliefs, remain uninterrogated within Mannoni's analysis.

Analysis of these will usefully also amplify his discussion of the deceptions carried by children. So this is where it is necessary to depart from merely explicating Mannoni's account to formulating a feminist, postcolonial, and intersectional analysis of it.

An intersectional reading of the 'mistake'

A first reading identifies class and property relations at play in 'someone who had taken a call for me', and '[t]he person who was to open the door', via the architecture of space narrated of the middle-class French household – the space, the corridors, the large rooms. A palpable sense of subservience and respect can be inferred via the way that people are only referred to in terms of designated function, as in the way 'was to open' naturalises the power relations of domestic activities and designated roles. Through this, the question of fault, or responsibility for the 'mistake', becomes blurred and even distributed. The implication is that this mistake would not have occurred had 'someone who had taken a call for me' not 'distorted the caller's name', and some element of reproach is discernible in Mannoni's comment that the 'person who was to open the door was informed of all this'.

Like the client who attributes both his pleasure and the false belief to his wife, rather than owning it as his own, Mannoni's projection of his slip reflects his presumption of privilege as master of the house. Such projection is significant since, as a psychoanalyst, Mannoni must subscribe to the view that one can never hear or speak except through one's own desire or investments. Hence such 'slips' must (also) be his. This intersectional analysis can be linked with the 'Brexit Street' stories discussed earlier, where what becomes more evident is how white, working-class interviewees are made to represent, or stand in for, forms of racist discourse that circulate much more widely. This shows how middle-class privilege enables the disowning and projection of unacceptable (racist) ideas onto the working class, who can then be vilified for this, rather than formulating analyses of racism as structural to current economic conditions (Burnett, 2016) and as also a feature of all classes (Meek, 2016).

Attending to classed and gendered relations returns us to the visitor who was expected but did not yet come. This is the 'black poet', through whom contemporary discourses of racialisation enter this text. By his description of this visitor, Mannoni presents both himself and the guest as cultured and liberal. Nevertheless, class and cultural markers elsewhere in the narrative invite the speculation of whether a 'black' person who was not a 'poet' would be met with as much interest and respect by the cultured, intellectual figure of the psychoanalyst. So 'friendly' is the visit that there should be 'time . . . for a pre-dinner drink' (also carrying gendered and classed significations, as well as markers of European civility, even civilisation). Hence, the delegated person, who opens the door, is 'a bit surprised despite himself' to find the client. The text suggests, then, that he was expecting the 'black poet'. Yet some kind of exceptional status is nevertheless still indicated via this curious designation (why not just 'poet', for example, or 'friend'?). Indeed, the key claim 'Monsieur, it's not a Negro, it's a client of yours' is not analysed for the assumptions at play in relation to racialisation and *which* kinds of people are assumed to be 'clients' undertaking psychoanalysis: 'Negro' and client are presented as mutually exclusive categories. Inscribed within the statement 'it's not a Negro, it's a client of yours', then, lies the history of the marginalisation of black and minority ethnic people from the theory and practice of 'talking therapies' such as psychoanalysis, rendered (as Fanon also argued) unanalysable, or insufficiently 'psychologically minded', in ways that resonate with the underserving of black and minority ethnic groups within psychological therapies today (Rogers, & Pilgrim, 2014; Fernando, 2010; Burman, et al., 1998; Maher, 2012).

The different terminology used by Mannoni and his servant to position the actual visitor merits attention. Mannoni calls him a 'patient', while the designation 'client' that is used by the 'person who was to open the door' suggests that this is a 'patient' who pays for his analysis. This further discloses the exclusionary political economy of the practice of psychoanalysis, in the sense that it relies on a set of presumed economic overdeterminations between class and racialised positions. By contrast, it is worth recalling that when Wulf Sachs attempted to psychoanalyze a black man in 1930s South Africa, not only did he offer this free of charge but also became involved in economic support of him and his family, which extended to political engagement (Sachs, 1937/1996). Furthermore, the class associations of psychoanalysis should also be read in relation to migration/refugee trajectories from Europe to the US that ended its earlier practice in free clinics (Danto, 2005).

Such classed and racialised assumptions also can be read alongside other intersectionalities relating to what can be surmised of the gendered divisions of labour in Mannoni's household. Such gendered considerations also recall the attributed gender of the deceiver, as well as the 'gull' or credulous one in his earlier formulation (76–77), which in turn can be read as reflecting presumed gendered arrangements surrounding those who most care and communicate with children. Indeed, Mannoni's 'clinical' example further indicates the psychic distribution of such gendered divisions in the attributed/imposed credulity of women reiterated by Mannoni's analysand.

Mannoni's failure

Mannoni highlights how he 'knows well, but all the same'. That is, he identifies his own participation in the structures involved in producing commitment to false beliefs. These beliefs extend to those mobilised by the 'Brexit Street' voters in believing that 'immigrants are taking our jobs', even when they are not allowed to work. Mannoni explicitly links his analysis to beliefs that produce anxious commitment, especially to (what he notes Freud calls) 'Throne and Altar' – that is, nationalism and religious commitments. Resonances of such anxious commitment can also be heard in the 'Brexit Street' interviewees' nostalgic complaints of loss of community as in 'come Christmas [and] New Year we'd be having parties in each other's houses' (Mark) and demands that 'our money should be spent in our country' (Carol). Other Brexiteers expressed a desire for 'sovereignty' or 'wanting Britain to be great again'. These claims were often at the expense of their personal, direct material benefit. Indeed, other 'Brexit Street' interviewees across the series were reported as having jobs that relied on the single market and open borders, such as truck driving across Europe, but nevertheless still espoused such views. Yet, as indicated, Mannoni, too, cannot quite extricate himself from, and so his text enables a disclosure of, a potent set of assumptions embedded in and maintaining key institutional relations. These include adult superiority over children, men over women, the rich over the poor, and the 'developed' over the 'primitive' (since, as we have seen, the 'Negro' is not constituted in the anecdote as a possible 'client').

In his text, Mannoni rebukes himself for not sufficiently analysing how the 'all the same' both secures and repudiates the 'I know well' (that the analysand was not in fact so invited). My analysis here supplements his own acknowledgement of the limits to self-knowledge. Building on his account of the dynamics structuring the investments in patriotism and nationalism as aligned to fetishism, I suggest that these commitments also rely upon intersectionally structured class, 'race', generation, gender, and (hetero) sexed relations, whose features Mannoni mobilises yet stops short of reflecting upon their significance. Thus, Mannoni reiterates the very dynamic he analyses: he knows well, but all the same.

Yet from his analysis, alongside Fanon's critiques, this unfinished project can be taken further to unpack the nested alignments between, first, the disempowerment of women (as a symbolic castration, or socially structured lack, arising from patriarchal relations, see Mitchell, 1974; Grosz, 1990); second, the institutional imperatives at play in both the deception – and so imposed/mandatory 'innocence' – of children; and, third, the investments at play in the elaboration of adult–child positions. This analysis further illuminates the notion of 'generational order', that is, the ordering of adult–child relations according to presumed natural life stages and roles that warrant sociostructural status differences (Alanen, 2009). In particular, it identifies the investments at play in elaborating and maintaining those generational positions, and shows how they also implicate other – classed, gendered, and racialised – orders. What emerges is how the fabrication of the (false) belief in differences between 'primitive' and modern/'developed' thought processes works alongside the performance of particular class and gender power relations – as with the servants whose job it is to open the door of Mannoni's house or to answer the telephone.

Beyond Idiotic child: Fanon with Mannoni

Mannoni therefore offers an analysis of the position of 'child' as a *specifically invested construction* securing certain societal as well as intrapsychic and inter-personal relationships. This can be applied to understand adherence to the socially sanctioned fetish of, for example, 'Nation' or even, within the cur-rent UK policy context, what are called 'fundamental British values' (a key trope of current British anti-radicalisation and counter-terrorism education policies). This reading of Mannoni enables a more fruitful engagement with Fanon's writings – alongside as well as against eachother. Combres (2016) has recently also suggested that Mannoni and Fanon's ideas may be less opposed than often presented, although she is discussing psychoanalysis rather than childhood.) Specifically, Mannoni enables a different reading of Fanon's quotation from Nietzsche (mentioned in Chapter 1) on how human tragedy arises from being 'once a child' (9 and 165), occurring at both the beginning and ending of *Black Skin*. While Fanon's claim here could imply the installation of an authentic or nostalgic rendering of the position of the child, this would seem untenable alongside his other constructionist models of societal relations.

Mannoni's analysis of the investments configuring this address to the child may help to situate Fanon's claims. So, for example, Fanon's denunciation of the childlike treatment of the colonised person ('a white man addressing a Negro behaves exactly like an adult with a child and starts smirking, whispering, patronizing, cozening', *Black Skin*, 23), can be read as indicative of anxieties that portraying the child as being like the 'Negro' wards off, rather than confirming the 'naturally' (inferior, unsophisticated, or limited) position of the child. Such a reading would also correspond with Fanon's analysis of children's games, and the racism of children's books and comics, which he highlights as functioning as a 'release for collective aggression' (*Black Skin*, 103) to install for the black child 'unconscious masochism' (*Black Skin*, 123). Indeed, underscoring the complex socio-political dynamics at play, Fanon further insists that this 'masochism' does not arise from a real, psychobiographical trauma, for example, 'the little black child see[ing] his father beaten or lynched by a white man'. Rather, he claims it is culturally installed, to 'drain these stories of their aggressive potential' (*Black Skin*, 123) such that they may disable the fostering of resistance. Even as he writes 'the black man has no ontological resistance in the eyes of the white man' (*Black Skin*, 78), Fanon also points out that this lack of resistance only occurs 'in the eyes of the white man', and so indicates that resistance is present and visible to other less privileged or oppressed parties. What this suggests is a reading of Fanon's statement on the 'tragedy of man' arising from being 'once a child' as oriented to specific, material locations and positions. Far from being naturalised, then, these can be read as intersectionally configured through and by not only racialised but also class, gender, and (hetero)sexed dynamics.

Idiotic child in 'Brexit Street'

This discussion of 'I know well, but all the same' as an analysis of racism relying upon particular conceptualisations and assumptions about children and childhood also returns us better equipped to reconsider the 'Brexit Street' radio broadcasts. For alongside the adult figures in this 'Street', as parents and carers of children, there are also children. Setting the scene, the Interviewer noted how 'little children are playing tag in the sunshine', also thereby subscribing to dominant childhood tropes confirming the innocence of children/childhood to signify that this is a friendly, safe area. Indeed, the area is 'nice, very nice', as Wayne (another Brexit interviewee, a landscape gardener) puts it. Meanwhile, Peter, a stay-at-home-dad described as off work with depression, is said to be unwrapping chocolate biscuits for his children (surely a trope of parental indulgence) as he offers the only Bremain story from 'Brexit Street'. Peter expresses concern about the harassment of his asylum-seeker neighbours extending to his family. This is where we can see how discourses of childhood confirming traditional notions of family and community, space and place, can nevertheless be compatible with others, in this case of the children enacting less 'sociable' sentiments such as daubing immigrants' houses with swastikas or worse. (As Peter put it, 'we all know where that leads, and it doesn't go anywhere good'.)

Mannoni's analysis highlights that the recourse to children's innocence is yet another imposture that we 'know well, but all the same', and so can recognise as not entirely true. There are key questions at stake that – within children's rights and childhood studies research – are typically discussed in terms of the problematic of agency (for example, Oswell, 2013). Yet, closer scrutiny of 'Brexit Street' suggests more is at play in the question of children's culpability or innocence. Mark is reported to 'shake his head in disgust at the abuse that the immigrants have suffered'. As if he had not earlier mobilised his own version of 'I know well, but all the same', he says: 'The kids here have decided to terrorise them. They're just children, they don't know any better. They're just brainwashed by their parents who are ignorant.' Claims of not-knowing reverse such that the children who 'don't know any better' appear to reflect the views of their parents who know nothing, 'who are ignorant'. Anticipating the interrogation of the relations between marginalisation through class position and racialisation below, we may note here how a further reading of this 'ignorance' could attend to an additional regional (and working-class) dialect northern English meaning that extends from unknowing to angry – with the links between these confirming the analysis of the affective basis of access to (self-)knowledge outlined here.

This is where Mannoni may offer some further help. Recall that, at the beginning of 'I know well . . .', he points out that once the need to disavow a belief is installed 'the reality that is observed does not remain without effect' (70). Indeed: 'Not only is the experience not eradicated, it is ineradicable. It leaves an *indelible mark* . . . . What is eradicated is the *memory* of the experience' (p.70, emphasis in the original). What this suggests is that the traumatic crisis (of authority, sovereignty and so forth) that is mobilised, but then warded off, by disavowal enters into the reality as it is experienced. The implications of this go beyond how 'but even so' only arises because of 'I know that'. For '[s]omething of the order of belief had to have subsisted . . . in order to be recognizable, despite its transformation' (71). This structural trace in the experience of reality is why 'but all the same' is not unconscious but rather indicates 'that desire or fantasy operates, as it were, at a distance' (72). It accounts for the felt sense that this dimly perceived something really is true. Once installed, then, the belief produces a changed engagement with reality that confirms it as so. This tricky, slippery terrain – of not quite known, nor unknown, belief – that can be understood to inform the structure of racist discourse accounts for why it is so difficult to contest. And, thanks to Mannoni, the origins of its cultural modes of articulation we now know to be tied to the deception of children.

Objectively or subjectively 'idiotic': agentic questions

Applying this once again to 'Brexit Street', children's supposed innocence or lack of knowledge, here attributed as the basis for their racist actions, becomes narrated as arising from the wilful 'ignorance' of their parents, while (in a double pathologisation) the latter is implied to be a question of culpability such that the ignorant (parents) should know better than the not-knowing children. Children are here rendered capable of 'decid[ing] to terrorise', that is, of engaging in deliberated courses of action. However, responsibility for why and what they are doing is portrayed as lying elsewhere – in the very 'community of practice' (Lave, & Wenger, 1991) whose terms of reference Mark, Wayne, and Carol are presented as outlining. Relevant here is Mannoni's claim that 'children, in their "ignorance", can serve as a support for the disavowed beliefs of adults' (87). This is what leads him to the conclusion: 'It is not the young Hopi who is responsible for the fact that he has been deceived, but the adults. He is *objectively deceived*; his subjectivity does not yet take any part in the matter' (ibid., emphasis in the original).

Whereas adults are seen to have in some sense 'chosen' to deceive themselves (through the psychic process of disavowal indicated by 'I know well, but even so'), and as such have subjectively produced this state of affairs, Mannoni elaborates a different subjective position for children who have been, in his words, 'objectively deceived'. He posits this objective deception alongside countering the 'myth' of children's innocence, indeed indicating this as an effect of the need to render the child as 'both present and an outsider' (77).

This invites the question that if their 'subjectivity does not yet take any part in the matter', are children less accountable or responsible for their actions – indeed whether considered as the consequences of or the motivations for their actions? Or should the interpretation be that their subjectivities may yet have taken *some* part in the matter, but not quite as much as – or of the same form as – adults? Yet to enter legal debates on responsibility, or quantitative answers (knowing more or less of or about something . . .), would seem to step too quickly away from the question of subjective configuration and psychic structuring by and within the social. Rather, at issue is the extent to which children are considered to be part of, and indeed shape, the sociocultural processes to which they are subject. To add a Foucauldian inflection (Burman, et al., 2017), this is the problematic of how the 'objective' becomes subjectified. At this point it must be acknowledged that, notwithstanding his important insights into the cultural role played by children's attributed ignorance, Mannoni was unable to address this question clearly. Adequate answers will have to be sought elsewhere.

In an evocative formulation, Fanon comments that the position of the child, read developmentally, historically, and biographically as 'man' 'at the beginning of his life' (*Black Skin*: 165) is 'always clotted, he is drowned in contingency' (ibid.). This occurs just before the final iteration of Nietzsche's trope, 'The tragedy of man is that he was once a child' (ibid.).

While 'clotted'-ness suggests density, perhaps also a viscosity that is not sticky, there is fruitful ambiguity about origins (for what is there before, or after, being 'drowned'?). To be 'drowned in contingency' functions as a claim about how what one becomes is overwhelmingly determined by historical and biographical conditions. This 'contingency', then, not only makes the child amenable to influence (or, in Mannoni's words, subject to 'the neurotic reactions of those around him', 1950/1964: 168), but this is also what makes possible Fanon's final humanist appeals (c.f. Hallward, 2011), discussed also in Chapter 1, to transcend racialised categories ('The Negro is not. Any more than the white man', *Black Skin*, 165). That is, it is the appeal to biographical history that enables Fanon to argue that

> it is through the effort to recapture the self and to scrutinise the self, it is through the lasting tension of their freedom that men will be able to create the ideal conditions of existence for a human world . . . to recognize, with me, the open door of every consciousness.
>
> *(ibid.)*

Idiotic child and pedagogies for decolonisation

In this chapter, the construction of Idiotic child has been shown to serve key socio-psychological functions whose practice needs to be contested as well as recognised. Drawing on but going beyond Mannoni's (1969/2003) paper, this feminist intersectional and postcolonial psychosocial analysis has indicated how generational, classed, gendered, and racialised attributions underlie claims to differential entitlements and inform the dynamics of exclusion. Both Fanon and Mannoni can be read as having some significant ideas to contribute to discussions of critical pedagogy and its role in and for antiracist educational practice. Although he avoided political discussion in favour of psychological processes, a chapter of Mannnoni's earlier text *Prospero and Caliban* (1950/1964) is significantly entitled 'What can be done?' (seemingly a mistranslated allusion to Lenin's 1902 pamphlet 'What is to be done?'). In this chapter Mannoni comments on the role of education in creating political conditions for change through making different ways of being possible, commenting: 'whatever one's favourite educational system, the most important thing to do is to save children from the neurotic reactions of the people round them' (168). Here Mannoni's account of children's amenability to influence points to the work that children do to process, rather than merely being subjected to, 'the neurotic reactions' of others.

Fanon, however, takes this line of argument further, ending his discussion of individual neurotic structures as 'simply the elaboration, the formation, the eruption within the ego, of conflictual clusters arising in part out of the environment and in part out of purely personal way in which the individual reacts to these influences' (*Black Skin*, 58). His account of these structures as framed through and by racialisation and colonisation thereby demands more than individual change: 'We shall see that another solution is possible. It implies a restructuring of the world' (*Black Skin*, 58). Central to Fanon's (as also Mannoni's) claims about the preconditions for that 'restructuring' is a move towards what educationalist William Pinar (2011) calls 'subjective reconstruction', 'for example, extricating oneself psychologically from interpellation by the colonial regime' (40), but, of course, as he points out, 'For Fanon, there could be no collective possibility without subjective and social reconstruction' (41). While theorists of decolonisation Tuck and Yang (2012) critique Freire on the basis that he abstracted oppression from material conditions and so rendered it an individual, mental state, I suggest that psychosocial theorists of colonisation, especially Fanon and even Mannoni in his 1969/2003 paper (discussed here), avoid such psychologisation by resolutely situating practices of racism and colonisation within relational and material contexts, while also insisting on their psychoaffective character (Oliver, 2004; Alessandrini, 2009).

The challenge, therefore, is to conceptualise decolonisation in similar terms. Tuck and Yang rightly caution against subscription to oversimplified notions of identity, highlighting how incommensurabilities inevitably structure relationships across diverse contexts, so rendering tenuous claims to identification as the basis for common action. Taking up this issue through what he calls a pedagogy of solidarity, Gaztambide-Fernández (2012) calls for a politics that emphasises interdependency, that does not ask for guarantees, and that understands provisionality of alliances as constitutive. Acknowledgement of such provisionality is of course what is precisely foreclosed by the paradoxical rigidity of orientation, or sentiment, but flexibility and mobility of object highlighted in Mannoni's essay: 'I know well, but all the same.' In line with this politics, my analysis here indicates some further necessary dimensions to solidarity, highlighting fantasised or scarcely conscious qualities, including feelings and assumptions that are socially embedded or normalised and so presumed. Such feelings include less 'pleasant' aspects of identification, including love, that also fuel attachment to racist and nationalist projects (Ahmed, 2004). Despite the (structural and psychic) power of such formations, the analysis here has aimed to highlight their provisional, geo-political character, mobilising the affective modalities of the 'pedagogy of failure' to open up possibilities of questioning and destabilising such formations.

Idiotic child as non-developmental anchor resisting social change

This attention to the role of the recourse to Idiotic child in securing the forms of belief that sustain racist discourse and practice invites both alternative formulations and contestations. I have also indicated how Idiotic child relies upon, intersects with, and performs those gendering, classed, and racialised relations (as well as – through a psychodynamic account – also necessarily involving affective dynamics). Mannoni's attention to the socially constructed but psychically determined function of the position of the child (as the repository for socially sanctioned myths or delusions) counters the dominant abstraction of the child/childhood from social relations. It also prompts further interrogation of sociocultural strategies of legitimation of gendered, classed, and racialised inequalities that this psychically determined position for children supports. Such analysis offers fruitful strategies to address what is at stake in 'protecting' children, thereby excluding them from social-political engagements that are belied by current inter-generational educational initiatives.

Other consequences should be noted. Idiotic child is not a developmental child, that is, it is not a child who transitions from this developmental stage to others, but rather a particular position designating a specific, albeit temporary, social status that is biographically transcended. Nevertheless, this status secures a social order structured around socially organised defences against constitutive lack and (corresponding) orientations to particular forms of socially structured enjoyment that are constellated around the abstraction and sentimentalisation of children. If all goes (normatively, developmentally) 'well', each unknowing/protected child is eventually – according to dominant pedagogical practices – permitted to know, to participate. This means that the developing subjects exit this status, but that the position (of Idiotic child) nevertheless remains for others. Indeed – as we have seen from Mannoni – it is necessary for others to occupy this. The cost of maintaining the illusion of children's 'innocence' is not only their exclusion from the socio-political domain but also precisely the constitution of its configuration as exclusionary in ways that prefigure other dynamics of oppression and injustice. Fanon, like other political theorists, needs to be read closely for the modes of temporality he mobilises as constitutive of his understanding of history and change (see, for example, Renault, 2011). As later chapters outline, his mobilisations of childhood traverse a wide repertoire but notably idiotic child, that is, the child separated from and (as we have seen) thereby securing the social order, is not one of them.

While this chapter has focused on how dominant cultural pedagogies of childhood support racist discourse, this is a specific – if urgent – example of a more general set of dynamics at play that this reading and application of Mannoni's analysis may explicate. Other applications could include the seemingly disproportionate anxiety often attending children's exposure (whether through curricular activities or everyday conversation) to discussion of non-normative sexualities, often supposedly warranted on the basis of avoiding confusing or worrying children. An indicative example would be the moment in Kip Jones's (2012) film *Rufus Stone* (directed by Josh Appignanesi), a research-based fictive reality story based on actual accounts of older gay and lesbian people growing up in rural Britain, when the 'outing' of the two male friends as (former or possibly current) lovers is accompanied by persecutory verbal and physical harassment with the chorus (principally from older women) of 'We have grandchildren!', as if the mere rhetorical existence of such children constituted the men as not only a direct but also an epistemological threat so precipitating the film's final tragic conclusion (Jones, & Appignanesi, 2012).

We may further note how reports of child abuse and sexual exploitation in the UK over-emphasise racialisation issues over class and gender ones, as indicated in the 2017 Birmingham prosecutions of a paedophile ring reported as composed of Pakistani men, rather than British Asian men – who were thereby rhetorically deprived of their native British status and racialised as 'other'. This is unlike the ongoing and interminably slow investigation of organised sexual abuse of boys perpetrated by men in the UK Parliament that is neither racialised nor even barely discussed (Seymour, 2017). Moreover, as Nizami (2017) notes, the response of the British state to this crisis around child sexual exploitation has been to not only consolidate its racialisation but also to import gendered, familial, and nationalist assimilationist and securitisation agendas (see also Shepherd, 2008) to propose that Asian women in Britain are not only responsible for the protection of their children but also that learning English will help them do this.

Other examples of what happens in the name of protecting children include the arguments made not to discuss climate change and sustainability challenges in school because this is claimed to frighten children (notwithstanding how children lead the way in demanding action on such questions, Brown and Lock, 2018). These examples highlight adult investments in securing a place of ignorance for children and young people such that the gambit of family and societal 'secrets' are secured and maintained. Moreover, this is part of the dynamic structuring debates about how best to 'protect' children from abuse, since a powerful argument has been that educating children is in some sense installing knowledge they should not know (Kitzinger, 1988). Yet not doing so renders children vulnerable because knowledge about abuse is with-held from them, and so rendered 'secret' (Warner, 2009).

Idiotic child, 'actional' pedagogies, and child as method

Idiotic child, then, works intergenerationally and bi-directionally, since this rendering of and for child will be shown to maintain not only their but also others' stupification within the adult social contract. That is, maintaining a docile and contained position for child helps to make adults similarly docile, and so less able to question received 'truths', too. These 'truths' include configurations of and positionings around class and gender, as well as those of generation and racialisation already topicalised, so also instituting an inter-sectional analysis that complements and reworks Fanon's (and Mannoni's) accounts. Particular, contingent, but widely subscribed to and so normal-ised, pedagogical orientations towards children emerge as central to key precepts that, through their circumstances of biographical construction, rely on buried or disavowed experiences that thereby render those assumptions unavailable for rational argument or critical interrogation. By such means, putting Idiotic child in question also helps expose key ideological dynamics underlying racism.

This treatment of Idiotic child works to exemplify child as method by showing how attending to the narration or positioning elaborated for child not only illuminates the power relations governing adult–child relations but also how these structure – in covert as well as overt ways – other discourses and practices of power and inequality. To unpick these covert processes the psychodynamic relations constituting the stereotype were discussed, such that the stereotype emerged as an unstable mode of knowing that fixes and abstracts what it describes in ways that the knower typically refuses to acknowledge. Idiotic child, then, contributes to critical social pedagogies that challenge presumed generational (adult–child) orders. Exemplifying child as method, this chapter's narrative has circled around the status of the child, moving from the problematic of racist discourse, to the ways the positioning of the child/children is implicated in this, as Idiotic child, exploring further conceptual-political consequences, before returning with correspondingly renewed resources to the question of adult–child relations and critical pedagogies.

As anti-racist pedagogy, then, Idiotic child highlights the defensive status of foreclosed knowledge, exposing what drives the 'passion for ignorance' that Lacan (2006a) identified (alongside the two other passions: for work and for love). Claims to faulty knowledge and belief cannot simply be 'corrected' but require a changed constellation of relationships around the definition of self and other that function outside conscious access or rational evaluation. In other words, we cannot mobilise 'reality' to challenge racist stereotypes, because (according to Mannoni) that reality has already been changed through the disavowal of the refuted knowledge. Rather, there must be a refusal of the positions that sustain these inequalities. Perhaps this is where we can engage with Hook's analysis of the forms of 'negation' that must inform antiracist strategies: 'we are left with a paradox in which the very inability to engage difference is what compounds it, what reverberates and extends its effects, reifying absolute racial categories in a vicious circle of racism and disavowal' (Hook, 2012: 201).

Implications arising from this chapter are as follows: While Idiotic child focuses primarily on the constitutive dynamics of others around children, the subjectivities of children are correspondingly polarised according to the boundary of social inclusion or exclusion identified earlier. This boundary is, as we have seen, formulated around the defensive dynamics preserving a nationalist, exclusionary, and so racist, social imaginary. Mannoni, it has emerged, attempted (rather inadequately) to resolve this difficulty by considering children as having been 'objectively deceived', but beyond this did not consider further the extent of children's complicities in this, which (as we have seen) leaves open the pedagogical question of how to engage the seemingly racist children of 'Brexit Street', as well as the adults. As far as the adults are concerned, we have seen how rational, economic interests neither account for, nor quite eradicate, the needs fulfilled by these defences. An antiracist approach arising from this analysis would address the ideological structuring of such dynamics to invite a different relationship to the totems and fetishes associated with nationalism, here in the form of its links with anti-immigrant racism as the index of social belonging. I consider below further interweavings of class and racialised dynamics discernible from 'Brexit Street'. For now, let us note one key question arising from this chapter: are the 'Brexit Street' children mini-adults who by their racist actions enact their inclusion within what, according to this chapter's analysis, we may now see as the racist social contract, or are there other ways of addressing them, and their parents?

'Brexit Street' pedagogies

Mobilised in the disjunction between the subject of enunciation (the documentary archive assembled by the reporter and received by us, the audience) and the subject of the statement (the Brexit Streeters), is a narrative that is at least as much about class as it is about the production of racism. Revisiting 'Brexit Street' through this analytical frame, other angles become available.

British listeners to Radio 4 only have to make a short semantic link to hear 'Brexit Street' through the genre of recent television series such as 'Benefit Street', whose assonance with 'benefit cheats' discloses everything about the pathologisation of the poor. Alongside global shifts to a neoliberal active citizenship approach to welfare, successive British governments have, in the name of 'austerity', cut welfare services and visited on the poor both the economic and moral responsibility for the worldwide international banking crisis of 2008. 'Scrounger-phobia' has been documented as circulating among the working poor to divisively undermine solidarity and add to the stigma and structural measures in place to prevent people accessing welfare services (Shildrick, & MacDonald, 2013). At play, at one step removed, then, 'Brexit Street' is a middle-class narrative about the poor (for Radio 4 engages and reflects British middle-class audiences).

So, as well as presenting racist sentiment and arguments as only associated with working-class, deprived communities there is another narrative at play. This is close enough to be present but deniable – yet another 'I know well, but all the same': This time it is 'we know the poor are not responsible for their "worklessness"' (the current policy term for being unemployed, itself an insidious psychologisation), 'but anyway . . .'. It takes merely a single linguistic reversal to turn the descriptors 'unemployed carpet layer' (Mark), 'caring for children' (Carol), 'off work with depression' (Peter) into 'benefit claimant' or (in the case of the landscape gardener, Wayne, at best 'semi-employed'), and the scene shifts dramatically.

Other reflections immediately become available, including the work done by the use of only first names to designate these protagonists. Surely this over-familiarity could be heard as betraying a stance of both (classed) condescension and presumed knowledge and understanding, structured within the journalistic device of summing up an entire person in a single phrase attribution of the form: gendered name, (sometimes) age, plus (former) occupation. As a contrast, Ken Loach's (2016) film *I, Daniel Blake* identifies its key protagonist with his full name, which in the course of its narrative is literally written large across the wall of the Job Centre as a final exasperated protest against the desubjectifying and de-humanising, indeed the structurally exclusionary, bureaucracy involved in accessing welfare support. It is a call for the restoration of dignity, of recognition as a fully human being.

Moreover, the 'Brexit Street' resident names are marked as English, rather than nationally or marked by indicators of cultural difference or minoritisation (how would it be different if a Sayid or Mohammed or Pavel had said those things, albeit that such have indeed been reported?). Already, then, whiteness is marked through class, and set against the racialised/ politically excluded other. Carol is reported as volunteering in a food bank (culturally marked as organised by the church). Such food banks are now widespread across the UK (as also across Europe) as an inadequate response to the mounting difficulties for poor people – in the context of vicious welfare cuts – to have enough even to eat. This clearly signifies both a community under economic pressure, and one that is making efforts to support its members. While how the lines of inclusion and exclusion for that support are drawn is clearly a key problem, this should not obscure others highlighting real struggle and need.

This, then, is the problematic of the ideological structuring of anti-immigrant racism as primarily or only a feature of poor, deprived communities (deprived not only of work but also support and resources, such that the very designation itself occludes key policy and political dynamics), which in the name of taking the concerns arising from those deprived conditions 'seriously' is mobilised in party political discourse through needing to 'pander to racism'. Could we not hear Carol's complaint as a displaced version of 'why should we have to pay back . . . why should we have to give . . .'? That is, as a recrimination of the oppression of the poor who pay for the mistakes of the rich. Rather than white privilege, then, we may hear this as a form of what Sullivan (2017) calls white priority, the complaint of poor white people to also have their needs attended to.

And then there is the 'they' who 'come' and who 'take take' (the repetition conveying emphasis, and contrasted with the demand to 'give') supposedly qualifying the 'immigrants'. 'They' remain even less subjectified. They are also completely nameless, known only through a designation of exclusion, of non-entitlement, and – even worse – of attributed misplaced or even fraudulent access to support and resources that is precisely the discourse to which the British poor are subjected. Are such tropes not another version of the stereotype, with its dual dynamic of essentialisation and reification? If so, what pedagogical consequences follow for the (re)building of solidarity across these constituencies depicted as divided by dominant ideology?

At least three pedagogies are depicted within the 'Brexit Street' scenes, and another in its narration. There is Peter's pedagogy, that of the 'stay at home', and so present and responsible, dad (the 'good father' of social policy, with its continual anxieties about absent working-class fathers reneging on their financial and moral responsibilities, Scourfield, & Drakeford, 2002). He treats his children *as* children (with chocolate biscuit treats, that he unwraps for them), within an intimated parental strategy of appropriate regulatory framing applied within a controlled, interior domestic space. Significantly, the new arrivals, the migrants, are figured by him as neighbours rather than foreigners, mobilising an emotional geography that positions them as proximal to, rather than outside, the home/community space. In terms of the pedagogical narrative of the reporter, Peter's is the 'best' or morally most worthy position. Then there is Carol, whose gendered ethic of care extends beyond her own immediate family to the food bank, but, in the name of such care, she seeks to impose boundaries on it by limiting who is entitled to access it. In this, we may add, she follows dominant social welfare policy, but the immediacy of the consequences identified makes her appear rigid and even unreasonable or cruel. Mark, in his account of the 'ignorant' children, appears aligned with the pedagogical stance of the narrator to criticise the parents who allow or encourage the children to harass the migrants, and whose 'brainwashing' of their children positions them – in the moral classed (and racialised) lexicon of developmental psychology – as authoritarian rather than appropriately sensitive and democratic (Walkerdine, & Lucey, 1989). We are close to the right-wing trope of 'feral children' mobilised to discuss the 2011 'riots' arising from British urban disaffection (Allen, & Taylor, 2012; De Benedictis, 2012). These parents are implied to be neglectful of their responsibilities, the 'bad' working-class parents, and this moral judgement extends somewhat also to Mark who – in his absence of engagement – seems to shrug and consider there is nothing he can do.

Finally, but only indirectly, the analytic gaze falls upon us – the listening public – exposing the lines of interpellation and presumptions by which we are characterised. Under critical scrutiny, every term of 'I know well, but all the same' becomes questionable. If the trope exists precisely to indicate the anxiety of uncertainty about the status of knowledge, the (ideological) constitution and specification of the 'I', the subject, the 'but all the same' seeks to shore up that uncertainty and indeed indicates something about the need that drives the attachment to certainty. The 'but' is perhaps a space of hesitation or moment of deferral, an acknowledgement of (at least potential) contradiction. How then to proceed if in fact what we know is very unclear, including what and who we are? Fanon's commitment to confronting that question in practical and politically meaningful ways is what makes his contribution so enduring. His refusal of the ways past certainties, including the legacies of oppressions that fix and so 'distort' (to use one of his terms) subjectivity, put both knower and known into question. Yet, instead, for Fanon, 'but all the same' perhaps translates into something more like 'as I am alive (I exist), I have to act'. That is, as a call to action, to engage with others and forge new subjective and political relationships.

Hopi children revisited: after Idiotic child

I return to some of these considerations in Chapter 5. But before leaving this chapter we need to consider a different 'child' inhabiting Mannoni's essay, albeit present only in subjugated form. As noted earlier, Mannoni's analysis is founded on the example of an experience of Hopi cultural practice that he sees as culturally authentic (since arising from a 'traditional' society) and therefore prototypical. In so doing, he is, of course, subscribing to a long-standing colonial anthropological trope. Yet Mannoni's prototypical example was drawn from the autobiography of Don C. Talayesva (1890–1985), the titular 'Sun Chief'. However, Talayesva's story of deception and enlightenment through initiation arises in the context of describing how, as a child, he transitioned between cultures as a Hopi in early twentieth-century United States (Talayevsa, 2013). A significant medium of and for the cultural tensions he both experienced and mediated was through education. From the age of 10 Talayesva went to white government schools, thus highlighting one of the key complicities of education within colonial-developmental practices. Schooling has long played a key role in the project of transforming indigenous populations via changing the subjectivities of children, so estranging them from their native languages and culture – hence giving rise to their description as 'stolen children' (Jacobs, 2006) or 'stolen generations' (Fournier, & Crey, 1997).

In *Sun Chief,* Talayesva narrates his eventual return to his community (in Hopi-land), and to its culture and religious practices. In the Foreword to the second edition, Matthew Sakiestewa Gilbert, whose grandfather attended school with Talayesva, criticises Robert Hine's Foreword to the first edition for its emphasis on cultural conflict and prefers to see Talayesva as forging his own personal blend of Hopi culture with and through his engagement with American culture. In fact, the episode that forms the focus of Mannoni's analysis occurs as a relatively minor incident comprising less than a single page (79–80) of a very long text that includes much more obviously traumatic material (including losing almost all vision in one eye from a childhood accident at the hands of his brother, and having near death experiences when very ill at school). At any rate, rather than as ethnographic example (of culturally authentic practice) anchoring Mannoni's account, then, we could read this incident from Talayesva rather differently. It could be understood as a redemptive (gendered) relational narrative of cultural pressure and oppression (sometimes described as genocidal, and certainly indicative of the barbarism of the civilisational process, Krieken, 1999), of both spatial and psychological dislocation produced through settler colonialist practices, in this case in the US. Quite why and how Mannoni came to know of Talayevsa's text, or how it acquired this iconic status (as he claims, for the French public), remains unknown, although Saskiestewa Gilbert (2013: ix) claims that 'the Hopi were among the most researched indigenous peoples in the Americas'.

Clearly a postcolonial reading of this text is available that would re-interpret the status Mannoni accords it instead in terms of Talayevsa's narration of the alienation from his family and community of origin produced through colonial education, read retrospectively from his account of returning as an adult to resume his place as Chief. That an entirely different, more socio-politically as well as psychoanalytically situated, reading is possible – of adults securing the illusion of the Katcinas as gods as a way of expressing pressures on familial efforts to retain and sustain cultural practices in the context of colonisation – does not, however, invalidate my analysis of Mannoni's use of this text. Rather, it vindicates this reading of Mannoni's essay through Fanon's pedagogy of 'failure'. (Equivalently, critical readings could be made in relation to other examples that Mannoni analyses in this essay.) Hence, we end Mannoni's narrative framing of Idiotic child with Talayesva's story, as a trace of other untold stories, including those of the unnamed 'immigrants' in 'Brexit Street', to bring us to Chapter 3.

3

TRAUMATOGENIC CHILD

'there is a retaining-wall relation between language and group.'
(Fanon, Black Skin*: 29)*

This chapter addresses what is undoubtedly the most famous depiction of childhood associated with Fanon's writings: the child who names him as 'Black' in *Black Skin, White Masks (Black Skin)* (Fanon, 1952/1970) – that is Traumatogenic child. It is this encounter that precipitates Fanon's account of the existential chaos produced by racialisation. Presented as an experiential, and therefore biographically specific, account, it is also read as a general, even logical (according to the prevailing racist order) depiction of the vilified and abject(ed) position accorded those excised from social norms. As is well known, this act of racialisation is described as having traumatic, irreversible impacts including not only rendering Fanon/the now black(ened) person separate from the white world and white people but also instituting an alienation that is bodily as well as psychic. It is on the basis of this iconic scene – perhaps the primal scene of racialisation, echoing accounts by other black authors writing at that time, including James Baldwin's (1955) *Notes of a Native Son*, Richard Ellison's (1953) *Invisible Man* but also later accounts such as Audre Lorde's (1982) biomythology *Zami* – that the racialised other is produced alongside the imposition of a fixed relationship with sets of traditions and cultures and secure a limited and dangerous essentialisation of qualities that Fanon succinctly parodies as being 'battered down by tom-toms, cannibalism, intellectual deficiency, fetishism, racial defects, slave ships' (*Black Skin*: 79). As Nancy Fraser (2017: 162) puts it: 'This was Fanon's great insight: that racialization imprisons people of color in their bodies; "race" itself is a form of bodily harm.'

This chapter revisits this account, discussing both how Fanon narrates this and also what commentators have made of this. Attention to selective character of its representation, both of the scene and the protagonists involved, is used to further analysis of the status of this child within this key event (or sequence of events). Far from diminishing the significance of this moment, this reading instead enriches it by attending to other intersecting classed, gendered, and sexed dynamics and specific geohistorical conditions, while also identifying moments of potentially fruitful underspecification.

While most commentators either fail to attend to the positon of child elaborated, or else either overlook this in favour of, or even elide the child with, other parties present at the scene (notably the child's mother), as part of the project of child as method the models of child subjectivity or agency made available in (readings of) this event, whether allowed for or proscribed, are considered. If 'child' speaks the vital 'truth' that others circumperambulate, as a kind of malign version of the Emperor's New Clothes story, what clues are offered as to intentionality or complicity? Is child here an effect of ideology, a conveyer of it, or a commentator upon it? Key ambiguities are identified that, in both Fanon's account and the various receptions of it, can be read also as reflecting prevailing models of social relations. These include not only the inscription of models of childhood within social relations, but also how these models institute and rely upon others, in particular gendered and classed relations, in ways that have key implications for social and political theory, as also for pedagogical possibilities.

Situating this reading methodologically

If Chapter 2 made the case for a psychoanalytic engagement in the service of engaging with Fanon's psychoaffective ideas, in terms of methodological and analytical frameworks mobilised for the analysis in this chapter, further philosophical discussions of recognition and misrecognition are revisited that require setting Fanon alongside other philosophers of the social, notably Althusser and Foucault. Building on discussions begun in Chapter 2, this involves further engagement with psychoanalytic accounts of the formation of subjectivity – although now focusing on the constitutive affective impacts of the encounter with child, rather than (as discussed in Chapter 2) on those sustained by creating that position for (the thereby idiotised, or rendered

Idiotic and separated) child. As this chapter's title suggests, this includes reviewing discussions of the notion of trauma, specifically (given the concern here with the ways child is inflected by and so reflects) models of temporality. Alongside this, we will also address the logical role that temporality plays within models of subject formation, including how the question of timing, or sequencing of the narrative, is important to understanding the status of Traumatogenic child within Fanon's broader arguments.

Given the iconic status of this version of child within Fanonian studies, a prime focus of analysis is how it appears within this field. Since virtually no account of Fanon fails to mention it, I have had to be selective in my focus here. Of particular relevance in informing the discussion below are feminist engagements that focus on the gendered characteristics of the scene, alongside those that read the depiction of racialisation intersectionally also through and with classed dynamics. Childhood studies of course imports a specific attention to the meanings accorded the intergenerational relations at play, as well as, together with queer theory, bringing conceptual nuance to the claims of capacity or possibility mobilised alongside those attending temporality.

This chapter therefore revisits Fanon's relationship with psychoanalysis that was begun in Chapter 2, here specifically with Lacanian psychoanalysis, via a close reading of his rhetorics of childhood – primarily as mobilised by the 'Look, a Negro!' scenario from *Black Skin*. Specifically, as a key contribution to child as method, this chapter explores the depiction of child with which Fanon is primarily associated, reviewing its various interpretations, including the perhaps surprising lack of analysis of his model of childhood. Areas of ambiguity are shown to qualify not only the processes of racialisation experienced by Fanon as a prototypical (but specific kind of) black subject, but also the ontological claims accorded child in this scenario. After reviewing the reception of Fanon in relation to this specific focus, I discuss Fanon's use of the ideas of the French psychoanalyst Jacques Lacan, in *Black Skin,* juxtaposing this with Lacan's own account of the constitution of individual subjectivities via the social field (in his 'Logical time' sophism), in which children also figure. This is then applied to the implied spatio-temporal field of Fanon's 'Look, a Negro!' scene to highlight some instabilities, or vacillations. Other receptions of this scene are read critically, and intersectionally, while further examples from Fanon's texts are considered, both to evaluate the adequacy of their account and the assumptions about sex/gender, class, and age (as well as racialisation) set in play. These are used to reconsider how Fanon's child(ren) figure in his model, ending by suggesting that the ambiguities and underdeterminations may in fact be political strengths.

Trauma and traumatogenesis

It is noting at the outset that Fanon's invocation of 'traumatogenic child', the scene evoking the felt experience of racialisation and de-humanisation, comes precisely after a chapter where he has not only dispensed with Mannoni's 'so-called dependency complex of colonized people' but also where he claims that

> it does seem to me that M. Mannoni has not tried to feel himself into the despair of the man of colour confronting the white man. In his work I have made it a point to convey the misery of the black man. Physically and affectively. I have not wished to be objective. Besides, that would be dishonest: It is not possible for me to be objective.
>
> (Black Skin: *61*).

He goes on, of course, in that chapter to show Mannoni's 'dishonesty' by unravelling his arguments, while here in Chapter 5, he presents this affective and physical 'misery'.

The notion of trauma evokes rupture, arrest, and wound. It is counter-developmental, in the sense that it is portrayed as the result of development going awry. Within a psychoanalytic model some trauma is (logically and developmentally) inevitable and necessary (such as that attending the Oedipal moment of the entry into language). This is the trauma of separation from the (m)other to join the social, or in Lacanian terms a move from the Imaginary to the Symbolic and so moving beyond a dyadic relationship to the group. The condition of becoming social is that surrender of the illusion of wholeness that institutes a sense of lack, of something missing, at the core of the subject (psychanalytically speaking, this is 'castration'). Yet what is traumatising can only be known retrospectively, via the dynamic that Freud named *Nachträglichkeit*, or deferred action. Thus, it takes two traumas to make a trauma, since the later trauma reactivates and so brings into the present the impact of the earlier one. The question of which trauma is at play, then, that is, the relationships between these successive but retroactively encountered traumas, and who or what does the traumatising, is very much the focus of this chapter.

Fanon's account of this traumatic encounter, of this encounter as traumatic, thereby not only offers a diagnosis of the structure of racialisation but also how this diagnoses other constitutive power dynamics at play. This is a traumatogenic statement of the problem, presented without the redemptive reassurance of a 'cure'. Traumatogenic child, then, is shown to work as a form of child as method by securing a particular model of time and development, in which the status of child poses specific as well as general problems. What is topicalised, however, is the meaning and effect of the traumatogenic encounter, that is, the trauma, rather than the position of the traumatiser. That is, we come now to attend to the position of the unnamed migrants as figured within the 'Brexit Street' text discussed in Chapter 2. We are presented with an account of the rupture of the subject, catapulted out of history into the timelessness or fixed time of trauma, a (psychoanalytically informed) understanding that has political as well as personal consequences. For Fanon, the recovery of subjectivity, of 'actionality', is equivalent to turning away from this subjective rupture to forging a changed relationship with past history – that is, psychoanalytically speaking, an active relationship that does not merely repeat the patterns of the past but consciously reflects upon these to change these. In this chapter I attend to instabilities and ambiguities, and the interpretive possibilities these afford, within Fanon's account of this encounter with Traumatogenic child whose significance, I suggest, has not yet attracted sufficient attention.

Fanon's Traumatogenic child

Translation has already featured as a topic in Chapter 1, as indicating socio-political aspects of the reception and circulation of Fanon's writings. Here some specific textual questions set in play by Fanon's account of the encounter with (what I am calling) Traumatogenic child should be noted. This scene occurs in Chapter 5 of *Black Skin* where *'L'experience vécue du Noir'*, in the first English translation, was rendered 'The Fact of Blackness' but commentators claim that this is better translated – in line with Fanon's phenomenological approach – as 'The lived experience of being black' (see Desai, 2014: 68). Indeed, Macey (2010; 2012) claims that there are many inaccuracies within Charles Markmann's first translation of the English edition, which he also argues (Macey, 2012) have contributed to the Americanised readings of Fanon and consequent occlusion of both the fact of, and specific features arising from, his Martinican background and political activism in the Algerian revolutionary context.

All versions of the text, however, convey his powerful responses to a child taking fright at the sight of Fanon, as a black man, which precipitates a traumatic installation of a racialised identity. I use Macey's (2012, 164) translation, for reasons outlined above (see also Macey, 2010). Macey also discusses how the French word *'négre'* is not equivalent to the English 'negro', and is (even) more insulting. Indeed, the chapter opens with the shocking exclamation: 'Dirty nigger!' Or simply, 'Look, a Negro!' (77).

This unattributed generalised statement, instigating his 'object status' (ibid.) comes to be specified two pages later within a more particular relational configuration. The famous passage goes like this:

> 'Look, a Negro!' It was an external impetus that flicked me in passing. I smiled slightly.
>
> 'Look, a Negro!' It was true. I laughed.
>
> 'Look, a Negro!' The circle was gradually getting smaller. I laughed openly.
>
> 'Mama, see the Negro! I'm frightened!' Frightened! Frightened! Now they were beginning to be frightened of me. I wanted to laugh till I burst, but that had become impossible.
>
> . . .
>
> Having come under attack at several points, the corporeal scheme collapsed giving way to an epidermal racial schema.
>
> *(79)*

Central to this account is Fanon's notion of 'epidermalization', that is, the way the skin, including skin colour, and the body become signifiers of alienation from self: 'Below the corporeal scheme I had sketched a historico-racial schema' (78). Fanon here draws on a Freudian notion of neurosis but develops this to show how a socially produced event instigates a narcissistic trauma and the interiorisation of inferiority. Or rather, as Oliver (2004, 51) puts it: 'the colonized do not internalize but rather epidermalize racist ideology. The values of racist imperialism enter the colonized through the skin.' The significance accorded the visual register, as well as the body, is also important, as discussed later in this chapter in relation to Fanon's use of Lacan's notion of the 'mirror phase' and the various forms and directions of 'looking' set in play.

As a depiction of traumatisation, Fanon presents its effects as cataclysmic, writing of dislocation, depersonalisation, and alienation: 'I took myself off from my own presence, far indeed, and made myself an object' (79). It is an experience of 'amputation, an excision, a haemorrhage that spattered my whole body with black blood' (ibid.). It is pivotal as instigating a confrontation with an image of himself that fundamentally distorts the relationship with his physical and psychological being, and his collective as well as individual identifications. This account has widespread resonances, across cultural and geographical arenas, describing the psychological impacts of racism (Oliver, 2004, 2005; Macey, 2010; Hook, 2012). Indeed, other significant black figures were also 'caught up in the "Look, a Negro" scenario' (Macey, 2012: 165). These include the Barbadian poet George Lamming, Léopold Sédar Senghor (future president of Senegal), W. E. B. Du Bois (founder of the US National Association for the Advancement of Colored Peoples) and African-American feminist theorist bell hooks, while the scenario itself bears a striking resemblance to incidents depicted in Ralph Ellison's (1953) US-based novel *Invisible Man*.

The 'Look, a Negro!' scene invites analysis of both the forms and stages of racial (mis)identification set in play. This includes the complex 'both–and' position of being subjected to a(n abjected) universalised and transhistorical black experience, but also as divorced from it – as the exoticised and discretionary *exception* to the racist rule: 'When people like me they tell me it is in spite of my colour. When they dislike me, they point out that it is not because of my colour. Either way I am locked into the infernal circle' (*Black Skin*: 82–3). (This is an aspect of the flexibility and rigidity I described in Chapter Two as racism's tolerance.)

General or particular interpellations: space and class

Whether or not this event really happened (Macey, 2012: 165, calls it 'the imaginary or recollected scene' while Bergner (1995) cautions against an overly autobiographical reading of Fanon's account), as an attempt to frame Fanon as a psychoanalytic theorist, it is often called a 'primal scene' (Bhabha, 1993). That is, it is a logical or epistemological moment in the violent imposition and constitution of a racialised subjectivity: a psychodramatic prototype conveying the emotional impact and consequences of such treatment, and so brings together 'an analysis of a given social-psychological situation and an affective articulation of that same situation' (Hage, 2010: 113).

Louis Althusser's account of how the subject is hailed or called into being through by the other, that is, how identifications are forged and sedimented in the ideological production and structuring of subjectivity draws on Lacan's theory of misrecognition. That is, recognition is always misrecognition, as the cost of accessing the symbolic order (the social) requires surrendering the ideal/imaginary relationship where one (mistakenly believes one) is known and understood (this is Lacan's Imaginary). Going beyond that Lacanian frame, Hage (2010) names the outcome of this vacillation 'mis-interpellation', a dynamic to which he regards elite racialised subjects as being particularly sensitive (and Fanon, the medical student in France, was certainly part of a middle-class elite): Fanon, he suggests, exemplifies 'cosmopolitan people with high capital who seem to be far more exclusively haunted by the desire for universality at the expense of particularity' (Hage, 2010: 118).

There is a lack of clarity over the status of this scene suggested by shifts of setting, as also narrated by commentators. Macey sets the scene in a park, while Hage's (2010), Hook's (2012), and Yancy's (2017) accounts mark the scene as in a train. Fanon's text in fact mentions both contexts, perhaps to suggest that the event or encounter is a composite of many insulting scenarios. Nevertheless, the specificity of arenas cited should be noted in terms of the classing of public space: these are ordinary, rather than privileged, spaces; ordinary encounters with ordinary people in modern urban contexts. Hage discusses wider political consequences of this (as he points out, classed as well as racialised) particularity that appeals to the universal, which sits alongside wider evaluations of Fanon's radical humanism (Hallward, 2011; Gilroy, 2010). He argues that Fanon

> exhibits not just a willingness to locate himself in the universal but a psychological fixation with that universal. Such an affective state cannot be understood simply in terms of class aspirations . . . it is also the product of a particular subjectivity grounded in a specific form of racialization that comes with this cosmopolitan fixation with the universal. It makes one paradoxically both fixated on, and fixated on transcending, the racializing force one is subjected to.
>
> *(Hage, 2010: 119)*

Important as such philosophical debates are, especially in highlighting what is at stake in the specificity of Fanon's scene (which, as we will see, extends to its relational characteristics), my focus here, however, is on how the question of vacillation, 'muddled perspectivism' (Hage, 2010: 119), or indeterminacy *qualifies the child* in Fanon's writings, as much as Fanon himself.

(Dis)appearing 'child' in (receptions of) Fanon

Notwithstanding its pivotal significance for Fanon's theory of subjectivity, the role accorded the child in this scene also remains unclear. Indeed, the word 'child' fails to appear in the Index of *Black Skin*, or in Macey's (2012) biography, or Silverman's (2005) collection. (Translations of Fanon's *Wretched* and *Dying Colonialism* that I have consulted do not have an Index.) Further, the word 'child' does not appear in the index of key collections that reprint and discuss this iconic encounter (for example, Evans and Hall, 1999). Most focus on the whiteness of the woman and the child, and the gendered, and certainly sexed, relationship between the mother and the hypersexualised black man.

Typically, as Lebeau (2005) comments in a rare treatment that does focus on the position of the child (albeit with problems I discuss below), accounts have interpreted the scene in general terms: 'Negrophobia as a symptom of sexualised anxiety, as sign of the hallucinatory sexual presence of black men in a phobic imaginary' (133). This strand of argument is clearly present elsewhere in *Black Skin*, meriting also the discussion of Fanon's sexism, heterosexism, and homophobia (Vergès, 1996), including his claims in the same book that white women fantasise about being raped by a black man, and that black women desire to sleep with white men (see also Bergner, 1995, 1999). The many interpretations of this include attention to specific impacts of Fanon's background and experience (Vergès, 1997). But what of portraying all this as instigated or precipitated by a child?

Indeed, Chow (1999) briefly considers another construction of the child offered by Fanon, that of the white girl whose erotic desires in becoming a woman (to be hurt) are the subject of his speculations. Chow's argument, addressing the model of collectivity this presumes, is pertinent to my topic here since I am tracing a somewhat equivalent argument in relation to child. However, Fanon's rather conventional psychosexual theorising at this point – although significant in many ways – elides the girl into the woman within a developmentalist reading that makes its mode of (inauthentic) psychoanalytic theorising of less interest to the other arguments being developed here.

Fanon's ambiguous claims to and for Traumatogenic child

For all its interpretive problems, Fanon's account offers an unconventional set of resources to interpret the figure of child and its role in models of both development and decolonisation. By reversing the now globalised model of childhood as innocent and authentic (Boyden, 1990; Steedman, 1995), through its cultural recapitulations of the exclusions and oppressions of the history of Western modernity (Levander, 2006; Taylor, 2013; Rollo, 2018; Meiners, 2016), Fanon emphasises the extent and complicity of European culture with racism.

Fanon's child in this scene is not the ideal-typical subject of narrative identification but rather the index or representative of pre-constituted racist/colonising culture that instigates psychic 'amputation', that is, the agent of colonising violence. The child (figured by Freud, 1914, as 'His Majesty the Baby', to characterise primary narcissism) confirms the ideological order on which imperialism is built. Lebeau (2005: 131) puts it (in her object relations psychoanalytic reading) as the child dealing with its existential fears through subscription to a racist symbolic order: 'Slavery, lynching, segregation: with a child's looking and pointing.' But in Fanon's account, as the repetition of his racialised attribution and its associations intensifies with the escalating fear of the child, so, too, does the child become increasingly qualified: first, as a 'boy', and then as 'the little boy', and then as 'the handsome little boy', and finally as 'the little white boy' who 'throws himself into his mother's arms' out of fear of being eaten (*Black Skin*: 81). I return to this sequence of attributions, qualifications, or (mis)recognitions later. But first some clarifications.

A closer reading: intersectional specificities

Returning to the question of interpellation, Pierre Macherey (2012) reads Fanon against Althusser via their relationship with psychoanalysis, and more indirectly also both in relation to Foucault. Foucault was, of course, suspicious of the notion of ideology but Macherey links Fanon's concern with what – after, for example, group analytic perspectives (Hopper, 2003) – may be described as (socially) unconscious or collective with Foucault's preoccupation with the constitutive powers of the norm. Acknowledging that both theorists address the question of what happens when the subject is hailed, Macherey argues that the 'hey you there!' of Althusser's (1971) formulation, and Fanon's 'Look, a Negro!' converge but also differ in significant ways. In common is a level of determination, that is, the *turning around* to assume a subject position – to become subjectivised. As Macherey (2012: 13) highlights: 'subjects are people who have turned around in response to the call to become what has been projected at them; the constitution of the subject is a matter of turning around.' He argues that Althusser's formulation of this paradigm from a religious context (of God calling Moses) invites a spurious abstraction and universalisation (presuming that all subjects are hailed in the same way). By contrast, Macherey proposes that Fanon's account, from the field of colonisation, highlights the 'there' – the field of spatio-historical material and interpersonal relations that structures what kind of subject is identified, and identified with: 'one is never only hailed/recognised as only a subject, but as a subject in a situation, in a colonial or imperial situation' (Macherey, 2012: 18).

So, let us consider in more detail the situation of Fanon's traumatogenic hailing. '"Look, a Negro!"' is uttered by a child to his mother, where the subject (the 'Negro') is spoken about, rather than to, but thereby qualified and so implicated. From this a subject position is created (as 'Negro/ black') via a process that is outside and beyond the intersubjective – that is, beyond a place of relationship. This place beyond the intersubjective is what marks Fanon's departure from a phenomenological frame in two directions: towards psychoanalysis and politics. This invites the question: who is the subject of traumatogenesis? Significantly, Macherey portrays the child as a social cypher, ventriloquised by her or his parents. Or even as the more generalised voice of a hostile society or culture:

It is an anonymous voice, which uses the body it possesses as a resonator, rendering in vain the attempt to assign responsibility to anyone in
particular: one may be tempted to say, in a language that differs from
Fanon's, that it is the voice of ideology itself that conveys the thoughts
and words to be expressed.

(Macherey, 2012: 17)

The descriptor 'resonator' is interesting for its focus on relaying prior impulses,
rather than specifying origins. In group analysis, an analytical model of group
processes that is committed to a model of the social in the psyche (Brown, &
Zinkin, 1994), resonance is the group equivalent of the individual dynamic
of identification, in the same way that free-floating discussion is the group
equivalent of free association in individual psychoanalysis (Foulkes, 1975).
However, group analytic investigations of resonance would always also
include attention to the specific nuances contributed by and interpreted by
the specific individuals in the relationships.

Thus, the key features set in play by Fanon are the body (or corporeal
scheme) and abjection/phobia produced by the installation of raced subjectivity. These rely on and derive from material co-ordinates of a particular
social field, alongside corresponding(ly ideological) fantasies with which the
body is invested – or, in Oliver's (2005) suggestive analysis, secreted. Yet
the fact that this is all generated by the encounter with a child has not been
sufficiently considered.

Lookings: intergenerational and gendered elisions

A closer reading of the text supports this, in the sense that the child –
although pivotal in both the plot of this story and its affective force – remains
elusive – its gender amenable to confusion (as will be discussed further later,
Bhabha, 1983, qualifies the child as female, a matter of significance discussed
by Bergner, 1995, among others), and its understanding of the significance
of its apparently spontaneous response far from clear. Indeed, although it is
the child who claims to be 'frightened' and fears that the black man will 'eat
me up' (80) (which is what sets in motion many of the sexualised interpretations, forging the links between orality and sexuality and bolstering the
many other elaborations of the links between racism and sexuality), Fanon's
accusation of attributions of responsibility are more generalised: 'Now they
were beginning to be frightened of me' (79). The child is amalgamated into
the mother, the 'they'.

While Cherki (2006) topicalises the child without mention of the mother,
as also Yancy (2012) in his sustained treatment, elsewhere child and mother

combine, and the subjects of this scene of misrecognition destabilise or are distributed, with uncertain ownership. It is worth exploring what is achieved by these instabilities of time, parties, and settings, rather than too precipitously resolving these, for such resolutions close down possibilities. First, asserting the culpability of the child assumes its separability from the relational context (with the mother, in the socio-political scene), an assumption that both installs the dominant discourse of individualism and also denies the complex affective networks of interdependency between caregiver and child, that make separate treatment an ideological fiction (Burman, 2008c). On the other hand, second, only focusing on the mother threatens a reproduction of the dominant ideological trope of positioning mothers as responsible for their children and how they 'turn out'. Not only would this rehearse the longstanding modes of misogynist mother-blaming (Caplan, & Hall-McCorquodale, 1985), it is also psychologising, that is, offering a philosophically unsatisfactory account of the production of the social by reducing the socio-political to the interpersonal (Gordo López, & De Vos, 2010; De Vos, 2013). Hence, either blending or over-differentiating mother and child has key political resonances and consequences.

It may also be pointed out that the act of racialised hailing of the black(ened) subject is not only enacted through but also simultaneously interpellates the woman as mother, as well as naming the child as *her child*: 'Mama, see the Negro.' While most accounts, then, address how mother and child are elaborated as 'they' in relation to the abjected other, Fanon, they attend less to how they *are produced as* an entity through this. Indicated here is the entire history of how imperialism has inscribed the bourgeois nuclear family (McClintock, 1995), with the absence of explicit reference to heteropatriarchy working perhaps both to indicate its vulnerability (the potential for 'fright', and how protecting the purity of and regulating the affectional bonds of white women and children were central to the imperial project, Stoler, 2002). Further, qualified as a boychild, this mother–child pair already form a couple prefiguring the heterosexual matrix, in which the other, now blackened, man appears as an intruder, as a threat or competitor with the child *for* the mother, ushering in the question of Oedipal dynamics taken up below. For now, though, let us note how the interpellations and corporealisations do not only concern racialisation but rather that this takes place alongside and through corresponding gendered and intergenerational hailings. Thus, we see the role accorded the visual field in constituting 'epidermalisation': bodily experience is constructed (and disrupted) through modes of intersubjectivity and symbolic interaction that forge or even impose identifications through (mis)recognition. These features lead Hook (2012: 114–15) to claim 'epidermalisation' as virtually a 'proto-Lacanian' concept, while all such aspects arise through the intersection of gendered, generational, as well as classed and racialised positionings. As Khanna notes:

> the *economic, historical, and biological* are not simply symptoms of the psychical universe described by Lacan. They are not shaped and produced by subjectivity; rather, they are what causes subjectivity. Effectively, castration, as the primary trauma, and importantly as a gendered trauma, is displaced by something else: the economic, the historical and the biological. While castration may perhaps figure as a structural factor in the constitution of subjectivity, it is given prime focus by Fanon neither in a more developmental Freudian model, nor in a more structural Lacanian psychical constitution.
>
> *(2004: 174, emphasis in the original)*

It would appear that, corresponding to his psycho*political* project, Fanon's psychoanalytic engagements are here addressed to the field of cultural, rather than specifically individual, meaning – although there is evidence within his 'case history presentations' in *The Wretched of the Earth* (an example of which will be discussed in Chapter 4) of working with metonymy to unravel and ease individual symptoms generated by torture and violence. Crucially, the question of what it is within the white child that prompts such terror is not Fanon's main interest (hence, as proposed above, the interiority or subjectivity of Traumatogenic child is not a prime focus). This appears to be for two clear reasons. First, as discussed in Chapter 2, because racism cannot be 'explained', and, second, because ultimately Fanon is concerned with sociogenesis rather than psychogenesis in order to elaborate his theory of conscious resistance (Hallward, 2011). For Macherey, the scene of racism/colonialism is not only played out via the white woman and child in relation to a (non-interactive) encounter with a (de-subjectified) other, who comes to find himself as black (and male). Beyond this, he suggests that this account emphasises the significance of attending carefully to the materiality and material differences of turning, turning around and looking, of being overlooked and underseen.

Like other commentators (such as Hook, 2012; and Hage, 2010), Macherey's key point is that Fanon's analysis invites us to consider more closely the materiality of the scene itself to highlight the complex and contested relations between class, gender, sexuality, age, and racialisation. I would add to this attending to Fanon's own account of the constitutively racialising character of adult–child relations, reading this as a model of subjectivity that is neither victimised nor entirely compliant. Far from being committed to a defined future or development, therefore, Traumatogenic child, that is, the child of "'Look, a Negro!'" is subjectively inscrutable, underwritten, and perhaps unreadable, even as 'he' also suspends dominant developmental narratives by positioning the child within a spatially contingent, 'development-free' (Motzkau, 2009) space.

Traumatogenic child: interim conclusions

To clarify, "'Look, a Negro!'" is a narrative that institutes a traumatic subject, Fanon as the black(ened) man – while the relational (if de-subjectifying) process by which this occurs is via Traumatogenic child. As a practice of child as method, such versions of child invite some interim reflections. First, notwithstanding its reproduction of various gendered and generational normalisations (for example, of mothers protecting vulnerable children), Traumatogenic child is neither abstract nor prototypical. Noteworthy as a contribution to the lexicon of childhood tropes, it is not a proxy for subjectivity. In this sense, Lebeau's (2005) account, already indicated as noteworthy for a rare attention to the position of the child, is, however, limited for two reasons: first, because it simultaneously generalises and limits Fanon's intervention as if it were only an additional or alternative psychoanalytic theory, rather than a challenge to both psychoanalysis and to social theory, while, second, psychologising and so de-legitimating his account as merely his.

Second, while Fanon mobilises and assumes the position of humanist subject for himself, that is, as traumatised subject, significantly, Traumatogenic child is not a specified subject endowed with interiority and reflection. While various possible narrative frames are mobilised, these are also suspended or left undetermined. Correspondingly, third, Traumatogenic child, *as agent* in Fanon's narrative of the constitution of racialisation, is not the child of developmental psychology advancing towards a presumed normative maturity – the definition and elaboration of which is complicit with historical and current colonialisms and imperialisms (Burman, 2008a, 2013a, 2017a) – alongside classed, sexed, gendered, and other pathologisations. Fourth, despite attempts to make it so, nor is it the child of psychoanalysis – as we shall see next.

Oedipal triangle, or racist symbolic order

Since Fanon's account of the psychological creation and consequences of an imposed black identity mobilises claims to subconscious and unconscious features of the black/colonised psyche ('I discovered my blackness, my ethnic characteristics; and I was battered down by tom-toms, cannibalism, intellectual deficiency, fetishism, racial defects, slave ships . . .', *Black Skin*: 79), his engagement with the work of Jacques Lacan comes into focus. This arises not only because of Fanon's own references to Lacan (to be discussed below). Nor even because Octave Mannoni's psychoanalytic formation was Lacanian (indeed Mannoni published a fictionalised account of his analysis by Lacan, Mannoni, 1969). Beyond this, through its attention to language, Lacanian psychoanalysis has been a particularly significant resource inform-ing critical theory, including both postcolonial studies (notably via such figures as Bhabha, usefully reworked – as we have seen – by Hook), but also via feminist (for example, Grosz, 1994; Copjec, 1994) and other critical psychological (Henriques, et al., 1984) and educational theorists (for exam-ple, Lather, 1992; Brown, et al., 2006) seeking a social theory of subjective formation. It should be noted that such theorists' use of Lacanian approaches often exceeds Lacan's own (since he could scarcely be considered a feminist, for example). Nevertheless, Lacan's linguistic reading of Freud, elaborating how 'the unconscious is structured like a language', has offered a route for social theorists to ground a psychodynamic account of subjectivity within the symbolic order, and more particularly within specific social and material conditions, that enable psychoanalysis to offer a critical reading of that order (as a racist, heteropatriarchal order, for example) rather than an endorsement of it (Mitchell, 1974). This takes us to a re-reading of Oedipal relations, as reworked by both Lacan and Fanon. For Lacan, 'castration', or the Oedipal context, is forged through the access to language as a social symbolic order, enabling a third position that institutes an irrevocable separation from the (pleasures and terrors) of the imaginary merger with the (m)other. The moves Fanon makes in '"Look, a Negro!"' from the dyad to triad echo this Oedipal transition, and open up questions about how the position of Traumatogenic child may rely upon this, not only to install a racist order but how that racist order may frame the symbolic coordinates of a subject's relationship with the social. As Fuss (1994: 33) notes: 'Fanon's effort to call into question the universality of the Oedipus complex may constitute what is most revolutionary about his theoretical work, a political intervention into classical psychoanalysis of enormous importance for later theorists of race and sexuality.'

This is where we may recall that the first chapter of *Black Skin* is entitled 'The Negro and language'. Here Fanon opens his (phenomenologically ori-ented) psychoanalytic account of black subjectivity by claiming that language is precisely what inserts the black subject into a racist social order. For if 'To speak is to exist absolutely for the other' (*Black Skin*: 13), and 'To speak a language is to take on a world, a culture' (29), then the question of access to and mastery of language comes to inscribe racism:

The Negro of the Antilles will be proportionately whiter – that is, he will come closer to being a real human being – in direct ratio to his mastery of the French language. I am not unaware that this is one of man's attitudes face to face with Being. A man who has a language consequently possesses the world expressed and implied by that language. What we are getting at becomes plain: Mastery of language affords remarkable power.

(13–14)

Hence, Fanon recognises the necessity of language both for subjectivity (Being) and access to the social (existing for the other), while also highlighting how this is what installs racialised meanings and inferiorised subjectivities.

It should be noted that, although sometimes mistakenly described as a psychoanalyst rather than a psychiatrist, Fanon had little clinical or theoretical experience of psychoanalysis. Indeed, authoritative accounts portray him as more influenced by phenomenology and especially existentialism, in particular by Sartre (Macey, 2012; Desai, 2014). More convincing, however, is the designation of his contribution as 'psychoanalysis of culture being conducted, quite literally, through an *interpreter*' (Gates, 1991: 468, emphasis in the original), as in Fanon's account of racialised sociogenesis, or the social construction of blackness and, in particular, black masculinity as 'phobogenic' (generating phobia). Both Gates (1991) and Macey (2012) disparage efforts to portray Fanon as a proto-Lacanian, notwithstanding the key role accorded visual (mis)recognition in the the separation between self and other (see also Vergès, 1997). Yet even as Hook (2012), among others, reads Fanon through Lacan, the direct line of influence is less clear, and certainly more ambivalent.

In his practice as a psychiatrist Fanon drew on ideas from therapeutic communities (which were known through British and North American psychiatric traditions, and to Lacan also, see Burman, 2012b). As discussed in Chapter 1, Fanon's psychiatric practice drew on the psychoanalytically informed 'institutional psychotherapy' he learnt from his internship at Saint Alban with François Tosquelles. As also mentioned there, Tosquelles escaped Fascist Spain. Moreover, there are claims that he carried with him over the Pyrenees a copy of Lacan's doctoral thesis, so informing the mode of group therapeutic practice he founded that combined political and psychological forms of asylum (including for those being hunted down by the Vichy regime) (Macey, 2012: 142–146). Indeed, Vergès (1997: 586, Footnote 26) goes further to suggest that Fanon had also read Lacan's thesis, although she provides no evidence for this. At the very least, what *Black Skin* indicates is

Fanon's engagement with Lacan from his position as a doctor, a psychiatrist and, from this, a particular tradition of radical psychotherapeutic practice can be traced (Giraldo, 2012).

Despite such indications of influence, notwithstanding Fanon's brief citations in *Black Skin*, there is little explicit engagement with Lacanian (or indeed much Freudian) theory in his texts. As I detail elsewhere (Burman, 2016d), what there is is poorly referenced, and often only mobilised in the service of furthering his critiques. (Confusingly, *Black Skin* includes both footnotes, which accompany asterisked portions of the main text, and a few numbered endnotes listed at the back of the book.) Of the four citations of Lacan indicated in the Index of *Black Skin,* a substantive one references Lacan's thesis as support in his critique of the notion of biologically determined 'psychic constitutions' of the kind subscribed to in the then contemporary colonial psychiatry being practised especially in Algeria. Yet notwithstanding mobilising Lacan for support, the endnoted references do not include Lacan.

Elsewhere, Fanon targets Lacan as part of his repudiation of the Oedipus complex (in a footnote on page 108): 'in the French Antilles 97 per cent of the families cannot produce one Oedipal neurosis. This incapacity is one on which we heartily congratulate ourselves', with a further asterisked footnote devoted to expounding how he is departing from psychoanalytic orthodoxy, taking Lacan as the paradigmatic example. So, while there is scant evidence to read Fanon, as Gates (1991) puts it, as a 'Black Lacan', as indicated above, some interesting lines of continuity can be noted. As will be discussed in Chapter 4, Fanon is perhaps at his most Lacanian through his methodology and pedagogy of failure in his psychotherapeutic practice.

Intersectional connections: gender, heterosex

Between the two terrors (ascribed to the child and to the black(ened) man who is increasingly frightened by the child's fear), an exchange takes place between the (black) man and the (white) woman, 'the mother', that is little commented upon. The mother says to Fanon, 'Take no notice, sir, he does not know you are as civilised as we . . .' (*Black Skin*: 80). This piece of patronising exceptionalism is presented as enraging Fanon further (after all, her apparent efforts to mitigate it in fact repeat the insult by the re-inscription of 'we' versus 'you'), but it could still be read as embarrassment at her son's response. Lebeau considers this 'a civility that reveals her to be an active participant in her child's fear' (2005, 132). Nevertheless, Bergner (1995: 86, Footnote 14) suggests otherwise, that 'the mother, at least in this instance, apologises for her son's outburst'. The mother's next turn is an indirect communication to Fanon, via a pedagogical address to her son: 'Look how handsome that Negro is!' (81). Rather than accepting this, he replies: 'Kiss the handsome negro's ass, madame!' Or in Macey's (2012: 165) translation: '"Look he's handsome, that nigger". The handsome nigger retorts: "Bugger you, Madame!" . . .' This marks a turning point. For the mother: 'Shame flooded her face' (81) and, on seeing this apparently more intersubjective response, Fanon claims to be 'set free from his rumination' to feel some measure of agency return, albeit one built on aggression: 'The field of battle having been marked out . . . I had incisors to test. I was sure they were strong' (*Black Skin*: 81).

Clearly, it is hard to go beyond this gendered and sexed encounter, alongside the manifold discussions of this visual scene of misrecognition, in which what is made through the impact of looking is clearly at issue. Moreover, we should note how these characteristics are also 'guaranteed' as heterosexed through the presence of the child (as queer theorists would claim, Edelman, 2004), the offspring of a previous heterosexual coupling. Also noteworthy is how this mobilises conventions about not engaging in flirtation or erotic activities 'in front of the child', while this presence is also what precisely wards off the encounter as primarily constituted by, but also recapitulating, the erotically charged positioning between the white woman and the black man. Much can and has been said about all this (for example, Doane, 1999), as also equally the absence of subject position accorded black women (Bergner, 1995; Fuss, 1994) with implications for black women's political mobilization (Xala, 2017). Lebeau continues:

> [i]n other words, that model of phobia – Fanon's attention to the trauma of sexuality, to sexuality as trauma – is bound to his struggle *not to think* the transfer of a white boy's fear, his mother's reason, into the black body, to refuse the fraught opening to the world that the Black comes to represent in *Peau noire*.
>
> *(2005: 135, emphasis in the original)*

For Lebeau, the child functions in the text not only to foreground Fanon's account of the development of racism, but also to tie this less to gendered and sexed dynamics than to separation. In her object relations analysis, it is the question of separation, the confrontation with difference, and its resolution via seeking out support and protection from a familiar figure, that is played out through the racialised and racialising encounter between the child and the black man, mediated (in multiple senses) by the boy's mother. Bhabha generalises this to develop its political implications:

the very question of identification only emerges *in-between* disavowal and designation. It is performed in the agonistic struggle between the epistemological, visual demand for a knowledge of the Other, and its representation in the act of articulation and enunciation.

(1994: 50, emphasis in the original)

I will return to this set of exchanges later to offer a different interpretation.

Logical time and the racialisation of subjectivity

Fanon's fourth, more favourable reference, to Lacan in *Black Skin* occurs as a longer footnote (on p. 114), offering an account of Lacan's mirror stage (which Fanon calls the 'mirror period') in relation to racialisation. The source for Lacan offered here is the (undated) *Encyclopédie française*, a text that anticipates Lacan's later development of the role of the mirror stage in relation to the imaginary, since Lacan first presented a version of his mirror stage in 1936, and published it with some modifications in 1949 (see Lacan, 2006b). Given the explicit relation made by Fanon between his own and Lacanian formulations, a more Lacanian reading of Fanon's account of Traumatogenic child may be warranted. Just as some commentators have discerned in this mise en scéne a sequential stage model of racialised identification (c.f. Hage's, 2010, account of Hardt and Negri's reading in terms of radical alterity), its chronology and spatialisation can be elaborated in another way via Lacan's (1946) discussion of the intersubjective, relational construction of subjectivity in the 'Logical Time' sophism (see Lacan, 2006c).

Associating these two texts is not arbitrary. Lacan wrote this paper as a direct counter to Sartre's (1944) portrayal in *Huis Clos/No Exit* of 'hell as other people' (*'L'enfer, c'est les autres'*), and both were responses to Nazi death camps. In the 'Logical Time' (first published in 1946) sophism, Lacan (2006c) discusses three logically distinct and necessary phases in the (gendered as male) prisoners' calculations as to their identities – identities that are interestingly figured as 'white' or 'black', according to discs placed on their backs, which they cannot see but that are visible to others. The warder, according to Lacan, tells them that if they can tell him which colour they are then they can leave. There is the 'instant of the glance', when the men look at each other; the second phase is 'time of comprehension' when each reasons that – since they have all been told that there are two black and three white discs – if he was black each of the others would have rushed to leave; finally, there is the 'moment for concluding' when, *precisely because* the others have *not* left, and as a function of the hesitation on the part of the other two, each man realises that they must all be white, and so they all get up to go to the door at the same time.

For Lacan, what is important is that each realises that he is white, that is, that this is the commonality between them; indeed, this recognition is vital to his account of the social constitution of subjectivity. As a 'logical sophism' there is no intentional engagement with notions of racialisation, even though such terminology could be suggestive, especially as the paper was written from the French colonial centre at a significant cultural-political moment in relation to precisely the anticolonial struggle that Fanon was to become engaged with. Indeed, the more salient context for both theorists was the Second World War, and perhaps here, too, we can see the importance of distinguishing Sartre's agendas from Fanon's, notwithstanding the former's influence on the latter (Kuby, 2015). This clearly invites a particular kind of misrecognition that we may also see, within a racialised, racist social field, as a kind of overdetermined 'mis'-interpellation. Especially, consideration arises of what would have happened *if they were not all* white (here, if they did not all have white discs on their backs). Or indeed that the resolution of the sophism *relies on* the exclusion or foreclosure of blackness in the production of subjectivity. Yet, contrary to Lacan, this is the scenario Fanon addresses, inhabiting and dramatising the position of the subject who is made-to-be black (the object rather than subject of abjection, Hook, 2012).

Nevertheless, Lacan's key point is that there is an intersubjective and therefore social logic to this temporal sequence; each is necessary, and one necessarily follows the other. The guard calls each prisoner to identify himself as the condition of their freedom, but the only way they can do so is via a *relational sequence* of interpretive inferences. Only on this group-relational basis can individual subjectivity be forged, assumed, and so identified with. Thus, contrary to the more individualist, phenomenological accounts to which Fanon more readily aligned himself (and that are of a piece with his radical humanism (Hallward, 2011; Gilroy, 2010, Hook, 2012)), individual identification is inevitably, necessarily, created through relationship with the other: one becomes 'individual' in relation to the social field. This is what makes Lacan's a radically social account of the construction of subjectivity, which – potentially – is more convergent with the kind of group/institutional psychotherapeutic practice that Fanon actually engaged in (Macey, 2012; see also Keller, 2007; Razanajao, et al., 1996; and Chapter 4).

Applied to '"Look, a Negro!"', what Lacan's logical time parable highlights is the mutual contingency of action and reaction. The first 'call' elicits a smile; the second a laugh and a sense of greater entrapment ('the circle was getting smaller'); and, finally, third, the moment of concluding, of assuming a toxic identification, when 'laughter . . . had become impossible'. Could we read this accumulation of incidents temporo-spatially ('having come under attack at several points'), as representing in a particular way what happens when the child colludes with the mother against the father, and how – within a heteropatriarchal paradigm – in this case this racialises the man/father as black?

In *Black Skin* Fanon continues by differentiating between acquiring a sense of oneself as other to an other (that is, what happens through the resolution of the Oedipal complex, or through symbolic castration as a condition of, and for, entry into the Symbolic) and being fragmented and, through rejection, unable to establish a relation, and so failing to be able to orient to what is happening:

> In the train it was no longer a question of being aware of my body in the third person but in a triple person. In the train I was given not one, but two, three places. I had already stopped being amused. It was not that I was finding febrile coordinates in the world. I existed triply; I occupied space. I moved towards the other – and the evanescent other, hostile but not opaque, transparent, not there, disappeared. Nausea . . .
>
> (70)

Far from generating a representational model of the relation between self and other ('not . . . febrile coordinates'), Fanon describes a process of splitting ('I existed triply'); he feels himself to be materially present ('I occupied space') but, precisely because his existence is not confirmed by the other it is the other that disappears, which is what produces existential nausea. This description clearly evokes a Sartrean, rather than Lacanian, model. Sartre's individualism is at least as troubling as Lacan's, if rather more revolutionary in tone. As Françoise Vergès (1997: 589) argues: 'Fanon's reading of Lacan through Sartre supported his theory of both a Lacanian understanding of desire applied to the colonial situation and a Sartrian consciousness that animated the struggle for emancipation.' Vergès develops her (influential) analysis in terms of tracing consequences of this occlusion of sexual difference for both Fanon's model of conscious/unconscious relations (what lies beneath the mask) and as covertly installing a pre-given subject. This conclusion is echoed in the only reference to Fanon in Judith Butler's (1990) *Gender Trouble* (note 20 on p. 152).

It seems we are far away from a mask whose masquerade is constitutive and performative (see also Naimou, 2013). Indeed, Fanon elaborates his account of 'Negrophobia' through explicit analogy with Sartre's account of anti-semitism, claiming that both share similar dynamics but give rise to different effects, while the 'phobia' appears at a 'level' that makes it seem 'instinctual, biological' (114). He starts by stating this thesis:

At the extreme, I should say that the Negro, because of his body, impedes the closing of the postural scheme of the white man – at the point, naturally, at which the black man makes his entry into the phenomenal world of the white man.

(ibid.)

Next, he alludes to some previous work:

This is not the place in which to state the conclusions I drew from studying the influence exerted on the body by the appearance of another body . . . What is important to us here is to show that with the Negro the cycle of the *biological* begins.

(ibid., emphasis in the original)

Jumping to conclusions: gender as racialisation

Yet between these two sentences there is a parenthesis in which Fanon depicts a scenario that, at least superficially, chimes more closely with the structure of Lacan's 'logical time sophism' than any other examples discussed, by him or other commentators (including Bhabha and Khanna). He writes:

(Let us assume, for example, that four fifteen-year-old boys, all more or less athletic, are doing the high jump. One of them wins by jumping four feet ten inches. Then a fifth boy arrives and tops the mark by a half-inch. The four other bodies experience a destructuration.)

*(*Black Skin: *114)*

This text is literally bracketed, in parenthesis between the two earlier sentences, but the illustration of the production of racism through a phobic response to inadequacy framed as a gendered competition in athletic performance between young men surely invites reflection. Fanon suggests that experience of being superseded produces a 'destructuration' or phallic castration. As this story lacks explicit reference to 'race', it seems Fanon uses this story of gendered competition and bodily prowess as an analogy to and illustration of the dynamics of racism. He embeds this within an explicit account of the 'biological danger' (117) posed to the Negrophobic white (man) by the Negro. Via this staged story of group relations, in which physicality is privileged, blackness acquires its associations with the body, its particular register of the biological: 'it is in his corporeality that the Negro is attacked' (116). 'The Negro symbolizes the biological danger . . . To suffer from a phobia of Negroes is to be afraid of the biological. For the Negro is only biological' (117).

Questions arise concerning the additional rhetorical features conveyed by the aged and gendered specifications of this high-jump competition, that is, its concern is not with adults, girls, or women. One relatively facile reading of this merely reiterates Fanon's gender chauvinism and inadequacy in relation to conceptualising (black) women's positions and experiences. Here a masculinist version of castration elides gendered positionings with race in a way that consolidates heterosexed as well as racialised identities in ways ripe for queer destabilisations (see, for example, Musser, 2012; Pellegrini, 2008). A different angle for commentary may be to consider further the status of the age and gender specifications: are they developmental in orientation (like Fanon's rendering of the mirror 'period', to which this account is proximal)? Or do they convey something more like 'the time before', the earlier ('younger') moment before a new transformative structure will come into play. And why does the fifth boy produce a 'destructuration' for all the four others? Butler's (2015: 190–191) discussion of the status of 'muscular power' within Fanon's *Wretched* is suggestive here. While acknowledging his allegiance to the European civilisational project, including its gendered hierarchies, she proposes that his formulations can be read as fantasised compensatory responses to oppression: 'When he claims that the oppressed dream of becoming the persecutor, he is giving us a psychosocial description of the fantasies that take hold under such conditions. He is not necessarily arguing for them' (190). That such questions remain unresolved may at least keep some political options open. But now we turn to how others have resolved Fanon's ambiguities in particular directions.

Misrecognising Fanon's Traumatogenic child

Given his widely cited contributions to this discussion, it is noteworthy that Homi Bhabha presumes the child in Fanon's iconic encounter in *Black Skin* to be a girl. As Bergner (1995) suggests, this indicates either a significant under-attention to gender or else subscription to the attributed transcendent feminised subject position of 'the child'. Specifically, Bhabha (1983) mistakenly claims that 'a white girl fixes Fanon in a look and word as she turns to identify with her mother' (28). As Bergner (1995: Footnote 14) comments: 'Bhabha's slip suggests that preconceptions of how race, gender and sexuality intersect run deep.' Indeed, Bhabha (1993: 28) maintains the gendering of the white child as female to differentiate the identificatory pathways – and (anticipating Macherey's 2012, analysis) 'turns' – of the white and black child, by continuing in the next paragraph:

The drama underlying these dramatic 'everyday' colonial scenes is not difficult to discern. In each of them the subject turns around the pivot of the 'stereotype' to return to a point of total identification. The girl's gaze returns to her mother in the recognition and disavowal of the Negroid type; the black child turns away from himself, his race in his total identification with the positivity of whiteness which is at once colour and no colour. In the act of disavowal and fixation the colonial subject is returned to the narcissism of the imaginary and its identification of an ideal ego that is white and whole. For what these primal scenes illustrate is that looking/hearing/reading as sites of subjectification in colonial discourse are evidence of the importance of the visual and auditory imaginations for the histories of societies.

(Bhabha, 1983: 28, emphasis in the original)

Here the gendered differentiation being girl and boy would appear to work to emphasise the racialised difference between black (boy) and white (girl).

Generative as Bhabha's account may have been for accounts of the social structuring of psychic subjectivities of colonialism, Fanon's text demands further scrutiny. For, contrary to the focus of most commentators, it is not the mother who is qualified as white, but the child – the child who is a 'little boy', a 'handsome little boy' and finally a 'little white boy' (*Black Skin*: 80). That is, the assignation of the white–black relation occurs as a function of *Fanon's reaction to the child's reaction* to him: in the visual scene, the child names him as 'a Negro' and is 'frightened', which produces in Fanon a rupture of worldview dividing him as black from the child as white, and from his previous understanding of himself. Thus, it is after this final (aesthetic, and age/size) qualification of the little, handsome boy as 'white', and his fear of being 'eaten up' that Fanon becomes aware of his black skin, that is, recognises this as identified with a traumatic and violent history and so also experiences a sense of burning and implosion from 'all this whiteness', that Macey (2012) specifically relates to the traumatic Martinican experience of colonisation and brutal enslavement. 'For the Martinican Fanon, the experience of coming under the white gaze reproduces the primal experience of the island's history: slavery and a colonization so brutal as to be a form of trauma or even annihilation' (166).

Indeed, for Fanon, as we have seen, in his most extensive engagement with Lacan (albeit in a – long – footnote), the mirror stage 'is basic: every time the subject sees his image and recognizes it, it is always in some way "the mental oneness which is inherent in him" that he acclaims' (*Black Skin*: 114). As we have seen in a rather significant developmentalist reading, he calls it a 'period'. This is of a piece with Vergès' (1997) analysis: 'It is a transparent ego.

Fanon's insistence on the cultural, as well as his conception of masculinity, lead him to finally embrace a notion of an unpolluted ego reached through stages of progressive development' (p. 593).

It is from this understanding of the 'structural harmony, a sum of the individual and of the constructions through which he goes' (*Black Skin*: 114–115) that Fanon builds his account of psychosis, specifically the sociocultural psychosis of the black person's failure to know their colour: 'Whenever there is a psychotic belief, there is a reproduction of self' (114–115, Footnote). As Bhabha (1994b) comments, 'Like the mirror phase "the fullness" of the stereotype – its image *as* identity – is always threatened by "lack"' (110, emphasis in the original). It is this psychotic hallucination of the 'neutrality' of 'colour' that Fanon then exemplifies with everyday stories from the Antilles, including from his own childhood: 'I contend that for the Antillean the mirror hallucination is always neutral. When Antilleans tell me that they have experienced it, I always ask the same question: "What colour were you?" Invariably they reply: "I had no colour" . . . It is not I as a Negro who acts, thinks and is praised to the skies' (*Black Skin*: 115, Footnote). This is also where he narrates the racist descriptions made by Martinican World War One veterans of the Senegalese soldiers ('They cut off their heads and collect human ears', ibid.), which include, from Fanon's own mathematics teacher, anti-Muslim comments (ibid.). Fanon reports that when the soldiers passed through Martinique in transit to Guiana, they were such objects of fascination that 'my [Fanon's] father went to the trouble of collecting two of them, whom he bought home and who had the family in raptures' (ibid.). This continues with the famous example of the institutionally sanctioned misrecognition of the colonised subject, as exemplified by the French compositions written by Antillean children in schools:

> Given as a theme 'My Feelings Before I Went on a Vacation', they reacted like real little Parisians and produced such things as, 'I like vacation because then I can run through the fields, breathe fresh air and come home with *rosy* cheeks'. It is apparent that one would hardly be mistaken in saying that the Antillean does not altogether apprehend the fact of his being a Negro.
>
> (Black Skin: 115, emphasis in the original)

Fanon, Lacan, and traumatogenic child-as-suspended-subject

Political evaluations of Fanon focus on his philosophical debt to Sartre, in particular in relation to his humanism and associated links with notions of individual and collective liberation, while some postcolonial theorists possibly overstate his Lacanian sensibilities. My purpose here is not to choose between these readings, but rather to explore what can be gained from their frictions. Fanon was neither a psychoanalyst nor a philosopher; he was a psychiatrist and political revolutionary, who drew on a range of political and intellectual resources to fuel his distinctive account of the formation of racialised subjectivities and the psychopolitical consequences of colonisation, in particular the links between psychic and social suffering. As well as Sartre and Lacan, he also cited Jung, Adler, and other psychological resources in the service of warranting his arguments, as also reproducing very extensive extracts from other popular and literary texts in *Black Skin*.

A clear contribution made by Fanon is the disruption and suspension of the romantic humanism with which the child is typically invested (this would be the traumatised, rather than the traumatogenic, child), showing how this is the offspring of historical relations of exclusionary racialisation (that carry, we may add, equivalently gendered, sexed, and classed features). Yet rather than staying with this figure of the child as transcendent repository of a racist culture, there is also a need for a more fully transformational account of subjectivity that can provide a socially situated reading. As Hook argues:

> A pressing research agenda comes to the fore: accounting for the intertwining of these registers of racism, of explaining the combinations of racism at the levels of symbolic functioning, imaginary meanings and identifications, and the libidinal investments of embodied passions.
>
> *(2012: 85)*

Given the child's long history as proxy for the modern humanist subject and, by exclusion, its 'others', s/he becomes a vital resource for such interrogations. Critics (such as McCulloch, 1983) debate whether Fanon succeeded in resolving the societal-psychological connection, but this misses his wider methodological and disciplinary challenges. Fanon's contribution is indicative rather than exhaustive.

Together, his analyses offer fruitful resources for a critical reading of childhood and models of subjectivity. Fanon's destabilisation and at times desubjectifications of the child (since the subjectivity of Traumatogenic child remains opaque) not only challenge humanist and developmentalist readings connecting child with individual, social, national, and international development. They also reinvigorate discussions of the psychopolitical stakes in contemporary social theory.

This is where, as discussed later in relation to pedagogical applications, Yancy's (2012) claim that the white boy is 'undergoing white subject formation, a formation that is fundamentally linked to the objects he fears and dreads' (3) while suggestive, also risks overlooking the intergenerational, gendered, classed, and other geopolitical conditions structuring the interaction. That is, Yancy portrays the child as a subject in development, a developing subject forged through the constitution of racialised privilege. He continues on this theme, generalising it to the constitution of the naturalisation of what he calls 'white ways of being'. Yet, for Lacan, as for any adequate readings of Fanon, all interpellations, as ideologically structured misrecognitions, are 'mis'interpellations, so making any claims to determine or claim subjectivity problematic. While Lacanian approaches frustrate the recuperation of psychoanalysis into a developmental psychology that would reinstate normativity and teleology, Fanon's underdeterminations surrounding the child leave ambiguous, or (in Hage's, 2010, terms) open to vacillation, aspects of its identifications and even agencies.

Yet Fanon may provide other resources, too. Desmond Painter (2012) discusses 'This is the Voice of Algeria' (in Chapter 2 of *Dying Colonialism),* which highlights not only the reversals of meaning that the possession of, or even listening to, a radio held for Algerians, but also, too, how its hiss – that is, even its undecipherable sound when lacking clear reception – came to signify revolutionary commitment. Importantly, like the ambiguities surrounding the subject position of the child, this moment of ambiguity is what makes Fanon remain a fruitful analytic resource. Butler (2000) comments: 'interpellation does not always operate through the name: this silence might be meant for you' (157), but here even the boundary between speech and silence is blurred.

Notwithstanding the many Fanons, and diverse contrary readings of Fanonian subjectivity, and acknowledging the paradoxically closed pre-social versions that linger within his model even as he strived to configure others, it is at these moments of resignification that Fanon is at both his most politically radical and most social. Whereas Hallward (2011) interprets Fanon's claim (on the last page of *Black Skin)* that 'The tragedy of the man is that he was once a child' (165) in terms of a political voluntarism arising from his radical humanism, the multiple temporalities implied by this description invite less determined and stable trajectories. This is no nostalgic celebration of childhood, nor only a claim about vulnerability leading to complicity. Nor is it an instrumentalised developmental child, whose current needs, desires, and aspirations are co-opted for the (national, racialised, individual, or even planetary) future, even if it clearly references a historical-biographical child influencing the adult to come. This final formulation from Fanon – one that encapsulates the questions explored in this chapter – sets in motion an ambiguous dynamic, of uncertain directionality, between child and adult. It foregrounds both the sociopolitical and the affectively invested character of the constitution of relations. In the midst of current superspecifications and exploitation of human resources – emotional as well as physical/material – such underdeterminations represent key spaces of political possibility.

Educational applications: dilemmas of colouring in whiteness

It should be noted that Traumatogenic child is not the predominant model of Fanon taken up in educational literatures that mainly attend to the experiences of disaffection and alienation produced through racialisation for learners and teachers. The primary focus of this educational literature, which is addressed in Chapter 5, has correspondingly been on those subjected to such traumatic experiences, rather than those (positioned as) responsible for producing them, with particular concern including how this produces both educational failure and wider societal marginalisation. That is, discussion of Traumatogenic child is used to warrant supportive educational interventions designed to counter the effects of the traumatisation, which will be discussed there.

Here, however, we will stay with pedagogical questions posed by the ambiguously implicated traumatogenic agent. There is a large antiracist and feminist educational literature that addresses what may be called 'pedagogies of the powerful' (Cornwall, 2016), addressing how educational and pedagogical practices reproduce racialised (as well as class and gender) privilege. These range from addressing the non-problem of (educational) arenas of privilege (Yancy, & del Guadalupe Davidson, 2014) to more active discussions of pedagogical responsibilities and possibilities.

While much of this work has been concerned with 'colouring in' implicit racialised and cultural assumptions informing educational curricula (both overt and 'hidden'), as well as inscribing policy and provision, a substantial literature does address those (presumably positioned as 'complicit') co-learners/peers and teachers/professionals positioned as able to access such privilege. Crucially, these analyses have relied on conceptions of identities as complex, plural, and relational (rather than as fixed or essential), as enabling the destabilisation of positions of privilege and so identification with the marginalised and oppressed (as in Fine, et al.'s, 1997, early collection *Off-White*, for example).

If the child who says 'Look a Negro!' speaks the voice of ideology that excises Fanon/the other from the social, that same voice also positions that child ambiguously as neither quite representing nor as separate from the relational and ideological context producing her/him. This is where the lack of subjectivity identified here within Fanon's traumatogenic child remains so significant, perhaps signalling key political disjunctions that lay ahead.

Debates on 'whiteness studies', which began in antiracist exploration of the conditions for the production of racialisation, highlight political dilemmas in attending to the subject of privilege as much as only attending to victimised positions (Leonardo, 2009). As Ruth Frankenberg (2001) notes, revisiting the reception of her earlier, 1993, key text, efforts to understand such subject formations risk offering justifications for them, or at least as being read as doing this, and so understandably critical pedagogues have been wary. Perhaps it is inevitable that such approaches attract claims of re-centring the dominant white subject of educational or social theory, as also through more recent neoliberal management discourse on 'diversity' that depoliticises and flattens out power relations of inequality into mere interpersonal or even intrapersonal dynamics (Ahmed, 2009; Dalal, 2009). This whitewashing or malestreaming pedagogical strategy, therefore, will always threaten recuperation, yet the status of Traumatogenic child, the subject producing or perhaps merely relaying the psycho-affectively definitive moment of oppression, must be addressed within educational discourse.

While clearly a normalised pedagogical object of address, or redress, is untenable neither should the subject be abjected, or excluded, from it. Yancy's (2012) persuasive account is distinctive in attending to the agency of the child. Yet, even as he acknowledges that '"Look, a Negro!" presupposes a white subject who is historically embedded within racist social relations and a racist discursive field that pre-exists the speaker' (5), he still perhaps overstates the child's agency and separation from those relations/that field. In this he moves beyond Macherey's account, that hovers in the space between 'innocence' and 'proxy', to name complicity. Yancy, however, appears to be addressing not merely Traumatogenic child as a position but also its corresponding developmental mode of subjectivation. Thus:

> The white boy's performance is not simply the successful result of a *superimposed* grid of racist ideology. Rather the white boy's performance points to fundamental ways in which white children are oriented, at the level of practice, within the world where their bodily orientations are unreflected expressions of the background, lived orientations of whiteness, white ways of being, white modes of racial and racist practice.
>
> *(Yancy, 2012: 3, emphasis in the original)*

What this leads to is a pedagogical counter-strategy of hailing whiteness, 'Look, a White!', as he puts it. This looking back, he claims, does not involve either essentialisation or dehumanisation. It is not meant to stigmatize white people as something aberrant or inferior. The countergaze is not meant to essentialize whites. Rather, 'looking back' signifies an act of agency, an act of counter-hegemonic seeing, of bringing attention to that which often hides under the category of normativity.

(Yancy, 2012: 4)

Hence, like other antiracist and black-centred educationalists, Yancy advocates acknowledging complicity and being willing to examine the ways in which white practices must be disrupted. Clearly these are important and useful educational points that can complement Yancy's related discussions, including fading out whiteness (Butler, 2017) and the dynamics of epistemologies of ignorance (Bailey, 2017). Yet we have not quite finished with Fanon's scenario and his staging of the emotional dynamics of traumatogenesis.

Logical time and the mother's pedagogy

Macherey's invitation to attend more closely to the materiality of the scene of (racialised) interpellation can be taken further by attending to its narrative sequencing and spatial distribution, and how this suggests both the temporality of duration but also the quagmire of timelessness and infinite space that composes trauma. I have already noted that 'Look, a Negro!', the exclamation that stands for racism, opens the chapter unattributed and only later comes to be instantiated and situated within the particular encounter with the woman and child. This suggests some distancing from attributions of specifically malign intentionality on their part, indeed even of specificity. While Fanon mobilises the spectre of the colonial woman as protector of the nation (personified by the child), he does not quite align her as primarily responsible for this. Clearly the mother–child pair both benefit from and are indeed a key index of white privilege, but Fanon does not quite subscribe to the elision that would render the woman as mother as bearer or symbol of cultural-racialised continuity for the nation (Yuval-Davis, 1997), and as such positioned as warranting *particular* moral responsibility for this. Indeed, attending more closely to the sequencing as well as the content of the interaction may further indicate the social architecture of pedagogical possibilities, even if some of these will be destined to fail.

Let us consider what we may call the mother's pedagogy. When the child objectifies Fanon, the mother does assume a position of responsibility to counter or mitigate this. She does not, for example, concur with her son or collude with him (by adopting a position of child alongside him). First, she addresses him, the objectified and racialised man insulted by her son, with 'Take no notice, sir, he does not know you are as civilised as we' (*Black Skin*: 80), then she attempts to reframe the boy's negative attention by offering a positive description: 'Look how handsome that Negro is!' (81). That is, inadequate as her efforts might be, she attempts both a reparative move towards the injured party and a corrective educational reconstruction.

That Fanon offers such a graphic depiction of the stream of associations violently evoked that it fills the page between the child's hailing and the mother's intervention (and much before and after this too) also highlights how and why he does not only hear what is said but much more, too, and can only hear the mother's (admittedly dreadful) attempt at mitigation as furthering the insult. This is not, of course to say that it does not do this, but rather that Fanon's narrative structuring of his account helps us to see how and why the mother and child themselves also then become to him desubjectified icons of a racist order. Nevertheless, as we have seen, it is her attempt at engagement that shifts him from abjection to the domain of some kind of possible relationship, that is, it detaches him enough from identifying with the torrent of collective traumas that comprise racism to be 'set free from those ruminations' (81) and so restores his position as subject, and an angry one at that.

Attending to this spacing, the distribution across the pages of Fanon's Chapter 5 of *Black Skin*, may offer some further useful insights. It is indeed in the middle of the book. The unattributed racist hailing opens the chapter, and as we have seen, this only becomes instantiated within the encounter with the mother and child two pages later, while it takes another page and a half of Fanon's 'ruminations', the associations provoked via the racist hailing, before it is concluded by Fanon rejecting the mother's 'compliment' by telling her where to go ('Bugger off . . .') still another one and a half pages later. Interestingly, the stream of associations has led Fanon from the 'whiteness that burns me', not only to 'become aware of my uniform. I had not seen it. It is indeed ugly' (ibid.), but also to start to reflect critically on this train of thinking in the very next sentences. 'I stop there, for who can tell me what beauty is?' (ibid.) The key point here is that this distance between the first racist interpellation and its instantiation within a supposedly specific interaction, with speakers attached to it, is, literally, the narrative space of the 'rumination'. *It is therefore portrayed as in part a construction of and by the racialised subject, even as it also a response to, and caused by, those racialising conditions.*

If this chapter has been about how that traumatic scene works, what can we learn from the mother's apparently futile or inadequate, but still significant, actions and responses?

The mother's shame (which 'floods her face', ibid.) comes, it must be noted, not at the boy's racist hailing, but at Fanon's rejection of her racialised 'compliment' on his appearance. Her attempt at reparation and even engagement has failed, indeed has confirmed her position as 'enemy', and it is not hard to see why. Public humiliation can of course be traumatogenic, too, although the audience here is also fruitfully ambiguous. If she feels shamed *in front of her child*, then this suggests a further embodied traumatogenic effect he (the boychild) embodies. But it would seem more likely that she feels shamed by Fanon. She is shamed by Fanon's rejection of her offer, but this at least acknowledges reciprocal impacts within a relational, intersubjective field. It is surely an improvement from having been excised from it. Indeed, the 'shame' flooding her face is what frees him 'from my ruminations. At the same time I accomplished two things: I identified my enemies and I made a scene. A grand slam. Now one would be able to laugh' (81). That is, it would appear that her attempt was productive in at least enabling the now blackened subject to respond, to act, in this case, to oppose and resist, to name her as 'enemy'.

We not only need to read Fanon's rendering of Traumatogenic child in the context of the social (gendered, classed, sexed, racialised, generational) meanings of the positions at play, but in the context of the argument he is developing in *Black Skin*, and in fact across his writings. For 'The fact of blackness'/'The experience of being black' is the middle of the story, or rather the middle of Fanon's story for this text. Yes, it is a story of excision, amputation from the social, and from the temporality of action and transformation (of self, with other), that is, of trauma. It is the cry of anguish of the abjected and exploration of strategies available to the subject of dealing with this, including affirming the very qualities that are the source of the rejection. Traumatogenic child names a problem, but Fanon will offer possible answers, other ways of proceeding later in this book.

The mother's shame

It is worth recalling that, under heteropatriarchal conditions, the mother's position is already one of shame. Recall that, as we saw in Mannoni's essay in Chapter 2, the fetish (of racism) that the child comes to protect, or secure, covers a constitutive lack. Psychoanalytically speaking, this is castration, or the mother's lack of a penis. Much psychoanalytic theory since has shifted focus from the actual organ (penis) as such to that which signifies power, the 'phallus' – that is, to phallic attributes of power as socially, rather than biologically, structured. Reading this as social rather than physical lack, as feminists engaged in re-reading psychoanalysis have done, opens up further questions.

In one way Fanon mobilises his gendered place in the socially structured discourse of masculinity to put the woman in her place, or even perhaps to ward off being in her place (of lack). It is an available response for him to the abjection generated by Traumatogenic child, but one that overlooks (or even mobilises?) the constitutive role of misogyny and and heterosexism within colonial relations. (While she does not specifically discuss this scene, Fuss's, 1994, critique is certainly relevant.) At issue then is how we understand the heteropatriarchal symbolic order, once it is admitted that this is also a racist symbolic order, and that, as Oliver (2001: 34) puts it, 'racist social structures create racist psychic structures'. (This is further developed by Nayak, 2014.) Put simply, how do we understand the relationship between racism and sexism? As Seshadri-Crooks (2002) cogently indicated, racism cannot merely stand for another kind of difference (that is, as analogous to gender), for that would subordinate it to that (sexual) difference and fundamentally erode the specificity of the dynamics – and the geopolitical, material histories – composing racialisation. This is both a challenge to psychoanalysis, to socially situate the role of gender (whether as or with racialisation), and of course a wider political challenge, which black feminists have posed both to white women (for example, Carby, 1996) and to black men in particular through intersectionality theory. As Lorde (1984) puts it, echoing but developing Fanon's analysis: black feminism is not white feminism in black face. Fanon, then, puts the white woman, the mother, (back) in her place of shame. But this is only a temporary, compensatory response. For in the end, at the end of *Black Skin*, having sorted through a range of arguments and reactions that include the denial of essential racialised differences, and the determinations of racialised or national histories, we see him denying the epistemological, political categories of black and white.

The mother's response, then, also invites consideration of the pedagogical risks as well as possibilities of shame. This is no simple matter, for, as feminists have long pointed out, women and girls have long been subject to shame as a mode of regulation and surveillance, with profound implications for the impairment of creativity and learning (Bartky, 1996), and with a core link to embodiment, since the body both expresses and is a source of shame, as Fanon suggests for the black(ened) man. Fanon's example can be read in relation to the more recent revival of interest in shame not only in psychoanalysis but also in feminist and queer theory (for example, Probyn, 2005). The role of shame in inhibiting social solidarity has also been a recent sociological concern (Chase, & Walker, 2013). As Lindo (2013: 212) points out: 'the dynamics between shame and the body are such that the most shame-inducing moments are in fact those when the body appears to have lost control'. (We will see more of Fanon's figuring of shame and the body in relation to the case of the daughter of a murdered policeman, in Chapter 5.)

Here the loss of control is the blush, which (as alluded to in Fanon's school essay example quoted earlier) is also what discloses the woman's whiteness: 'Shame as an emotion carries a biography of the body that is specific to the individual and the cultural context from which the individual originates' (212). While the link between femininity and shame appears to hold across cultural contexts, such that 'oppressive ideologies damage, cripple and distort female subjects precisely because they function as *shaming* ideologies' (Johnson, & Moran, 2013: 3, emphasis in the original), nevertheless this does not prevent it having communicative, political, and even educational purposes:

> [S]hame is a non-dialectical flow between and within individuals. It can bind or divide. It can distort reality or serve as a moral compass. Significantly, shame can function as a tool of critique, for does the critic not shame the perpetrators of patriarchy, homophobia and colonialism in his/her parsing of such ideologies?
>
> *(ibid.)*

Risking shame?

Notwithstanding the civilisational hierarchy historically associated with the division between shame and guilt (with shame-based societies portrayed within the orientalist imaginary as developmentally more 'primitive'), we should note how this formulation by anthropologists was initially in the service of colonial and, later, cold war agendas (as exemplified by Ruth Benedict's, 1935, 1967 classic texts). While the binary between shame and guilt is largely now questioned (Price Tangney, & Dearing, 2002), even Benedict (1967) herself came to question this image of simplicity or uncommitted reasoning because, as she noted, it is the *fantasised* anticipation of, rather than an actual encounter with, humiliation that works as the prompt for shame:

> Shame is a reaction to other people's criticism. A man is shamed either by being openly ridiculed and rejected or by fantasying to himself that he has been made ridiculous. In either case it's a potent sanction. But it requires an audience or at least a man's fantasy of an audience. Guilt does not.
>
> *(157)*

Guilt has been understood as a more 'mature', complex emotion, associated with Western societies and Christianity (also discussed in Burman, 2007). Yet as we have seen, shame can also galvanise change. Indeed, insofar as their relationship remains tenable, cultural psychiatrists now tend to interpret cultural interpretations and distributions of the shame/guilt opposition in terms of an East/West difference in relation to societal cultural differences:

> [T]here is a cultural difference, and some people are brought up to be more other-directed and less inner-directed, so this is not a simple moral issue. A practical consequence is that guilt is not a reliable indicator of depressive illness in every culture, and we should not expect to encounter it everywhere.
>
> *(Rack, 1982: 109)*

As we will see in Chapter 4, in the case of Fanon's discussion and intervention within B—'s depression, such cultural allocations around lack of guilt are highly questionable. As Richards (1997) also notes of other binaries such as collectivism versus individualism, these risk reification and psychologisation that, even if they were ever tenable, are undermined through globalisation and transnational relations.

At any rate, we can do something to rectify public opinion, and as such shame can be an important incentive towards both individual and collective reparation. By contrast, guilt, with its cycle of spiralling associations, can often never be assuaged. In so far as such a distinction is tenable, alongside the variable and conflicting ways people use these terms there may be aspects of shame, rather than guilt, that offer a better position from which to formulate strategies for antiracist education. (The psychoanalyst Helen Bloch Lewis (1987: 22), for example, claims a typology for distinguishing them that crosses rather than corresponds with my discussion here (Lewis, 1980; Zarem, 2006).) Shame is, at least, something we all have known, and have been recognised as experiencing by others, if only through our bodies, whereas guilt is silent and invisible.

Significantly, Fanon opens *Black Skin* by claiming its status as 'a clinical study' (11) not only in diagnosing certain pathological conditions but also in aiming to prompt a therapeutic change, a change to be prompted by shame at racialisation processes. He continues:

> Those who recognise themselves in it, I think, will have made a step forward. I seriously hope to persuade my brother, whether black or white, to tear off with all his strength the shameful livery put together by centuries of incomprehension.
>
> *(Black Skin: 11)*

This may help inform the status of Fanon's claim when he names shame as the mother's emotion 'flood[ing] her face' (81), and shame is also what he identifies as his own response: 'Shame. Shame and self-contempt. Nausea' (82). But even so, shame presupposes an intersubjective relationship, in the sense that it not only involves a devalued perception of oneself but also the intersubjective sense of being devalued in the eyes of the other, and so betrays how the self cares about how the other sees one (Lewis, 1987). Nevertheless, two shames, exchanged or added together, neither cancel the hurt nor necessarily usher in solidarity or rectification (Locke, 2016). At issue, then, are general as well as specific questions concerning thresholds of comfort and discomfort necessarily at play within any educational (as also therapeutic) project (see Burman, 2016b; Britzman, 2003), even as accounts of antiracist education have come to topicalise pedagogies of discomfort (Bailey, 2017; Brooks, 2011; Zembylas, 2015a).

Emotions in learning

Notwithstanding their reflections of particular national histories of racism and racialisation, that (as Macey, 2010, and also Batchelor, 2017a: note) produce correspondingly distinct readings of Fanon (some US accounts could invite the impression that Fanon was a civil rights activist, for example), key educational precepts emerge that reflect those guiding this book. A central theme is affect or emotion: terror, fear, and (as we have seen) shame, as well as what that terror instigates for the racialised subject subjected to it. (Indeed, a recent account suggests that Fanon's account of the white child's reaction of fear is no different from the US now, 50 years later, Zack, 2017.) A considerable literature addresses dilemmas of engagement, of speaking out (to name not only oppression but also privilege) and how (often in the name of institutional or interpersonal claims to being 'colour blind') silence over racialisation – including whiteness – can function either as an escape or as a lower risk space to encounter the challenges this may pose (Ahmed, 2004; Yancy, 2017; Applebaum, 2012; Swan, 2017). The longstanding psychotherapeutic literature in this area is also a surprisingly undermobilised resource (Cooper, 1997; Treacher, 2004), whose relevance is attested by the discussion of psycho-affective and relational features of challenge, defensiveness, and avoidance. What is largely assumed and so underanalysed is how the educational space of the group – whether in the classroom or playground – is necessarily a site of reworking Oedipal challenges – here explicitly racialised. That is, outside a one-to-one, dyadic, relation, we are – each of us – all othered to others around us, as 'they' (see also Burman, 2015).

What this chapter's focus on Traumatogenic child adds to these discussions is a strategy of resisting the resolution of 'child' to a singular, abstracted, or separated child, the latter understood as itself as ideological a construction as the racist symbolic order it is depicted as issuing forth. Methodologically, it has attempted to stay with instabilities and ambiguities of reading the position of 'child'. Or, after Lacan's logical time puzzle, to wait, hesitate, and deliberate, before claiming to determine what this is. This practice wards off precipitous readings prompted by the recourse to the figure of the child, whether, as we have seen, resolved in favour of individual, interpersonal, familial, gendered, or racialised dynamics. The reading undertaken here has attempted to foreground how class, generational and gendered dynamics intersect with, and so complicate, those of racialisation and sexuality. While generated from Fanon's writings and the commentaries this has inspired, it is also motivated from a commitment to a pedagogical strategy that follows from an acknowledgement of such intersections that itself crosses discussions of pedagogies of solidarity. So, reading the 'Brexit Street' interviewees' reproduction of racism as narratively situated within an ideology of pathologisation and vilification of the working class offers some sites for coalition and mobilisation, even as also working-class communities have always been more mixed and diverse than middle class ones. This does not rely on a dynamic of common identification, but rather on analysis of the ideological processes structuring the formulation and reception of racist discourse that implicates every reader and speaker. This is a pedagogy of failure, of humility and partiality, but one committed to failing better next time, rather than giving up, to learn to 'do whiteness otherwise', through practices of solidarity and collective mobilisation as Butler (2017: 59) proposes. We make mistakes all the time: if psychoanalysis highlights the ease with which we repeat them, the educational question is (what) can we learn from them?

And how can we best enable educational environments where such learning can occur, that is, without either colluding with privilege and oppression but also without recapitulating the 'kind of violence that marginalizes the emotional selves of all participants in the room' (Brooks, 2011: 57). As psychotherapists know all too well, learning and change involve being discomforted, and – as we have seen from the mother's response as well as Fanon's (de-)subjectification, at the very least, from an acknowledgement of necessary inter-relatedness. As Zembylas, drawing on Butler, puts it:

> discomfort is inescapably tied to others: we always live in discomfort in this sense. Pedagogical discomfort, then, is the feeling of uneasiness as a result of the process of teaching and learning from/with others; insofar as the others 'de-center' us in this process, namely,

they challenge our cherished beliefs and assumptions about the world, pedagogical discomfort seems to be a necessary and unavoidable step in pedagogical actions.

(2015a: 171)

This chapter has indicated how Fanon's humanist commitments coexist with his psychoanalytic engagements. Across his writings, his model of the subject is psychoanalytic in that it is as much internally conflicted as externally driven and constrained, albeit that the former arises through the latter. His commitment to addressing those external constraints to liberate the individual from those conflicts is what makes him a humanist (and social constructionist), albeit that he understands clearly how internal barriers can still persist even after the external conditions have changed. As both politician and clinician he was committed to addressing both. If this chapter has reviewed what holds the subject back from change, from being able to act, as generated through Traumatogenic child, Chapter 4 offers some clues on how he went about doing something about this. In this, the moment of hesitation, that we have seen is necessary for the assumption of subjectivity and action within Lacan's 'logical time' sophism, is echoed by the suspension or underdetermination now seen here to characterise the subjectivity of Traumatogenic child. This is also what enables this child/subject to escape the determinations and fixity wrought by the position of the traumatised.

Traumatogenic child as a modality of child as method

This chapter follows child as method as a way of reading child into as well as from social relations. Here we have seen how intergenerational relations implicate others constellated around racialisation, class, and gender. The mother adopts her position of generational seniority, as someone 'who knows', and mobilises the claim of her son that 'he does not know'. Clearly one could, of course, suggest that he should know and that she should be responsible for this 'knowing', but this claim would merely recapitulate the reduction of the social to the interpersonal that was understood earlier as to be avoided. That aside, it is interesting that Fanon figures her response not in terms of 'he's only a child', nor even 'he does not *yet* know'. 'Child' here exercises a subject position that is accorded an epistemological and relational significance both equal to, but perhaps also beyond, any other. There is a curious multiplicity and instability here: there is no diminished responsibility on the basis of age, even if the racialised interpellation is also presented as experienced as all the more cataclysmic or foundational precisely because it is identified by the child who (as also marginal social subject) is not yet sufficiently 'civilised' as to have acquired the habits of politeness suited to his racialised and class position.

One final point brought to the fore by the perspective of child as method is that there is no equivalent of 'Look a Negro!' in relation to a child, except perhaps to indicate a child in a hazardous or unusual situation in need of help or intervention. Rather the trope would be 'Ah, a child!' – an attitude of indulgent presumption that indicates a different relationship to the social order: not one of excision from the social (as was the case with Idiotic child), but of only partial participation in it – that is, involving presumption of what a child is. This is what warrants the affective stance of assumed knowing, of spurious inclusion rather than marking of difference. Such are the fruitful underspecifications at play within Fanon's Traumatogenic child. Rather than banalising or sentimentalising, we should be attending to how 'Look, a child!', like 'Look, a Negro!', names a potent space of non-relationship.

4

THERAPEUTIC CHILD

If the prototypical image of child within Fanonian studies is Traumatogenic child (as discussed in Chapter 3), this is perhaps all the more remarkable given that the dominant iconography of childhood in culture is Therapeutic child. That is, a rendering of child and childhood as aligned with the self. This sentimentalised child, relentlessly mined by modern consumer capitalist culture (for both adults and children), relies on the conception of a period of ontogenetic vulnerability commanding indulgence and protection that is vital to sustain an experiential narrative of personal change. The 'inner child', that in current times is called upon to be nurtured, stands as a metonym for the adult self. But this is not all it achieves. For it can only occur as a corollary of the damaged child. It is this damaged or spoiled child that demands repair in order to facilitate a transformed personal (and political) future. Think of social policy discourses of 'early intervention', for example, which offer a particularly concrete line of thinking on this, and of course attract criticism from childhood theorists of subordinating and instrumentalising children as beings into mere becomings (Qvortup, 2005; Lee, 2001). Here Therapeutic child can be seen to link the personal and the political, and the individual and the social. And Fanon, no less than other writers, mobilises such notions, albeit in varying modalities and – according to what particular point about colonialism and racialisation he is making – with varying outcomes. Here we see Fanon at work as psychiatric and psychoanalytic practitioner, as witness of the distress caused by violence and injustice, and as political advocate of revolutionary change.

This chapter, therefore, evaluates the narration of Therapeutic child within Fanon's corpus. It does so through a close reading of one of Fanon's case histories in *The Wretched of the Earth* (*Wretched*), in the long chapter cataloguing the brutalising psychological impacts of colonial war. Recalling Kuby's (2015) analysis discussed in Chapter 1, it is where Fanon's analysis of trauma can be seen to diverge from Sartre's, and where Fanon emerges as a critic of violence. Focusing primarily on a detailed reading of Fanon's depiction of his most complete case history in *Wretched*, of the FLN fighter he calls 'B—', we see how child works in this account as signifier of colonial damage, that can then be mobilised to warrant a project of (personal and national) development. Perhaps surprisingly, this particular case has attracted little discussion from commentators on Fanon, and it is discussed here because it offers a narrative of therapeutic development, rather than (as with many of the other 'cases') merely asserting irreparable damage. Other similar examples are identified from this and others of Fanon's texts. Damaged children populate Fanon's texts as indictments of the evils and brutality of colonial oppression and repression, as well as complicities with it. (As further discussed in Chapter 5, Fanon describes the colonial bourgeoisie as 'spoilt children of yesterday's colonialism', *Wretched*: 37.)

To recall his trajectory (since this sets the scene for the analysis below), having trained as a psychiatrist in Lyon, France, Fanon worked as the clinical director of Blida-Joinville, a psychiatric hospital outside Algiers. Here he applied the 'institutional psychotherapy' approach he had learned from François Tosquelles at his internship at Saint Alban, radically reforming the care of the distressed (see Gendzier, 1973; Macey, 2012; Keller, 2007; Razanajao, et al., 1996; Khanna, 2013; Menozzi, 2015; Sikuade, 2012). As discussed previously, Tosquelles had been involved both professionally and politically in the antifascist struggle in Spain.

Murard (2008) traces the origins of this approach to developments in Britain around war-traumatised soldiers. Here it is relevant to note that these developments in the UK (see Harrison, 2000) were different from the US. While the US origins of group psychotherapy lie in Trigant Burrow's sermons or moral lectures to distressed and alienated people (Scheidlinger, 2000) that had strongly individualist as well as prescriptive orientations (Van Schoor, 2000), in the UK – notwithstanding their technical and theoretical differences from each other – the emphasis shared by such pioneers of group psychoanalysis as Bion and Foulkes was on rebuilding the social bonds and everyday functioning through group activities and discussion. From Tosquelles Fanon learned a similar psychopolitically informed psychoeducational practice, which Gibson (2013) claims also links to his model of revolutionary organisation. Moreover, beyond his clinical responsibilities, Fanon harboured political dissidents and gave psychological help to the casualties of war. These casualties included both the tortured and the torturers, giving rise to increasingly unmanageable situations as therapist/doctor in maintaining doctor–patient confidentiality alongside his attempts to use his apparently detached situation to propose negotiations. Eventually, Fanon resigned his post in 1957 leaving Algeria for Tunis where he continued to work as both psychiatrist and political spokesperson for the National Libration Front (FLN).

As a psychiatrist, but also political revolutionary and psychoeducator, Fanon's account is read in this chapter as indicative of his pedagogical address in motivating for socio-political as well as personal change, as well as an example of how this informed his therapeutic approach, albeit that this is in need of a feminist re-reading of the gendering of violence, including sexual violence. Indeed, as we shall see, the Therapeutic child at issue here, perhaps counter-intuitively, names the male subject in therapy, 'B—', rather than either his raped wife or abjected/'rotten' daughter. The chapter concludes by suggesting that, consistent with his psychoaffective model, Fanon's therapeutic as well as political analysis highlights, first, how resistance and transformation are simultaneously intrapersonal, interpersonal, and socio-political, but also that, second, attending to their shifting unstable and relational features may renew and reinvigorate perspectives informing psychological and pedagogical activisms.

The arrested, or childlike, status produced by the colonial condition is narratively evoked by Fanon both through depictions of children but also, crucially, through the depiction of *others' perceptions of* them. Here the failure to provide for children, or to recognise (let alone indulge) their childhood status works to signify the deprivations and brutalisation created by colonialism. Fanon mobilises dominant iconographies of childhood in the service of instigating anti-colonial sentiment. Once again in this chapter we will see the need for an intersectional analysis that attends to gendered as well as classed and generational relationships. It is also worth noting that the case histories discussed in the catalogue of – mostly irreparable – damage produced by torture and occupation in *Wretched* largely concern young adults, as well as children (under 18 years). Nevertheless, the rhetorical impact of such cataloguing of damage works not only as a damning reproach but also as a way of indicating the possibility of psychic and political change (that will be taken up in the next chapter, as Extemic child).

Analytical and methodological orientation

This chapter sets in play feminist and – albeit to a lesser extent – Foucaultian analyses as resources for reading Fanon's case histories in the service of reinterpreting models of the relations between psychoeducation and political change. These inform a model of the psychosocial that is political, in the sense of conceptualising the sociohistorical constituents and determinants of the domain of the (individual or collective) psyche (Frosh, 2003, 2010; Frosh, & Baraitser, 2008; Burman, 2008b). A reciprocal claim can, however, be made that therapeutic practices of (what in Foucault's terms are called) the care of the self or technologies of subjectivity, which are also (variably) political in their effects, can be mobilised transformatively as well as repressively (Foucault, 1988). This analysis will illustrate how Fanon's psychoeducational and psychopolitical project of anti-colonial mobilisation was practised as much through his clinical as his more overtly political activities. Indeed, Fuss (1994: 39), concluding her critical evaluation, proposes: 'What Fanon gives us, in the end, is a politics that does not oppose the psychical but fundamentally proposes it.' Clearly putting feminist, Foucaultian, and Fanonian perspectives together is not merely an overambitious project; it is also bound to fail. However, as already indicated, failure – or lack of certainty – informs this book's method as well as topic. Rather than a triumphal, harmonious narrative traversing the psychic and the political, the therapeutic and the educational, following Fanon's own line of argument, the methodological approach taken explores their tensions and ambiguities. These are used to invite further readings of Fanon, as part of a project of elaborating critical theory (and practice) in education and psychology.

Fanon's methodology of failure

Fanon's anti-colonial project was clearly informed by Marxist perspectives (although as we have seen to call him a 'black Lenin' would be to overstate this, Gates, 1991). As a passionate advocate for national liberation movements, his analyses (especially in *A Dying Colonialism* and *The Wretched of the Earth*, both texts I will be drawing upon in this chapter) addressed the building of mass political consciousness and popular democracy, as well as explicating and critiquing the complicities of the colonial bourgeoisie.

Fanon's reference to Nietzsche's trope of how 'the tragedy of the man is that he was once a child' at both the beginning and end of *Black Skin* has already been discussed. To that discussion we can add that it can be read psychoanalytically and developmentally as emphasising the role of early experience, albeit to claim that such psychobiographical determinations can be transformed. Indeed, Fanon outlines his project as aiming 'to eliminate a whole set of defects left over from childhood' (*Black Skin*: 9). Fanon's psychoaffective account (Hook, 2012, 2005) of colonial experience also offers resources for understanding dynamics of internal colonization (Oliver, 2004)

and its perverse or conflicting effects (Oliver 2005). So, notwithstanding
Fanon's sweeping criticisms of psychoanalysis and colonial psychiatry, as in
dismissing the existence of the Oedipus complex in the Antilles in *Black Skin*
and his indictments of the ways that colonial psychiatry treats the native as a
backward child in *Wretched*, he draws on psychoanalysis in order to elaborate
both his theory and method.

Significantly, for Fanon, this theoretical and methodological engagement
arises via the question of language and power. This starts in *Black Skin*:

> all these inquiries lead only in one direction: to make man admit that he is
> nothing, absolutely nothing – and that he must put an end to the narcis-
> sism on which he relies in order to imagine that he is different from other
> 'animals'. This amounts to nothing more nor less than *man's surrender*.
>
> *(17, emphasis in the original)*

The method put forward to counter this disastrous 'narcissism on which he
relies in order to imagine that he is different from other "animals"' (*Black
Skin*: 17) is to analyse what he calls 'failures':

> Having reflected on that, I grasp my narcissism with both hands and
> I turn my back on the degradation of those who would make man
> a mere mechanism . . . . I am willing to work on the psychoanalytic
> level – in other words, the level of the 'failures', in the sense in which
> one speaks of engine failures.
>
> (Black Skin: 17)

Fanon's pedagogy of failure has already featured in earlier chapters. But,
for this chapter, two points of significance arise: first, that the 'mechanism'
may 'fail' but is still a worthy project, and, second, that this failure, or rather
the admission, the *speaking of* its failure, is the place to begin. This focus on
failure will be taken up as offering a different reading of Fanon's revolutionary political and therapeutic practice, through a close reading of primarily a
single case, the fullest and perhaps almost only 'successful' case reported in
Wretched, albeit that this 'success' remains contingent on the political victory
of anti-colonial struggle.

Disrupting linearity: Fanon with Foucault and feminisms

There is a second methodological point on which Fanonian perspectives
converge with both Foucaultian and feminist arguments (even as these
frameworks conflict elsewhere). All three trouble conventional models of

method, and, as such, make an important intervention in educational and psychological debates. Feminist theory asserts the key connection between ontology (being) and epistemology (knowledge) as central to challenging masculinist, spurious objectivisms to show how theory and method are inextricably linked (Harding, 2004, 2006; Haraway, 1988; Hekman, 1997, 2010). Similarly, Foucault's 'toolbox' imported a hermeneutic of suspicion: hence, his notion of the history of the present to describe the telling of history as a practice of legitimation of current conditions, rather than simply an account of the past (Scheurich, & McKenzie, 2005). Fanon also offers some provocative methodological comments in the early pages of *Black Skin* that can be read as anticipating discussions of 'methodolatry' in qualitative social research as diversionary, in its mimicking of quantitative research's preoccupation with methods (Chamberlain, 2000). With characteristic derision, he writes:

> It is good form to introduce a work in psychology with a statement of its methodological point of view, I shall be derelict. I leave methods to the botanists and the mathematicians. There is a point at which methods devour themselves.
>
> *(*Black Skin*: 11)*

Taken together, these critical frameworks topicalise questions of temporality. As a project of socio-political transformation, feminisms of all kinds are engaged in practices of both critique and prefiguration: or, what has been called, the future perfect tense (Kristeva, et al., 1981). As Jardine (1981: 5) writes, this is: 'a modality that implies neither that we are helpless before some inevitable destiny nor that we can somehow, given enough time and thought, engineer an ultimately perfect future'. By contrast, Foucault is often quoted as saying 'to imagine another system is to extend our participation in the present system' (1977: 230), expressing his suspicion of alternatives/utopias, as being framed in relation to – even if precisely because attempting to transcend or end – the present conditions (Pickett, 19996; Hartsock, 1990; Hekman, 1996). This has also been heralded by feminists as usefully cautioning overambitious political claims (Ferguson, 1991).

As a political revolutionary within the Algerian liberation struggle, Fanon was explicitly and actively committed to a project of political transformation, as well as to attending to the psychopathology caused by racialised and colonial oppression. It is, therefore, not surprising that in his later books he subscribes to a developmentalist account of (national) progress towards mass mobilisation and popular democracy (although as discussed in Chapter 1, this nationalism can be read as being in the service of a wider internationalism). However, his comments in *Black Skin* on temporality are surprisingly close to feminist and Foucaultian analyses. Of course, some of this comes from the phenomenological commitment to struggle and transcendence of the past: 'Ideally the present will always contribute to the building of the future' (*Black Skin*: 12). This converges with a Foucaultian caution, since this future can only be built by attending to current conditions: 'In no fashion should I undertake to prepare the world that will come later. I belong irreducibly to my time' (*Black Skin*: 12). The project of personal and political change is not only to make a new world for others. Rather:

> It is for my own time that I should live. The future should be an edifice supported by living men. This structure is connected to the present to the extent that I consider the present in terms of something to be exceeded.
>
> (Black Skin: 12)

Of course, it needs to be noted that there is also a trenchant feminist critique of Fanon that, first, highlights the incipient misogyny, androcentrism, and homophobia of his discussions (in *Black Skin*), as well as in some receptions of his writing (Bergner, 1995); second, interprets these as a displaced version of his own biographical anxieties as an Antillean man (Vergès, 1996, 1997; but see also Chow, 1999; Khanna, 2004); third, interrogates his nationalist romantic investment in the Algerian woman (Haddour, 2010; Fuss, 1994; see also Chapter 5); and, fourth, notes how he offers little in the way of a critique of the family, even if he critiqued some patriarchal practices within the peasant family, especially in attending to women's labour in rural Algeria. Nevertheless, it should also be noted that Fanon's work informs and supports challenges to (especially second-wave Euro-US) feminisms in terms of taking colonialism seriously (Thompson, 2015); while as discussed in Chapter 3, it has been suggested that Fanon may provide a better, in the sense of more specifically situated, account than Foucault among others of subjectification. As I shall argue below, in his accounts of his clinical practice he is much closer to both a Freudian and Foucaultian approach to temporality.

At issue then is the subversion or disruption of notions of linearity, including the route, direction, and outcome of intervention. This ushers in more complex, psychopolitically attuned temporalities mobilised by diverse arenas of political practice. Indeed, the attention to narrative, rather than logical or historical, order is reflected in the structure of this chapter. I present and then re-present Fanon's account of this case, offering additional and successive readings and re-readings to attend to and explicate his psychopolitical and psychoeducational methodology.

In terms of relevance to psychology and education, Fanon is emphatic:

> The analysis that I am undertaking is psychological. In spite of this it is apparent to me that the effective disalienation of the black man entailed an immediate recognition of the social and economic realities . . . It will be seen that the black man's alienation is not an individual question. Besides phylogeny and ontogeny stands sociogeny.
>
> (Black Skin: 11)

His claim to offer 'a sociodiagnostic' (ibid.), offers resistance to the individualising and pathologising (ab)uses of psychology, albeit also highlighting the psychological consequences of social relations of oppression and exploitation, and – as both mental health practitioner, and political spokesperson – making practical his support for revolutionary change.

Reading psychoeducational and political change against the grain

The notion of 'psychoeducation' topicalised here not only links psychology and education but also highlights pedagogical features of psychological technologies and practices, including psychotherapy. Indeed, the term 'psychoeducation' is frequently associated with modes of psychological therapy that involve the transmission of prescribed educational messages, whose (linear) pedagogical purposes are associated with social adaptation (especially, but not only, of misbehaving youth) as well as with group therapies (Scheidlinger, 1994), which are often heralded as offering 'corrective emotional experiences' to resocialise and re-integrate both marginalised experiences previously rendered unutterable and also marginalised or socially isolated individuals (Foulkes, 1975). The notion of psychoeducation is, however, also mobilised in relation to therapies around trauma and war (Litwack, et al., 2015).

I want to subvert adaptationist readings of 'psychoeducation' (that is, the project to adapt individuals to prevailing social conditions, rather than critically engaging with or changing them) through attention to the connections between therapeutic and sociopolitical project evident in Fanon's psychiatric practice, the significance of which has only relatively recently been given serious reconsideration (Giordano, 2011; Khanna, 2013; Khalfa, 2015; Menozzi, 2015; Sikuade, 2012). This critical approach to psychoeducation owes much to feminist and Foucaultian arguments, in particular those that demonstrate the reach of pedagogical and psychological discourses outside schooling and therapeutic contexts to inform state and transnational policies and practice

(Pykett, 2012; De Vos, 2013; Jones, et al., 2013). These accounts of the so-called pedagogical state highlight the indirect forms of governmentality installed by the educational mode of address, including 'nudge economics' whereby the subject is guided towards a 'correct' behaviour, and so feels themselves to be choosing to do it voluntarily, rather than being explicitly (as a more authoritarian mode of regulation) told what to do.

The attention to Fanon's therapeutic practice not only offers new per- spectives on Fanon but also on the psychoeducational project of psychosocial (that is, social and personal) transformation, too. While treatments of Fanon's political and psychiatric practice are often separated, this chapter's focus on a psychopolitical reading of (one of) Fanon's 'clinical' cases is used to argue for both the necessity of, and critical engagement with, the ways that psy- chotherapeutic as well as political pedagogical forms are linked. As Gendzier (1973) notes: 'It was an exposé of what colonialism did to people and what colonial wars accomplished' (104).

In particular, the genre of the 'case history' demands some critical reflec- tion since this is the pedagogical mode Fanon adopts in the last third of *Wretched*. As Gendzier comments, perhaps there is something 'obscene' in making case histories out of political atrocities (ibid.). Yet, clearly this is where Fanon the medical doctor is teaching his readers about the devastat- ing psychological impacts of colonial oppression and war – and his examples range from the trauma of witnessing loved ones being murdered (including, as a special form of torture for both the murdered and their loved ones, being forced to watch them being butchered), to a systematic catalogue of the outcomes of torture for (presumably the subset who survived of) those undergoing it, as well as some indications of the brutalising effects on the perpetrators. Fanon, the psychiatrist, is teaching his audience in the sense of warranting a particular moral-political lesson to be learnt – about the evils of war and colonial repression. It is a powerful way of using his specific profes- sional authority as a clinician for political purposes. As Turner comments,

> Fanon's method of engaging the intersecting spheres of domestic pri- vacy, the medical (il)legal privacy of the torture chamber, and the privacy of the psychiatric session was to rend the veil of privacy by publicising his case studies as a revolutionary act.
>
> *(2011: 120)*

If this seems an extreme application of psychiatric authority, it is in line with the general pedagogical purpose of the case history within psychotherapeutic and clinical practice. The genre of the case history, the history of clinical intervention in a 'case', has long inhabited medicine and psychotherapy, just

as psychology, psychotherapy, and psychoanalysis have also long been implicated in and benefit from war (Roberts, 2007). The very language suggests a
studied, dispassionate, and expert gaze. Indeed, the expert's authority is typically predicated on the supposed objectivity of the narration of the case. The
case history is often mobilised to tell the story of a clinical problem as if this
narrates the natural history of the problem rather than the record of formulation of and then intervention in it. Every therapist in training learns how to
tell these histories, oriented according to whichever model of practice they
are learning. Case histories, therefore, function for the case presenter as a
largely implicit pedagogical apparatus to perform their therapeutic compe-
tence, as much as to tell triumphal or redemptive developmental stories of
clients' psychological transformation.

Notably, for Fanon, the primary framework for and of the problem is
colonialism, and his account of his work with his patients becomes a lesson
about its abhorrent impacts on and in their lives. The main moral of the
story, then, is to document how bad colonialism is, rather than to do what so
many doctors and therapists find themselves doing, which is to risk servicing
those oppressive conditions by enabling people to cope better with them.
Hence, Fanon's case histories in *Wretched* are largely documents of psychological devastation and damage, narrated without therapeutic hope because
the 'cure' has to be political as well as personal. In response to authors who
have criticised Fanon as supplying insufficient biographical or contextual
information to allow evaluation of these 'cases', Gendzier (1973) suggests:

> For Fanon the connection between such acts and the environment of
> war was so obvious he no longer felt it necessary to record the detailed
> history of each man under conditions of stress. If his descriptions of the
> individual case histories, insofar as they were meant to be that and not
> merely descriptions, were inadequate, his more generous image of the
> Algerian situation and its impact on the human environment was ample.
>
> *(108–109)*

Yet since such performative projects are intrinsic to the genre of the case
history, the selective character of their presentation should be assumed. On
a practical note, much has been made of Fanon's lack of facility in Arabic,
although it should be recalled he in fact only lived and worked in Algeria for
three years, in which time it is said that he tried hard both to learn Arabic
and other regional varieties and idioms. Indeed, Harding (2017) explicitly
connects Fanon's translation and interpretation efforts with his project of
both psychiatric reform and (as with any antipsychiatry intervention that is
psychiatry-led) its anti-colonial tensions. As she comments:

Fanon and his colleague at Blida-Joinville, Jacques Azoulay, deliberately set about to increase their knowledge of local cultures, social
practices and socio-economic circumstances and, in response, worked
self-critically to modify their psychiatric practice (see also Cherki
2006; Shohat 2006, 257–258). Part of this included the novel recruitment of (local) male nurses to act as Arabic and Kabyle interpreters,
a practice which garnered their loyalty to the reforms that Fanon was
attempting to introduce into the hospital and facilitated communication between doctors and patients, but nevertheless, as Fanon and
Azoulay observe in the (French) article they co-authored on their
efforts, also served to reinforce the social and linguistic hierarchy of
French-colonised Algeria.

(207–208)

Hence, the apparent dialogical exchanges within the accounts of the cases,
in particular the one I focus on below, arise from sessions that were likely
to be conducted through interpretation (and may even have been initially
written up by nurses, Fuss, 1994; Gendzier, 1973). While Fuss (1994) questions how psychoanalysis could be possible across such modes of linguistic
and interpersonal translations and mediations, it is nevertheless possible to
read the text of such case histories as performative narratives indicative of
therapeutic problems and possibilities. Further, it should be noted that by
the time he wrote these case histories for publication in *Wretched* Fanon
had already left Blida, and indeed was in exile from Algeria, that is, he had
already acknowledged the failure of his therapeutic project there in favour of
political activism. Extending his explicit repudiation of colonial psychiatry as
offering an intellectual apology for or even rationale for colonialism, Fanon's
cases, therefore, offer a pedagogical narrative of the necessary failure of colonial psychiatry, of psychiatry under colonialism, even as conducted under his
clinical watch. Yet, we should also recall that Fanon was not only politicised
through his therapeutic commitments, but he also remained active as a psychiatric reformer in both Tunisia and Morocco, where he combined political
activism for the FLN alongside teaching and instituting psychiatric reforms.

Fanon's case histories: psychiatry amid 'a veritable Apocalypse'

As is well known, the question of identity looms large across Fanon's work, as
a feature of claiming subjectivity for those who have been denied it through
dehumanisation and subjugation. Fanon opens the section on 'Colonial
wars and mental disorders', which comprise the last 50 pages of his final

(1961/1963) book, *The Wretched of the Earth,* with the statement 'colonialism forces the people it dominates to ask themselves the question constantly: "In reality, who am I?"' (200). But here it is clear that this is also a question about the claim on the world, on reality, on the demand for a different reality – a glimpse that this, current, reality is not all there is.

Notwithstanding his sometimes conventional psychiatric practice (for example, there are reports that he used drugs and even Electro-Convulsive-Therapy, Macey (2012), Gendzier (1973), as is also indicated by recently published translations of some of his clinical papers, Fanon (2018) – although this would not have been uncharacteristic for that time), here Fanon documents rather than diagnoses. He presents the cases as 'eloquent' (*Wretched*: 201) evidence of the 'total war' (ibid.) on Algerians. So, he offers his 'socio-diagnostic' (*Black Skin*: 11) as a critique not only of the ways that colonial psychiatry serviced the occupying regime and legitimated the '"pacification"' (*Wretched*: 200) (his term) of the 'natives' (also his term) but also how this 'pacification' itself produces pathology.

His argument was that a 'cure' could not be found merely in interpersonal therapy, even as he was also demonstrating the psychic distress of colonization. So, Fanon writes of particular forms of (what he calls) 'mental pathology' that arise even during relatively calmer periods of (apparently successful) colonization. These include the aggressive boredom of enforced inactivity or suppression it produces, with ennui masking seething resentment that sometimes erupts destructively and displaced in relation to those close by, rather than directed to the source of the oppression. Brilliantly echoing Fanon's account, is the scene in Elia Suleiman's (2002) poignant film, *Divine Intervention,* where neighbours in a West Bank town in Israeli-occupied Palestine feud with each other over where the rubbish is placed on the street for collection. Just as colonialism seeps into the psyche, so the diminished and disturbed forms of subjectivity produced by precarity and poverty invite consideration, including how this works to dismantle the sense of a joined, if not even joined up, connection to a broader social collectivity. Or even where collective membership is offered only on a pathologised and dehumanised basis (see also Chase, & Walker, 2013). As Fanon puts it: 'The colonized people find that they are reduced to a body of individuals who only find cohesion when in the presence of the colonizing nation' (*Wretched*: 237). Here Fanon also presciently anticipates some of the subjective challenges to be faced following decolonisation, including the attachment to the connections with others forged through violent deprivations and struggle (see Lazali, 2011).

In *Wretched,* Fanon presents a systematic account of the psychic impacts of colonial subjugation. Notwithstanding his claims to 'avoid all arguments over semiology, nosology or therapeutics' (201), he explicitly repudiates the conventional psychiatric distinction between intrinsic and reaction-oriented explanations:

> It seems to us that in the cases here chosen the events giving rise to the disorder are chiefly the bloodthirsty and pitiless atmosphere, the generalization of inhuman practices and the firm impression that people have of being caught up in a veritable Apocalypse.
>
> *(202)*

He later formulates this as irreducibly combined psychic and political responses deriving from a specific context: 'These are reactionary psychoses, if we want to use a ready-made label; but here we must give a particular priority to the war: a war which in whole and in part is a colonial war' (202).

Fanon mobilises his psychiatric authority to offer an extensive catalogue of distress. There are four 'Series' of cases reviewed in *Wretched*, and each 'Series' subdivides into different 'cases'. Series A has five cases of the 'reactionary type' (204); Series B addresses cases arising from 'the atmosphere of total war which reigns in Algeria' (217), which includes another five cases, including the widely discussed case of the two boys who killed their 'European friend' ('European' here meaning French colonial, or *pied-noir*) (217–218) that will be discussed further in Chapter 5. Series C documents cases of psychological distress after torture (in which he also notes the numbers of cases encountered), which is then organised around the impacts of particular forms of torture (electricity, 'truth serum', brain washing – the last subdivided into effects on 'intellectuals' and 'non-intellectuals' since this status appeared to demarcate specific responses). Series D concerns 'psychosomatic disorders' of ulcers, colic, menstruation problems for women, muscle stiffness, hair turning white, insomnia, and more. The final section discusses the supposed 'criminality' of the Algerian, not only as a racist myth but as 'experienced on the narcissistic level as a manifestation of authentic virility, and [to instead] place the problem on the level of colonial history' (*Wretched*: 246). We may note that these cases are reported as having been encountered across hospitals, among his private patients and in the health services of the Army of National Liberation (204) – to which Fanon was also providing professional support.

I now offer a reading of one of Fanon's cases, in which questions of method, of temporality, of political and professional practice come into play. Consideration of these requires detailed explication – attending *both to the case and Fanon's narration of* the case. My account here correspondingly alternates between account and comment, importing especially some feminist reflections alongside an evaluation of Fanon's tale of the treatment.

'B—': a story of lost potency

Fanon titles the first case in Series A of *Wretched* 'Impotence in an Algerian following the rape of his wife' (204). This title, therefore, already proposes an explanation for a problem, yet even more will emerge as at play. The initial presenting problems of the man, who is referred to as 'B—', are described as anxiety, headaches, insomnia, and lack of appetite – all features, Fanon notes, of generalised depressive symptomatology readily recognisable in oppressed groups. Yet, and this is crucial to his psychoaffective commitment that combines attention to individual nuance of political conditions, Fanon is at pains to highlight that specific personal histories as well as political events are at play. What emerges is that this Algerian man, a former taxi driver, who then supported the Front de Libération National (FLN) as a driver, came to be caught up in a fight between the FLN and French forces and so was forced into hiding for three further years with the Maquis (armed resistance), away from his family. During this time his wife was taken away by French forces, where she was beaten and raped.

Fanon reports that on admission to the hospital

> the surface . . . screen of optimism melted away, and what we saw in front of us was a thoughtful, depressed man, suffering from loss of appetite, who kept to his bed. He avoided political discussion and showed a marked lack of interest in everything to do with the national struggle.
>
> *(205–206).*

Unravelling his story involved a complex set of associations linking his expressed problem of sexual impotence (in relation to a woman who was not his wife) to the report of a dream 'in which the patient saw the rapid rotting away of a little cat accompanied by unbearably evil smells' (206). The man's account of his efforts to overcome this impotence included that 'a few seconds before the act, he had an irresistible impulse to tear up the photo of his little girl' (ibid.) due to the overwhelming feeling that there was 'something rotten about her' (ibid.). This is where (notwithstanding the problems of translation and mediation noted earlier) a key connection is made. For in the act of narrating this, Fanon notes, the key disclosure of the underlying problem occurs: he 'spoke to us for the first time about his wife, laughing and saying to us: "She's tasted the French"' (ibid.). It is worth noting that Fanon and his colleagues – referred to as 'the Service' – report initially that they considered the possibility that 'irresistible impulse' (ibid.) to tear up the photo may indicate incestuous desires – or rather, it is implied, efforts to repudiate them. However, the dream and subsequent interviews 'led us to take quite another course' (ibid.).

So not only do the personal and the political emerge as intertwined with gender and sexual relations, including sexual violence, but they are specifically constituted through war. Recall that this man was referred to the hospital 'on the advice of the Health Service of the F.L.N.' (204) because he had become an unreliable fighter: 'In 1958 he was entrusted with a mission abroad. When it was time to rejoin his unit, certain fits of absence of mind and sleeplessness made his comrades and superiors anxious about him. This was when we saw him' (205).

Two key points should be noted. First, notwithstanding the referral on the grounds of questionable military function, the sources of the man's presenting problem appeared to lie in his marital relationship rather than directly with the military scene. Second, an important matter for the argument of this chapter is that, significantly, there is no account of his relationship to his daughter. Rather, only to the photo of her. Fanon describes how in further sessions 'B—' reports that his was an arranged marriage and that he had preferred another 'girl' who had been promised to another:

> 'I married this girl although I loved my cousin . . . I wasn't very attached to my wife. And with the troubles, I got further apart than ever. In the end I used to come and eat my meals and sleep almost without speaking to her.'
>
> *(206–207)*

The marital relationship had not been close, then, even before the enforced separation when 'B—' went into hiding. The development of the man's symptoms appears to arise through 'B—'s' recognition that the rape of his wife by the French forces was a direct result of her protecting him and the Maquis, in refusing to betray them, leading to a re-evaluation of the relationship. Even before he was able to return home, he resolved to be reunited with her:

> 'That wasn't a simple rape, for want of something better to do, or for sadistic reasons like those I've had occasion to see in the villages; it was the rape of an obstinate woman, who was ready to put up with everything rather than sell her husband. And the husband in question, *it was me*. It was because of me that she had been dishonoured. And yet she didn't say to me: "Look at all I've had to bear for you." On the contrary, she said: "Forget about me; begin your life over again, for I have been dishonoured." It was from that moment on that I made my own decision to take back my wife after the war.'
>
> *(207, emphasis in the original)*

Still he reported that 'often, while I was looking at the photo of my daughter, I used to think that she too was dishonoured, like as if everything that had to do with my wife was rotten' (ibid.).

The implication here is that distress needs to be situated not only within its sociopolitical context but also that this has preconditions. In relation to 'B——'s own psychobiography, his problem was not only 'caused' by his reaction to the rape of his wife as a (sadly widely used) deliberate and brutal colonial-patriarchal strategy of 'dishonour'/disturbance (Bourke, 2007; Fuss, 1994). Implied, though not stated, it is also as a response to 'B——'s dawning awareness of his own previous disregard for her. Tracing back the links, this lack of care was prompted by the psychic conflict he had experienced by not marrying the woman he had wanted, which now resurfaced as further conflicted through the struggle to overcome his sense of revulsion that her body, his marital space, had been invaded and occupied.

Therapeutic child as gendered proxy for trauma

Having presented the 'case', some reflections are needed. In particular, Foucaultian and feminist/queer analyses offer some interpretive resources. Further, the significance of the photo of the daughter standing in for the mother calls for consideration. This relies on a key chain of associations between sexuality and gender, as well as the longstanding connections between rape and war. A precondition for such linkage is the intersection between gender and childhood, here indicated by how the girlchild is made 'rotten' as a (gender aligned) substitute for/equivalent of the husband's affective orientation to her mother. Yet the trope of the girlchild may also express something else: an equivalent possible offspring as the outcome of her mother's rape. A third association (recalling here how the condensation function of the unconscious allows a single association to carry several meanings simultaneously) appears as a (perhaps accurate) anticipation of the stigma the girlchild may encounter because of what has happened to her mother. This interpretation is also supported by 'B——'s distress being focused on his daughter as now dishonoured through association with the 'rotten'-ness of the mother.

So, the girlchild emerges as some kind of focal proxy for other injuries and problems. This is made even more striking by the specification of this 'little girl' as being aged 'a year and eight months' (204) at the time of 'B——'s going into hiding. It would appear that this image of the (girl)child had become connected with the violent creation of a (dystopian) national futurity (French opposition to Algerian independence movements). This could only occur because of her representative status as a material sign of reproductive heteronormativity, as a girlchild presumed to become a woman, like her mother (Edelman, 2004). Yet not only did this case not involve a 'real' (historical, embodied) child, nor even a narrative account of the presenting 'patient' *as* a child. Rather the child in question was a *representation* of the analysand's daughter. All this psychic work was occurring around a photograph of a child, a photograph that does indeed depict this man's daughter. Yet his distress was not directly associated with his relationship with this child, but rather this appeared to mediate other dynamics. This suggests four key points.

First, Fanon is here indicating how the work of substitution and association (metaphor and metonymy) is facilitated around gender and generation. While (given the limitations of his analyses of gender and sexuality) he may not have explicitly topicalised this, it can be noted that this, in turn, could occur only because of heteropatriarchal discourses of the family, in which women and children are positioned as objects of 'natural' ownership. Moreover, this is also precisely the discourse through which, by analogical extension of such 'natural authority', colonial domination was legitimised (McClintock, 1995).

Yet, second, what Fanon also offers, through the depiction of this association, is a material example of how modern technology enters into psychic life, precisely through the complications of temporality and identifications set in train. It should be noted that this is not the only example Fanon provides – see 'The Voice of Algeria' in *A Dying Colonialism* that discusses the shifting and ambiguous political significations carried by the radio (see also Painter, 2012). That the inventor of the camera, Oliver Wendell Jones, described it as 'a mirror with a memory' (cited in Raiford, 2009: 112) prompts some more psychodynamic readings of this visual medium, as reflecting aspects of the subject. The photograph is an image that is invested with fantasies whose associations and temporalities shift according to moment and context of viewing. Recall that the birth and so existence of 'B——'s' 'little girl' (206), his 'little daughter' (ibid.), pre-dated his going into hiding. She was not, in fact, the outcome of a rape by French soldiers. Yet, she seemed now to be associated with and so functions as a reminder of this, after the event; alongside perhaps how she may now also be dishonoured through her relationship with her mother. This echoes Barthes' (1981) discussion of the photo as *punctum*, 'the laceration of the spectator by a detail' (cited in Scott, 1999: 24). This is what appears to fuel the desire to tear up the photo – as if by such action he could thereby destroy or erase the traumatic event. As Barthes put it:

> The trauma is a suspension of language, a blocking of meaning. Certain situations which are normally traumatic can be seized in a process of signification but then precisely they are indicated by a rhetorical code which distances, sublimates and pacifies them.
>
> *(ibid.)*

Third, remarkable also is the role fulfilled by the photograph in facilitating the transition of psychic association from mother to daughter. This is despite the fact that there is no information on whether the 'little girl' resembles her mother (nor do we know how old she was in the picture, for while he had been separated from her since she was a baby, according to the dates provided by Fanon and the interval noted, at the time of 'B—'s narration she is now at least 4 years and 8 months old). All this work was accomplished through assumed common gender transcending generation to link daughter with mother. It may also be relevant to note that there was no indication of how old 'B—'s wife was when they married – although it is implied by the designation of his wife as a 'girl', alongside the fact of it being a match arranged by both sets of parents, that she was young. Since 'B—'s current age was reported by Fanon as being only 26, this could, in current contexts, be interpreted as an early marriage.

Yet, fourth, what emerges as critical is how the sequence of the reported narration works in relation to the topography of the distress. 'B—' is reported as saying: "'So I decided to take her [his wife] back; but I didn't know how I'd behave when I saw her. And often, while I was looking at the photo of my daughter, I used to think that she too was dishonoured, like as if everything to do with my wife was rotten'" (207). That is, there is a series of steps: first, there was the decision to 'take back' his wife. Second, there was his anxiety of managing his own response: 'how I'd behave when I saw her'. Third, both the decision and the uncertainty/anxiety about this were constellated by looking at the photo, all of which gave rise to a sense of the 'dishonour' migrating from the mother to the daughter.

Therapeutic child as mediation, representation, and index of shifting temporalities

Unpicking this curious and complex set of associations reveals another level of representation. Just as Fanon's account of the case history requires a shift of temporal frame from the present to the past and back again, so this scenario of ambivalent reconciliation takes place only in fantasy. Crucially, at the time of this therapeutic encounter, 'B—' *has not in fact yet returned* to his wife. Indeed, it emerges that he learnt of his wife's rape indirectly, reported to him while he was in hiding. It is made clear in the text that, having consulted with her mother, 'B—' received a message from his wife while he was in hiding 'in which she asked him to forget her, for she had been dishonoured and he ought not to think about taking up their life together again' (204). It is reported that 'B—' was refused permission from his commander to return home secretly to see her, and instead a member of the FLN was sent to see 'B—'s' wife and parents and thus a 'detailed report reached the commander of 'B—'s' unit' (205), and from this 'detailed report' 'B—' learnt what had happened. So, what was being expressed here via the relationship to the image of his daughter was his response, and conflicted *anticipations of* his response, of what might happen when eventually he *might* return home, alongside the fact that the 'dishonouring' of his wife had been reported in detail to the Maquis. This further layer of mediated reporting invites three further points for consideration.

First, since he learnt of the detail of the rape through the report from the FLN operative to his commander, which was then passed onto him, as is well-known from legal practice (Crowe, 2015), the public character of this chain of reporting may well have had a (re)traumatising impact. Yet, second, unravelling the story indicates that 'B—'s psychological difficulties only emerged some two or three years after he had received this report. This was when 'B—' was called to undertake another mission, as well as (so to speak) attempting other emissions (a relationship with another woman). Therefore, third, this would suggest the model of temporality informing Fanon's analysis of trauma, of *Nachträglichkeit*, whereby the second event (of being called to do another mission) re-evoked the earlier one. However, *quite which is the earlier traumatic event* remains crucially underdetermined. Or rather – given the overall context of war and socio-political dislocations at every level – perhaps it would be better to say that this was overdetermined by other sociopolitical conditions.

Without saying so explicitly, Fanon implies that it is psychic conflict (whether comprising guilt, anger, shame, or something else is not specified, nor who this is directed towards) that is causing the presenting problem of impotence. After all, this man acknowledged that he had not particularly valued this woman as his wife; it is made clear that at an earlier point he had intended to divorce her. Perhaps – echoing his designation that she was 'an obstinate woman' (207) – her fidelity to him even in the context of physical and sexual violation is now presented as an obstacle even (or, significantly, exactly) as he also attempts to be unfaithful to her in having sex with another woman. Thus, it would seem he cannot help directing some anger towards her. Notwithstanding how he reported his initial response to hearing of her rape ('Then I said, "Oh well, there's not much harm done, she wasn't killed'", ibid.), the discourse of rape as wilful dishonour installed by the French works. As he reported, the message his wife was asked to relay to him was: "'If ever you see your filthy husband again don't forget to tell him what we did to you'" (ibid.). And, so, he reflects: "'But that thing – how can you forget a thing like that?'" This appeal to try to block out or repress the impossible, however, is also followed by the complaint: "'And why did she have to tell me about it all?'" (ibid.), although of course 'she' did not tell him, but rather it was reported to him.

Mother and daughter: subjugated and absent subjects

While 'B—'s' wife appears only indirectly in this case, her presence functions powerfully in 'B—''s account. Indeed, considering that her 'dishonouring' was a direct result of protecting (refusing to disclose the whereabouts of) both himself and the organisation, his derogatory description of her as an 'obstinate woman' is perhaps an expression of his resentment at this power she exercises. In the narrative, therefore, she is also a speaking subject, and it is her speech that works traumatogenically: first, through the message sent to her husband releasing him from their marriage because of her 'dishonour' and, second, through the information provided of her imprisonment, torture, and rape for the 'detailed report' that is taken back to the commander, and then relayed to 'B—'. All of this precipitates 'B—'s' deliberations about whether he should return to her, how he feels about this, and whether he will be able to deliver on his personal and political commitment to resume his responsibilities for and intimacies with her.

One telling silence, the absence of which speaks meaningfully in this text, is whether the wife wants to be 'back' with him, and crucially whether this will be a return to how things were previously between them, or a newly forged relationship. This resonates with 'B's' complaint about what cannot be forgotten (his neglect of her in the past?) and what he would prefer not to know ("'how can you forget a thing like that? *And why did she have to tell me about it all?*'" (207, my emphasis). However, he hasn't been 'told' it 'all' *by her* at all, but via various intermediary reporters.

Clearly, this invites other questions, including other matters he may not want to consider, most evidently that of her desire(s). Recall that (in Fanon's words) the 'moment' that permits 'the reconstruct[ion] of the whole story' (206) is not the report of the tearing of the photo, nor of the dream, but when 'B—' first mentions his wife, which is in terms of saying, 'She's tasted the French' (ibid.). This formulation transposes rape into an active oral-sexual claim. Aside from condemning 'B—'s stance as classic victim-blaming, as the little literature citing this case seems to consider it (for example, Holmstrom, & Burgess 1979), it would seem that this rape, metonymically connected to the question of 'B—'s' own sexual potency, poses questions about not only his wife's, and by extension women's, function as an indirect conduit to hurt and terrorise Algerian militants, but about her (and by extension other women's) desires.

By contrast, the (girl)child, 'B-''s daughter, appears not as a subject but as a logical node in the network of associations that build the therapeutic narrative. She is, literally, a two-dimensional surface, the photograph, through which the chain of (unpalatable) meanings from 'B—' to his wife are connected. Significantly, there is no sense of 'B—' wanting to return to or take back his wife for the sake of the child, let alone to become acquainted with his daughter or to support or witness her growing up. Yet rather than hear this as a morally reprehensible position of the neglectful or abandoning father, Fanon is perhaps also reminding his reader that this is a time of war, and wars involve disruption of normal codes governing relationships and associated commitments, as well as geographical separations and dislocations, and often involve the rupture of traditional familial ties and obligations.

The pedagogical puzzle: reconfiguring 'the problem'

The 'problem of [his] wife', then, was not only a matter of whether 'B-' is willing to accept her again, even though he acknowledges that he is 'shaken' by seeing these other men comfort and embrace their raped wives. Nor was it even the question of managing his uncertainty over his capacity to overcome his (unnamed) responses to her 'violation' (of disgust, perhaps, as implied by the 'rottenness' of his dream). Rather, one aspect of 'B—'s difficulties appears to concern his belated recognition of his neglect of his wife – indeed, of not merely having not considered her, but also of not having taken her seriously.

Fanon is explicitly pedagogical in his writings, to 'help' build the process of conscientisation:

> The important theoretical problem is that it is necessary at all times and in all places to make explicit, to demystify, and to harry the insult to mankind that exists in oneself. There must be no waiting until the nation has produced new man; there must be no waiting until men are imperceptibly transformed by revolutionary processes in perpetual renewal. It is quite true that these two processes are essential, but consciousness must be helped.'
>
> (Wretched: 246)

In this case, then, Fanon narrates a strong political lesson, as learnt by 'B—', who reports seeing other men 'drying the tears of their wives after having seen them raped under their very eyes' (207). In a second, even clearer, reference to the child as issue/outcome of rape – with female gendered youth now designating the victim of violence – Fanon notes 'B—' acknowledging his astonishment at seeing men 'proposing marriage to a girl who was violated by the French soldiers, and who was with child by them'. It is such experiences that prompt 'B—' to 'reconsider the problem of my wife' (ibid.).

The interpretive possibility arises that the little girl, or, rather, the effort to undo or destroy the available material evidence of her, represents something more. Structured within Fanon's account of this case, and of a piece with his wider political analysis of the wider transformational political possibilities generated through the anti-colonial struggle, especially for women's greater emancipation as discussed in *The Wretched of the Earth* and *A Dying Colonialism*, is an implication that 'B—'s struggle arises from having to consider the existence of his daughter, via his 'reconsideration of the problem of my wife' as the outcome of his lack of sexual care for his wife. If his daughter may have come into existence via a kind of rape, this would then identify 'B—', retroactively, with the rapists of his wife (in a different, but just as damaging, way from the one they had intended). It would align 'B—', the injured husband, with the very colonisers he is fighting. Fanon appears to mobilise the analogy, even the parallel metaphor or identification, between French domination of (feminised as colonised) Algerian men, with (Algerian) male domination of women.

If Fanon as presenter of this case is also a didact, teaching by such narratives of distress colonialism's crimes, he is also in pedagogical mode offering a working through of the process for Algerian man to welcome back rather than reject his loyal wife who has survived rape and torture for him. That is, he provides an exploration and evocation of the challenge and struggle of overcoming traditional discourses of shame and dishonour that had characterised Algerian (as many other) societies. We can see this as part of Fanon's modernising discourse of anti-colonial struggle and national development that he eulogises in *Dying Colonialism*.

But, as a therapist, Fanon is concerned with 'B—'. Hence, it is not his place to moralise on how 'B—'configures his parental responsibilities. Noteworthy also is how the child is not figured as a developmental subject, as future citizen of post-independent Algeria. Instead, child here is a necessary but not subjectified position insofar as it expresses aspects of 'B—'s' therapeutic development. While not quite the romanticised site of authentic subjectivity typical of modern, Western narratives of 'child', nevertheless it still partially partakes of this as the index of something precious that has been spoilt or made rotten. That rotten-ness, as a symptom of personal political stagnation or decay, however, is expunged – at least in fantasy – once the question of the reorientation of this marital relationship is resolved, and the child dissolves into a position of normalised absence – that is, absorbed into and as an extension of 'B—'s' relationship with his wife/family .

Therapy as (ir)resolution and revolution

This reading of this case arises from the four and half pages presented by Fanon – the first in his catalogue of misery, anguish, and sometimes murderousness that comprise the section on 'Colonial War and Mental Disorders' in *Wretched*, where Fanon adopts the medical discourse of psychiatric case history and trauma to convey the damage produced by colonial oppression and violence. Two other features warrant attention before leaving it. First, Fanon stays close to the man's own account and observations of his responses and condition. Much of the text is presented as his quoted account. I should acknowledge that the emotional attributions (of conflict, shame, or guilt) that I have suggested are my own. Fanon's text leaves much implied, rather than stated. This can perhaps be interpreted as a key narrative strategy, that is, both political and psychoeducational, of evidencing or witnessing, rather than diagnosis or 'treatment'.

Since Fanon was actually a psychiatrist, who engaged in psychotherapeutic practice, this presentation as a psychiatric case history is not merely tactical. Indeed, unlike other cases presented in *Wretched*, 'B—'s' is also narrated as a history of a *relationship* of consultation, of help-seeking, and receiving. Fanon's account of the interventions made and interpretations offered is not extensive. He initially notes some – apparently unhelpful – use of medication at the beginning that merely heightened the concern about the man's agitated state. Rather, the focus is composing a connected narrative, on how 'we reconstructed the whole story. The weaving of events to form a pattern was made explicit' (206). As we have seen, this pattern seems to involve the (girl)child as a key link. Given Fanon's pedagogical project to publicise the psychic impacts of colonial war, the rendering 'explicit' seems not necessarily to make all this conscious only or specifically to 'B—' but rather to provide a space for its articulation.

Yet notwithstanding the few textual traces of therapeutic approach, Fanon's account does indicate a therapeutic turning point. The narrating of this case shifts from how the psychiatric team saw the patient on initial consultation, to a (smaller print) first-person account written in the patient's voice. However, Fanon's (psychiatric and authorial) voice returns to report the final conversation:

He then asked me if his 'sexual failing' was in my opinion caused by his worries.

I replied: 'It is not impossible.'

Then he sat up in bed.

'What would you do if all this had happened to you?'

'I don't know.'

'Would you take back your wife?'

'I think I would . . .'

'Ah, there you are, you see. You're not quite sure.'

He held his head in his hands and after a few seconds left the room.

(208)

Fanon's professional expertise is first mobilised to affirm the diagnosis that, in his medical typology, he has classified as a 'reactionary psychosis' (202). As he had earlier emphasised, this is no less devastating or enduring in its damage for this 'reactive' status. However, here he is addressed as a man, a heterosexual man, or rather as someone who is invited to identify with one ('What would you do . . .?'). In his response, Fanon first topicalises uncertainty, perhaps not only that of the ethical practitioner not wanting to 'lead' his patient. When 'B—' presses him a second time, Fanon suggests that he would anticipate 'tak[ing] back' the wife.

It is noteworthy that 'B—', the patient, is portrayed as finding comfort or validation in Fanon's seeming lack of certainty ('Ah, there you are, you see . . .'), as if this legitimates his ruminations and fantasies. This suggests that, contrary to his question, it was not direction he sought but rather an acknowledgement of the dilemmas he faced. His holding of his head perhaps implies further deliberation, and then he is said to leave. This is portrayed as the end, or culmination, of the therapy. It would seem that the symptom has been socialised, rendered into speech; it has become communicable and so perhaps bearable, so 'transforming hysterical misery into common unhappiness' (Breuer, & Freud, 1893–1895/1955: 305). Or, to offer a more socially based psychoanalytic model that topicalises language:

> The language of the symptom, although already a form of communication, is autistic. It mumbles to itself secretly, hoping to be overheard; its equivalent meaning conveyed in words is social. This process of

communication is the medium of all other therapeutic agencies . . .
Thus there is a move from symptom to problem, from dream to the
conflict underlying the dream.

(Foulkes, & Anthony, 1957: 259–260)

As is characteristic of his writing, Fanon offers an almost pictorial description
of a set of stages in the decisive installation of a transformed psychic structure,
that I suggest recalls Lacan's account of the creation of the intersubjective
social bond discussed in Chapter 3. Indeed, the last lines of the 'case history'
comprise Fanon's account of 'B——'s' recovery, a recovery that – significantly –
concerns political re-engagement as well as the gradual disappearance of his
psychotic/psychosomatic symptoms:

> From that day on, he was progressively more willing to listen to politi-
> cal discussions and at the same time the headaches and lack of appetite
> lessened considerably.
>
> After two weeks he went back to his unit.
>
> *(208)*

Far from failure, this would seem a triumphal story. Fanon, the revolutionary
psychiatrist, has done his job whereby a psychologically wounded resistance
fighter has been able to resume his role in the military struggle. But this
is to oversimplify the story. Fanon's intervention did not merely patch up
a soldier so that his psychological problems no longer endangered himself
and others. Rather, Fanon's narration of the therapeutic journey illuminated
intimate connections between the public and private, the domestic and the
national, in which are at play the complex interweavings between the heteropatriarchal domination of women and national identity, including how
some versions of sexuality are sanctioned or mandated (that is, marriage) and
institutional arrangements (such as the family) correspondingly organised.
Gender, generation, and parent–child relations figure powerfully, not only in
connecting daughter and mother in the formation of the symptoms. While
not explicitly a therapeutic narrative about 'B——'s' childhood, his position as
son (and son-in-law) is at play via the various roles parents play in this story –
as arrangers of marriages, privileged advisors in contexts of adversity, and
holders of community reputation. Violence – physical, sexual, emotional and
economic – is shown to be instigated by and as mediating the re-negotiation
of interpersonal relationships and the relation with the state, even as the
proto-state apparatus of the Maquis is offering a model of modernisation and
change. Fanon's account shows how all this was at play in this man's sexual

problems, the undermining of his potency. In relation to the socio-political as well as personal meanings of sexual potency, it is worth noting that when the first psychoanalytic clinics opened in the 1920s and 1930s in Berlin and Vienna – which were, significantly, provided at no cost – not only were the major proportion of the clients young working-class men, but their main presenting problems concerned sexual potency (Danto, 2005). Given the volatile political context, of possibility (this was the time of Red Vienna) as well as what was later to turn into repression and fascism, a psychopolitical as well as psychobiographical account is surely as relevant to Fanon's account here as to there. Perhaps the question is whether, in the context of the Maquis authority coming to replace that of the traditional family (a development that Fanon elsewhere celebrated), and that was now mandating the re-acceptance of his wife, 'B—' could feel able to make this as a free choice, rather than another mandated arranged marriage.

It is noteworthy that Fanon, as therapist even more than political agitator, appears didactic but not explicitly directive. I suggest that this can be read as an instantiation of working psychoanalytically at the level of 'failure', of men's failures, including in this case what lies behind a supposed 'sexual' failure. The case finishes with: 'Before he left he told me: "When independence comes, I'll take my wife back. If it doesn't work out between us, I'll come and see you in Algiers"' (208). 'B—'s reported words, closing the therapy, semiotically link political and personal autonomy. Fanon here appears to be suggesting that liberation from colonial rule will create the conditions not only for 'B—' as an Algerian achieving national independence, but that this will correspondingly promote liberation from his previous compulsions and mentality. Indeed, it would appear he envisages that this 'independence' will empower 'B—' to forge a new relationship with his wife that is less patriarchal or colonial. This is a project he will willingly work for, alongside Fanon's support.

In relation to Fanon's relational pedagogy, it is significant that this 'independence' is *relationally defined even as it is also precisely relationally incited*, rather than recapitulating the traditional masculinist model of detached, rational autonomy. While, military commitments aside, deferring the moment of marital reconciliation until 'when independence comes' may recall the familiar 'after the revolution' postponement to wait for socialism before granting women's rights (Rowbotham, et al., 2013), 'B—'s reported narrative voice suggests commitment. Moreover, it is 'B—', rather than Fanon, who proposes a symbolic or psychosomatic interpretation of his symptoms. Similarly, Fanon's uncertainty (or 'failure'?) appears to work to prompt or provoke this man's own sense of certainty about the future. This is so, *even if only at this point it is only an imagined certainty* – for at the current moment, the moment of the conclusion of the therapy, 'independence' is still some way away.

The unresolved question, reverberating powerfully with what is known about women's involvement in revolutionary struggles and what happens to their 'independence' afterwards, from Algerian women in the liberation struggle (Haddour, 2010; Turshen, 2002; White, 2014) to feminist Kurdish freedom fighters in Syria now (Cockburn, 2013; Mojab, 2009; see also Staudt, 2010), is that of how much 'independence' or freedom the wife will have to decide whether to take 'B—' back, or not. White suggests that

> Fanon's failure to address the gendered struggles of African men under colonial subjugation as thoroughly as their race and class struggles contributed to his overly optimistic expectations concerning the transformative power of the Algerian revolution. Patriarchal convictions that preexisted independence struggles were further entrenched by war and militarism.
>
> *(2014: 864)*

Other feminist commentators including Fraser (2017) and Fuss (1994) critique his neglect not only of the colonised/black women's subjectivity but also how this limits his analysis of colonialism, including also the failure to address how such inequalities become played out in other political struggles (for example, Xala, 2017). While Fanon does not quite topicalise such questions, nor also the wife's psychological condition – a rather significant absence – at least room can be found in the reading of 'if it doesn't work out between us' that there is a relationship, some 'between us' to be negotiated. This could, perhaps, be read as leaving open the possibility that the relationship will not be a mere 'return' (for we know it was not much of one before). Attending to the complex intersections of the individual, interpersonal, and political revolutions at stake involves going backwards in order to go forwards. Here Fanon as a psychotherapist frustrates his Foucaultian critics, for he is no longer so subject to modernist progressivism, nor statism.

As will be discussed further in Chapter 5, this is also Fanon's narrative of women's increasing empowerment and liberation through the revolutionary process, with examples of the Maquis substituting for the peasant family to sanction marriage. This also includes the famous discussion in his earlier – 1959 – book, *A Dying Colonialism,* of Algerian young women carrying out military raids and bombings – in the course of which they gain confidence and access to spaces and travel that they had previously been excluded from. As White (2014) comments: 'Fanon broke new ground in suggesting that revolutionary violence held transformative potential for women as well as for men' (860).

Indeed, Fanon typically follows his depictions of the misery and internal aggression produced by colonial subjugation with examples of the psychically and socially beneficial effects of anti-colonial mobilisation. To take an example, in his paper 'Criminal impulses found in the North African which have their origin in the National War of Liberation' he describes how the war shifted the site of aggression and conflict away from the oppressive regulation and treatment of women: 'There are no longer explosive outbursts of rage because my wife's forehead or her left shoulder were seen by my neighbour. The national conflict seems to have canalized all anger, and nationalized all affective or emotional movements' (247). Indeed, 'Colonial War and Mental Disorders' concludes with a key claim about the intersection between psychic and social autonomy, liberation and self-determination. This is what 'independence' means for Fanon:

> Independence is not a word which can be used as an exorcism, but an indispensable condition for the existence of men and women who are truly liberated, in other words who are truly masters of all the material means which make possible the radical transformation of society.
>
> *(250)*

Therapy as transformational pedagogy

This treatment of Fanon as a clinician has focused on questions of pedagogy, identification, temporality, and subjectivity. It has involved bringing feminist and Foucaultian perspectives alongside, against, and in relation to a close reading of Fanon where he is at his most 'clinical' and therapeutic, but also (it emerges) his most political, and where the relations between intrapsychic and political, in relation to both conflict and change, are also both topic and process. Moreover, from Fanon's own analysis, in the apparent resolution of 'B—'s' case such processes of conflict and change emerge as unstable designations. Radically indeterminate, their status ultimately resolves – as Foucaultian, Fanonian, and feminist analyses each emphasise – into a question of perspective and commitment. That is, the orientation towards an 'end', a goal, can only be relationally defined, and is an ethical question. Fanon here joins with Foucault and feminists – all with their Marxist and Freudian inscriptions – to emphasise the intrinsic and simultaneous relationship between the affective, interpersonal, and political. Such relations also imply embodiment, and movement. This is why we need to attend to them in clinical and educational practice and activisms beyond. In the end,

'B——' becomes active, his capacity for activity and activism are restored: he 'takes his head in his hands' and, after this, not only 'leaves the room' but rejoins his unit, and looks forward to a renewed relationship with his wife.

Naming Fanon as a psychoeducator works here to highlight his pedagogical project of national as well as subjective liberation. This reading also corrects a dominant representation of him as programmatic. Far from demanding or presupposing specific responses or outcomes, Fanon's account of his clinical practice in *Wretched* indicates a subscription to a much more open philosophy of education: an ethical practice of enabling self-authorisation. This pedagogy of uncertainty insists on a radical openness of contingency as the route to agentic action (Pinar, 2011; Gaztambide-Fernández, 2010). Fanon's pedagogy of failure, of refusing to prescribe future outcomes can be seen also to align with his critiques of negritude that were also foreshadowed in *Black Skin* in refusing the model of a fixed past:

> In no way should I derive my basic purpose from the past of the peoples of colour. In no way should I dedicate myself to the revival of an unjustly unrecognized Negro civilisation. I will not make myself the man of any past. I do not want to exalt the past at the expense of my present and of my future.
>
> *(161)*

Fanon's psychoeducational practice, then, in addressing his readers as much as his 'patients', goes beyond asserting that individuals are not merely empty social cyphers. Rather, the account of 'B——'s' therapy demands accepting that the meaning of sociopolitical events and the possibilities for activity within these are inevitably shaped by specific biographical histories that are necessarily both sociohistorically and idiosyncratically structured. Beyond this, Fanon's pedagogical practice in his narration of 'B——'s' case, which – it is worth noting again – is the only specifically therapeutic account in *Wretched*, is not about fixing a soldier to return to action, or even advising on marital reconciliation. Rather, like any good psychotherapist, Fanon is focused on bringing about new capacities for relationship, and so change. In this sense, since it appears to rely on the mobilisation (if not explicit interpretation) of unconscious conflicts, associations, and patterning of meaning that appear to compose 'B——'s' depression and disable him, this is a psychodynamically oriented psychotherapy. It is not a Marxist or feminist or any other 'political' branded variety of therapy (psychoanalytic or otherwise) – for direct inscription of such political projects into the psychotherapeutic process always risks becoming authoritarian. (Indeed, debates about feminist therapy, for example, have largely arrived at this conclusion, too, Seu, & Heenan, 1998; Burman, 1992, 1995, 2001a). Instead, there is an ethical commitment to enabling the client, patient, here 'B—', to make his own political and relationship choices, albeit also that Fanon does not withhold his own opinion when pressed to offer this. But again, we may note, he is addressed and responds as a man, not as a medical/clinical expert. Even if he cannot, of course, deny the power and responsibility of his position, he nevertheless offers a space of hesitation, of deferral, to hand the decision back to his client. Crucially, then, this therapeutic project refuses social reductionism, instrumentalisation, and a naïve voluntarism. This is notwithstanding, or perhaps precisely because, Fanon portrays the therapeutic and political-pedagogical moment as intrinsically linked: his refusal to respond to the call to prescribe, to tell 'B—' what to do, prompts the installation of a radical openness or contingency such that the subject must act and decide for themselves how to act.

Similarly, my account here of reading 'against the grain' between and against Fanon's account, mobilising also Foucaultian and feminist perspectives, is neither morally relativist, nor progressivist (in the sense of committed to a presumed outcome). As a specific intervention within Fanonian analyses, this reading owes much to intersectionality theory by exploring mutual configurations and interdependencies, as well as conflicts within and between, competing axes of gender, racialisation, and generation (McCall, 2005; Phoenix, & Pattynama, 2006; Winker, & Degele, 2011). The intersectional links identified here include how the (girl)child is aligned with her (raped but loyal) mother; how the problem initially presented as 'sexual failing' (impotence) aligns with a political project of anti-colonial struggle; and the re-enactment but then interrogation of heteropatriarchal family relations. Fanon also discusses how traditional class relations are pressured under anti-colonial struggle, as also acknowledging the dangers of de-railing the revolutionary project through simply replacing a colonial middle class with a 'native' one. Significantly, Fanon links colonial brutalisation and violence against women – for both coloniser and colonised. Indeed, later, in Series A, Case Five of *Wretched* he discusses a European police inspector, whose daytime job as a torturer of Algerian insurgents spills over into torturing his wife and child. Fanon, here, does not provide any account of therapeutic relief but rather makes an analytical intervention by enquiring: 'What happens to you when you are torturing?' (216). That is, he offers the man a place of subjectivity outside the place of horror and dehumanisation, from which to view his actions.

Nor are the relations between these intrapsychic, interpersonal, and political domains mere repetition (as Butler, 1997, has helpfully clarified).

Rather, I would suggest this movement or critical reading between levels of analyses and across theoretical planes and narrative levels of pedagogy, which include topic, process, referent, and addressee, can work to promote understandings of subjectivity that are sensitive not only to constraints and limits in their formulation and framing, but also to the dynamic possibilities set in play by the complexity of their mutual relations and so dynamic instabilities.

Therapeutic child as a practice of child as method

If therapy is as much pedagogical process as discovery, in the pedagogy of this case Therapeutic child names not the 'learner' but what has to be learnt (known, acknowledged) and assimilated. In this case, this knowledge appears to be various meanings and associations of gendered and sexual violence, with the patient, 'B—', positioned as both helpless (indirect) bystander, proxy victim but also crucially proto-perpetrator. What is frustrated, then, by this perhaps counter-intuitive figuring of Therapeutic child, is the subjectivation *of* the child. What emerges from Fanon's account of 'B—'s' therapy is how a photograph of the child anchors a traumatic set of associations; that is, the meanings surrounding the daughter do not concern her as a subject (indeed her subjectivity is woefully absent), but rather 'she' functions merely as an object, a relay of other dynamics and affects, which – in the end – are returned to their rightful place.

While there are key links between Therapeutic child and Traumatogenic child (since both concern trauma and symbolic racialised violence), Therapeutic child topicalises the trauma, rather than what caused it or even the subject of the trauma (which is, since this is his therapy, 'B—'). In relation to the various other 'child' modalities discussed in this book, a reciprocal relationship can be identified between Traumatogenic and Therapeutic child. Whereas Idiotic child marks or secures a key structural position in relation to which full subjectivity is organised, and Traumatogenic child hails the subject as exclusionary agent or representative of that social order, Therapeutic child marks the place of externalised vulnerability that, in the course of development, becomes subjectified. The gendering of child as a girl(child), in this case history, then, is polysemic. The 'needy little girl' of therapeutic discourse (c.f. Eichenbaum, & Orbach, 1983) not only names a space of thwarted needs to be addressed, nor only a space of victimisation. In indexing these, it reflects denied aspects of the therapeutic subject, the subject in therapy, that only engage childhood through particular culturally contingent sets of associations, as a site of feeling to be acknowledged and integrated. In this sense, this quasi-psychodynamic trope is recruited into a discourse of personal growth. Rather than merely an act of withholding or denying subjectivity, I suggest that attending to such opacity can perhaps enable a more rigorous attention to the claims made for, to, and about child and so also children.

Therapeutic child, therefore, works as child as method to show how child and children are invoked within a developmental model, as positions within history (whether utopian or dystopian). Fanon can be read as invoking Therapeutic child within his narrative of socio-political transformation. The damaged child as signifier of the perverting effects of living under colonialism/racialisation can be aligned with Fanon's repudiation of fixed notions of the past, both individual and collective. As he asserts in *Black Skin*:

> I am not a prisoner of history. I should not seek there for the meaning of my destiny.
>
> I should constantly remind myself that the real leap consists in introducing invention into existence.
>
> In the world through which I travel, I am endlessly creating myself.
>
> *(163)*

Therapeutic child, however, not only ascribes the victims rather than (perhaps) the perpetrators of racism (as discussed in Chapter 3); it personifies these as evoking a model of recovery that also 'heals' both political and personal injuries. As such it ushers in a developmental model. This is because, for Fanon, the project of 'disalienation' is aligned with that of 'time':

> The problem considered here is one of time. Those Negroes and white men will be disalienated who refuse to let themselves be sealed away in the materialized Tower of the Past. For many other Negroes, in other ways, disalienation will come into being through their refusal to accept the present as definitive.
>
> *(Black Skin: 161)*

Fanon's model of time here is transformational and transitional on a number of levels, moving from trauma to recovery/action, and aligning individual subjective with national development, albeit now oriented to a different (national) end.

In relation to the status of time, development, and the role of Therapeutic child, this account of 'B—'s' case can usefully be contrasted with Fanon's account just a few pages later of a 19-year-old man presenting with 'anxiety psychosis' who had killed European women after learning that his mother had been shot by the French, and his sisters had been abducted (and presumably raped if not also murdered). Commenting on the detailed attention to the sequence of events, Gendzier comments:

> There is no inevitability in this tale, and had Fanon's notes on the individual in question been complete we might have known more about the nature of the man's attachment to his mother, his cultural and socioeconomic background, his commitment to the FLN, and his action vis-á-vis the woman who reminded him of his mother. There is much that is evoked by the brief study: the question of responsibility, the motivation of the individual, and the guilt he bears. What does it mean to 'cure' such a man, and such a case? Fanon offered little discussion of this except to explain that he had treated the young man for several weeks and that the most obvious symptoms, such as his recurring nightmares, had disappeared. But the associations that returned to haunt him did not.
>
> *(1973: 106)*

Rather than offering any possibility of recovery or 'cure', Fanon concludes that this young man's 'disrupted personality' (212) can perhaps only be helped by 'time alone' (ibid.). That is, we may surmise, he can envisage no Therapeutic child to be integrated into a narrative of development. The mobilisation of 'time alone' perhaps suggests that the prospect of decolonisation may offer some solace, but mainly it would appear to suggest a sense of helplessness on the part of the therapeutic practitioner. As Gendzier (1973) concludes: 'It is questionable whether time is enough, or indeed whether it ought to be enough, by itself, to produce a "cure"' (106).

This rendering of Therapeutic child can perhaps be considered alongside other images of ('innocent') children populating Fanon's text, who function as expressive objects indicating the psychological limits of others, rather than according the children particular subjectivities. This would include the description of children whose crying causes disproportionate irritation because it stops the desperately exploited labourer from sleeping, alongside other examples of how colonial oppression turns the colonised against one another: 'the natives fight amongst themselves. They tend to use each other as a screen, and each hides from his neighbour the national enemy' (*Wretched*: 248). Another (often cited) example of Fanon's repertoires of children includes his recalling having seen children in Oran concentration camp fighting among themselves ('with anger and hate', *Wretched*: 248) over the scraps of bread thrown to them by soldiers. Here, however, the children themselves are topicalised as subjects, with their own Therapeutic child in need of attention.

There is a sting in the tail of Therapeutic child, however, or – as with Fanon's methodology of 'failure' – a narrative position of 'existential irony' (Gordon, 2015: 3) to bear in mind. Therapeutic child is expressly *not therapy of* the child – that is, the child in therapy. Rather it designates the position of child as discursive object within another's therapeutic narrative (albeit that this could also be of a child's therapeutic narrative, too). 'Child' here is not the object of therapeutic intervention but rather functions as an object or entity, specifically as an index of developmental arrest or problem, within a narrative of therapeutic process. Implications for antiracist/pedagogies of solidarity may include how addressing emotions (shame, guilt, complicity) are central to restoring a sense of actionality (to use Fanon's term). As he puts it, this is not merely a matter of 'self esteem' (*Black Skin:* 109). Therapeutic child testifies to a reification and displacement of distress, attention to which enables an integration and corresponding restoration of agentic capacities.

5

EXTEMIC CHILD

Children figure in complex and contested ways within Fanon's anti-colonial analyses, including the affects mobilised and exercised around them. As with other cultural practices and commentators, Fanon portrays child as a site of resistance to colonialism as much as the raw material for colonial exploitation or as vulnerable to the distortions of the brutalities of repression and war. Discussing the US context, but drawing on influential British and European analyses, especially Rose (1984) and Steedman (1995), Karen Sánchez-Eppler (2005: xxiii) notes: 'The relation between childhood as a discourse and childhood as persons has proven so entangled because American society has so frequently employed children to give personal, emotional expression to social, institutional structures.' In this chapter I take up the 'personal, emotional expression' of child to consider not only child as *standing for* the social, but also child *as* social structure – that is, not (as in previous chapters) either separate from or (so) securing (Idiotic child), or alternatively absorbed into (Traumatogenic child), or as a feature of the self to be saved from or integrated into the social (Therapeutic child). By attending to Fanon's rich and diverse mobilisations, we can attend to the work done by such rhetorical appeals. So, despite, or rather precisely because of, the abstraction from specificities of culture, history, and nationality that surround dominant mobilisations of childhood, their status as a vital repository for the maintenance and reproduction of particular gendered, classed, and cultural norms can be illuminated.

As a final contribution qualifying child, then, we come to Extemic child. The term 'extemic' is a neologism ascribing a position that is as much outside as inside and, correspondingly, inside as outside. I borrow the term from the French psychoanalyst Jacques Lacan who coined it (as the French, *extimité*) to describe how that what is apparently most interior to the subject is actually exterior to them, as with the Moebius Strip that has both a single surface and edge (Pavón-Cuéllar, 2014; Parker, 2005; Miller, 1994). This works to emphasise how what is social is also individual, and vice versa. Instead of a binary opposition between the social and individual, inside and outside, then, we can envisage a process of looping between these that is seamlessly connected – indeed as a unitary entity the societal or individual features of which arise only from the point of view from which they are perceived. Developing these ideas for a critical social psychology, Parker (2005) discusses 'extimacy' (*extimité*) as the 'intimate exteriority of the subject in discourse', thus rendering as discourse that which is 'the most intimate to the subject', which is 'outside' or 'extimate to the subject, not reducible to it' (Parker, 2005: 172).

In this chapter, therefore, I use the term Extemic to qualify child as simultaneously (in the sense of being within the same topological space) included *and* excluded within societal practices, its specificity both under- and overdetermined by such co-presence. While the various other forms of child discussed in earlier chapters were either rendered purely as other, as outside, the social symbolic practice of their representation (Idiotic child) or as assimilated into it (Traumatogenic child), or recruited into the developmental narrative connecting individual and social (Therapeutic child), what Extemic child brings to the analysis here is an understanding of child as subject of and within the social; as agentic, and even resisting.

This chapter therefore explores a further range of childhood and educational motifs occurring across Fanon's writings to suggest that these not only illuminate more of Fanon's distinctive analysis of decolonisation, but also offer resources for addressing current debates on the political ambiguities of discourses of childhood, gender, education, and development. In his various works, Fanon mobilises a wide repertoire of child associations, including referring to children as subjects and agents in their own right, sometimes (as discussed earlier in his first book *Black Skin, White Masks* (Fanon, 1952/1970) (hereafter *Black Skin*)) even drawing on his own childhood and schooling memories to indicate complexities of racialised colonial subjectivity and identification in Martinique. Unsurprisingly, given Fanon's commitment to a model of subjectivity that is capable of acting as well as reacting, of transcending socio-political and historical determinations, his writing offers various depictions of actively engaged children. As we shall see, some such agencies may not be deemed 'positive', in the sense that they imply dystopic rather than desirable political outcomes. But this is where Fanon is perhaps at his most prescient and relevant for our contemporary challenges and dilemmas surrounding children and young people. It is also where he offers the widest range of conceptualisations of children.

Consistent with the precepts of child as method, which is informed by Fanon's ideas, these children are not the prototypical children of normalised, globalised models but rather children who are at the margins, marginalised by (in his descriptions) racialisation, political allegiance, class, and gender. These children are described by Fanon, for better or worse, as full political subjects – with their childhood status only sometimes marked within this. That is, the fact of being a child, of occupying the biographical or chronological status of childhood, neither diminishes nor exceeds societal membership. Questions of responsibility are posed, in various directions (but often no more than would be the case for adults). Thus, Extemic child is not structural, in the sense of subjecting and subordinating children to a political dynamic of either (affective) deference or exoneration (through some special status of childhood as not fully social). Nor is Extemic child, alternatively, developmental, in the sense of being subject to a dynamic of deferment or instrumentalisation that renders their subjectivity temporally postponed (and correspondingly only provisionally or discretionarily allowed). Fanon is here addressing the child of now, produced within the current cultural-political moment and in relation to which s/he is recognised to both react and act in personally and politically meaningful ways. As we shall see, this is also Fanon at his most intersectional, as would be expected from a socially situated and relationally constituted account of subjectivity.

Methodology: beyond child as metaphor

Unlike other chapters, which have focused on a particular scene or case history described by Fanon, in this one I draw on the whole corpus of Fanon's writing. Analytically, I use forms of discourse analysis to classify and identify the forms of child inhabiting his texts, assembled from iterations of close and critical reading (see also Burman, 2017b). The children that I identify here sometimes appear as explicitly metaphorical, their positions expressing other features of colonial and anticolonial relations, while at other times they appear as political agents – as apparently historical or empirical, rather than figurative, children. Nevertheless, perhaps only exaggerated by, rather than staged through, the performative character of Fanon's writing, all such mobilisations of child have to be understood as metaphorical. Indeed, given the societally as well as intrapsychically invested character of childhood, all appeals to child carry metaphorical status (Stainton Rogers, & Stainton Rogers, 1992), while most rhetorical deployments of childhood mobilise metaphor to further, covertly, their mode of argumentation. This is where we have to attend to what is being done with such metaphors. As Massey (1976: 192) put it: 'Unlike metaphor, which leaps to contact, interpretation recognises the inaccessibility of its object.' Hence, Lesnik-Oberstein (2010) notes that presuming a clear distinction between 'the historical child' and 'the image Child' not only conflates two different domains of description, but doing so also disguises this move. This gives rise to two problems: 'first [it is] fundamentally founded upon a split here between the historical child and the image Child, and then, again, in a figurative status which is acknowledged and addressed as not permitted to be acknowledged and addressed by us ('we')' (311).

Extemic child traverses both domains, and rather than (to continue with Lesnik-Oberstein's formulation) opposing historical child and image Child, its looping into and as the social discloses more about their mutual relationships. Indeed, different versions of the social order produce different models of child, as we shall see. Even as he sometimes subscribes to a romanticisation of child as subject of (personal, political and national) development, Fanon also subverts dominant iconography made available by discourses of childhood in critical and surprising ways to take forward his political analyses.

The analyses below may invite the charge of over-interpretation, as either making claims of, or even going beyond, what Fanon could be presumed to 'intend'. Yet this rather misses the key analytic point of child as method, or as Adorno (1951/2005: 29) put it in relation to a related domain: 'Nothing is true in psychoanalysis except its exaggerations.' I attend closely to the nuances afforded Fanon through his mobilisations of childhood and associated motifs precisely both to indicate more of the subtlety and complexity at play, and how these better identify the insidious character of colonial dynamics, as also to figure how these may be resisted, but also how the recourse to the various types of child promote this. Fanon's richly allusive characterisations often work in counter-intuitive ways; indeed, they work precisely to throw those intuitions into question. That is, the sometimes startling formulations he provides demand some work to unravel their meanings, or to interpret them, in Massey's sense noted above. Similarly, the forms of child entitling each chapter of this book resist easy or quick interpretation, even reversing these (such that Idiotic child is not about children as idiots, and Therapeutic child is not about the child in therapy . . .) as an analytical strategy topicalising the sets of political assumptions that lie unaddressed within banal childhood tropes. Hence, as a key expression of child as method, we will see how the positions accorded child implicate others within the gendered, generational, classed, and sexed – as well as racialised – orders.

Extemic child under colonial rule

Early in *Black Skin,* Fanon comments on the child-colonised elision: 'A white man addressing a Negro behaves exactly like an adult with a child and starts smirking, whispering, patronising cozening' (*Black Skin*: 23). Yet in repudiating this comparison, he does not warrant demeaning treatment of children (rather than black people) but rather criticises such modes of address to both. We can see this as a version of Extemic child in the sense that the child is relationally engaged with as part of colonial order, albeit occupying a specific position within it, rather than set apart from it.

As discussed later, Fanon's (1961/1963) final book *The Wretched of the Earth* (hereafter *Wretched*) offers both more diverse and nuanced accounts of both childhood and violence than Sartre allows in his Preface to this book. This, however, is in largely gender-free terms – with the generalised child figured as masculine (while as we shall see, Fanon reserved gendered specification for particular treatment in his representation of the anticolonial subjects). The first essay, 'Concerning violence', not only discusses the violence of the colonialist, rather than the revolutionary, but Fanon's iconography of childhood equates the figure of the child with incompetence and irresponsibility – that is, with being undisciplined, and greedy. These undesirable qualities, which are presented as childlike or associated with (bad) children, are applied primarily to the colonisers and those who emulate them. He describes the colonialist bourgeoisie as 'spoilt children':

> We find intact in them the manners and forms of thought picked up during their association with the colonialist bourgeoisie. Spoilt children of yesterday's colonialism and of today's national governments, they organize the loot of whatever national resources exist.
>
> *(*Wretched: 37)

Nor do the colonised escape these negative childhood associations, for he endows those subject to colonial rule who feel themselves deprived of material goods with 'a childlike process of reasoning' (58), commenting: 'The masses by a sort of (if we may say so) childlike process of reasoning convince themselves that they have been robbed of all these things' (ibid.). Here Fanon reverses the presumed universalised romantic repertoire of childhood innocence associated with modern European thought to position childlike qualities, and by extension children, as expressions of colonial power.

This critique extends to material artefacts associated with childhood and education. As is well known, in *Black Skin* Fanon discusses children's stories and folktales to highlight their pedagogical role in structuring racialised subjectivities and relationships for both the colonised and the colonisers, as in Tarzan and Brer Rabbit stories. He comments: 'all those "comic books" serve actually as a release for collective aggression. The magazines are put together by white men for little white men. . . . these same magazines are devoured by the local children' (103). Yet he critiques the appropriation of the narrative voice of the child to portray the individual investments in racialisation as foundational, as in his analysis of Mayotte's psychohistorical account in *Je suis Martiniquaise*:

> From the first this is how the problem appeared to Mayotte – at the fifth year of her age and the third page of her book: 'She took her ink-well out of the desk and emptied it over his head.' This was her own way of turning whites into blacks.
>
> *(34)*

The theme of whitening persists, as he discusses how she later works as a laundress. Here Fanon disrupts the move he himself is sometimes read as making in 'Look, a Negro!' (see Chapter 3), by troubling the attribution of racism as originating from a child, albeit in this case it is the internalisation of racism by the colonised subject: 'Looking eagerly for external reasons for his Cinderella complex, Jean Veneuse projects the entire arsenal of racial stereotypes onto a child of three or four years' (55).

Extemic child as feminised subject within the heteronormative romance of colonial rule

Fanon also engages more complicated descriptions of 'child' to invoke a deeper historical and logical interweaving between inside and outside, and between child and the social order. In the only reference in *Wretched* to a cultural artefact of childhood, a fairy tale, he figures the European who refuses to see that colonialism is over as a child caught in the world of make-believe. 'Concerning violence' ends with a call (addressed to the European coloniser) to recognise their complicities: 'To achieve this, the European peoples must first decide to wake up and shake themselves, use their brains, and stop playing the stupid game of the Sleeping Beauty' (84). The sleep, or lack of awareness, of the European, is portrayed as 'stupid' while the dual discretionary and trivial characteristics of 'playing' and 'game' are brought into question. Play, as the quintessential activity of childhood (that is opposed to the work that non-normative, poor children undertake), here masks a 'serious' intent – indeed masks a different peda-gogical lesson. Fanon here joins other critics of play (Sutton Smith, 2001) to identify the dominant discourse of play as suppressing its coercive, less 'adaptive' characteristics, albeit that here Fanon is here challenging the playing (coloniser) subject to see this.

Even as play is a pedagogy (as in the now ubiquitous 'learning through play'), Fanon mobilises its supposedly enjoyable, voluntary characteristics ironically not only to identify how its pleasures or privileges for the coloniser are at the expense of coercion of the colonised, but also to put into ques-tion the European perception as make-believe, as fiction. As players of a 'stupid game', he also unsettles the superior brainpower usually claimed by Europeans as part of the paternalist rationale for colonial rule. The narrative frame of the fairy tale, Sleeping Beauty, with its cultural presumptions and, in particular, performance of classed, gendered, and heterosexual privilege, is both mobilised and ruptured. As a final queering, the reversed allusion to Sleeping Beauty (with the coloniser figured as the girl waiting for her des-tined male lover) could even be extended to indicate the presumed violence of heteronormativity, since the 'waking up' of the coloniser from their long sleep (signifying lack of awareness, or presumed privilege?) by the coloniser may involve more than a kiss.

Extemic child in/as postcolonial national development

While it is sometimes suggested that Fanon's mixture of critical socialist analysis and economic development discourse provides a better Marxist reading of processes of decolonisation and redevelopment (Rabaka, 2011), at times Fanon mobilises a traditional progressivist model to transpose the narrative of individual development onto that of the new postcolonial state. Within this narrative, the category 'youth' appears as a synonym of newness, or of something insecurely established, as where he develops an image of 'the young national bourgeoisie', as gang-related dynamics: 'The behaviour of the young national bourgeoisie of certain under-developed countries is rem-iniscent of the members of a gang, who after every hold-up hide their share in the swag from other members who are their accomplices' (*Wretched*: 139). Fanon also writes about the problem of 'young nations' (who 'do not attract much private capital', *Wretched*: 81) and, and notwithstanding his extensive references to education as a process of mass democratic mobilisation, he even discusses the racial prejudice of the 'young national bourgeoisie' as an effect of the subjective psychopolitics of decolonisation (*Wretched*: 131). Indeed, the only time he qualifies another child or youth-related category in

Wretched invoking a chronologically older category, 'adolescence', is in relation to an account of misplaced revolutionary defiance. While presented as understandable in a context of desperation and deprivation (indicating some developmentally implied indulgence), this is seen as foolhardy:

> The flagrant refusal to compromise and the tough will that sets itself against getting tied up is reminiscent of the behaviour of proud, poverty-stricken adolescents, who are always ready to risk their necks in order to have the last word.
>
> *(Wretched: 65)*

At times Fanon's recourse to traditional chronological age (and, as we shall see, gender) categories and status seems surprisingly conservative. Adulthood is portrayed within a traditional developmental discourse as a valued state of maturity, and also as a consciousness that can be taught, as in: 'The political education of the masses proposes not to treat the masses as children but to make adults of them' (*Wretched*: 146). (Recall, as discussed in Chapter 1, this formulation of 'political education' was the translator's English version of the French 'politiciser', and so may now be better understood as 'politicisation'; see also Batchelor, 2017b.) In terms that now resonate with neoliberal development discourse, he claims: 'The Algerian people is today an adult people responsible and fully conscious of its responsibilities. In short the Algerians are men of property' (*Wretched*: 155). Similarly, the chapter 'On national culture' discusses how 'these new forms are linked to the state of maturity of the national consciousness' (*Wretched*: 196). Some commentators have addressed these masculinist mobilisations in psychobiographical terms, making claims about the investments guiding Fanon's engagement with the Algerian revolution and for the gendered character of his focus. Hence, Françoise Vergès proposes that

> Fanon's notion of masculinity presupposed a modernization of the Creole male through his entrance into a 'responsibilized' patriarchy. The Antillean male was weak; he danced and sang, mimicked the white man, when he should have seized a gun and fought.
>
> *(1997: 594)*

If such mobilisations are psychobiographically informed they cannot of course occur without wider cultural-political supports. Indeed, they are common tropes of development discourse. Yet, Fanon did not merely uncritically reproduce this linear, lifecourse equation between individual and national development. Far from celebrating this as triumphal or inevitable, Fanon turns it around by invoking a discourse of the unnatural or impairment within his political critique. In Chapter 2 of *Wretched,* 'The pitfalls of national consciousness', he ridicules the incipient national bourgeoisie for wanting to be like its Western counterparts, suggesting that this reverses a natural ontogenetic path: 'We need not think that it is jumping ahead; it is fact beginning at the end. It is already senile before it has come to know the petulance, the fearlessness or the will to succeed of youth' (123). Fanon mobilises this normative depiction of the chronological life-course to highlight its deviations. Even as he destabilises youth and old age from their usual chronological associations (of precisely the kind that queer theorists of childhood disrupt through the discourse of 'growing sideways', Stockton, 2009), he also reinstates these precisely by reinscribing the very developmental path that has been departed from. Yet, we may also note that, even his mobilisation of senility is not within a fixed frame that is without subjectivity, for here it has been deprived not only of its childhood but also its vigorous youth. We may also note how, in Chapter 1 of *Black Skin,* Fanon indicates how a reflexive moment in clinical consultation with a 'seventy-three-year old woman, whose mind was never strong and who is now far gone in dementia' (24) corresponds to the 'absence of wish, this lack of interest, this indifference, this automatic manner of classifying him, imprisoning him, primitivising him, decivilising him' (ibid.) that comprises the everyday racism experienced by black people. That is, he recognises this process not because it is one he, too, can be subject to, but precisely by virtue of this:

> I was suddenly aware of the collapse of the antennae with which I touch and through which I am touched. The fact that I adopt a language suitable to dementia, to feeble-mindedness, the fact that I 'talk down' to this poor woman of seventy-three; the fact that I condescend to her in my quest for a diagnosis, are the stigmata of a dereliction in my relations with other people.
>
> *(24–25)*

Once again, then, we see Fanon's pedagogy of failure, as an ethic of political struggle, at play.

Finally, Fanon also mobilises child to ward off a pre-colonial narrative of postcolonial development. A rare reference to child labour in *Black Skin* occasions an early anticipation of his later critiques of 'negritude' and romanticisation of pre-colonial cultural practices. Fanon comments:

I should be very happy to know a correspondence had flourished between some Negro philosopher and Plato. But I can absolutely not see how this fact would change anything in the lives of the eight-year-old children who labour in the cane fields of Martinique or Guadaloupe.

(164)

That is, he questions the relevance of recovering such histories for addressing contemporary forms of exploitation, here personified by child labour.

Gendering and generationing the colonial relation as unnatural

In a particularly rich and dense set of images that reverse the conventional modernist trope of the birth of the nation, Fanon mobilises an accusatory image of the coloniser as a bad mother to the colonised nation in his call for decolonisation. He presents an (arguably misogynist) image of the heteropatriarchal, mother–child relation under or as the colonial order:

On the unconscious plane, colonialism therefore did not seek to be considered by the native as a gentle, loving mother who protects her child from a hostile environment, but rather as a mother who unceasingly restrains her fundamentally perverse offspring from managing to commit suicide and from giving free reign to its evil instincts. The colonial mother protects her child from itself, from its ego, and from its physiology, its biology and its own unhappiness which is its very essence.

*(*Wretched: *169–170)*

The 'unhappiness which is its very essence' of course recalls Fanon's earlier project of documenting the 'despair and the misery of the black man' (61) in *Black Skin*. Noteworthy is the elision of woman to nation here, the mother as colonial power, depicting how 'her' care suppresses expression of distress and protest, and alienates the colonised (her child) from 'its very essence'. By such means the perversions of colonial oppression are transferred from the coloniser into the colonised, and the 'evil instincts' to resist colonisation now turned into suicidal tendencies from which it must be 'protected'. Fanon is here a 'psychoanalyst of culture' (see Gates's, 1991 and Macey's, 2012 critical evaluation) as well as revolutionary theorist.

Conventional gendered discourses of presumed natural maternal protection are here subverted in the complex turns and connections forged between the individual, interpersonal, and the political through a critique of the evils of colonialism. Yet also significant is how Fanon is depicting how its rule (here rendered as maternal, alluding to the motif of the 'mother-country') does not position the child as innocent, or at least it is not innocent in the eyes of the coloniser. However, precisely through the unconventional reversal of portraying the child as always-already evil in the eyes of the colo-niser ('evil instincts') insofar as it strives to understand its condition and so confronts its own misery, Fanon could be read as indirectly restoring instead a discourse of child innocence. This characterisation of the (bad) colonial mother's perversions could appear to invite the restoration of a child who is free of such suicidal provocations. Yet Fanon stops short of this.

This move should be seen in the context of Fanon's broader political perspectives. His trenchant criticisms of both nostalgic claims to a precolo-nial past or appeals to some mythic common 'negritude' correspond with his opposition to spontaneism (the focus of Chapter 2 of *Wretched*). Fanon's rhetorics of childhood, then, corresponding with his perspective on decolo-nisation, were less concerned with romanticising or returning to what went before than with transforming current conditions of oppression, exclusion, and exploitation. Hence, Fanon's claims to 'belong irreducibly to my time' (*Black Skin*: 12), so resisting teleological accounts of political and subjective transformation: 'The future should be an edifice supported by living men. This structure is connected to the present to the extent that I consider the present in terms of something to be exceeded' (ibid.).

Extemic child as dislocated, separated, and exploited innocent securing European bourgeois subjectivity

As discussed below in relation to educational engagements with his writings, Fanon's primary address was to convey impacts of the violence and distortions *done to* the oppressed/colonised. Correspondingly, his address is to the colo-nised to encourage them to oust the insults and inner psychic reproductions of the colonial state. He discusses the condition of the 'native intellectual', who through colonialism (including colonial education – as in the 'rosy cheeks' example of Antillean children's essays discussed in *Black Skin,* which offer the colonial counterpart to the racialising moment of the mother's blush discussed earlier in Chapter 3) is oriented to Western culture. Fanon mobilises a discourse of misplaced 'adoption' not merely to advocate for the reinstatement of natural-ised biological kinship (aligned to national belonging), but rather to foreground the dynamics set in play by insecure roots or foundations: 'Like adopted children who only stop investigating the new family framework at the moment when a minimum nucleus of security crystallizes in their psyche, the native intellectual will try to make European culture his own' (*Wretched*: 176).

Reflecting Fanon's socialist commitments (Rabaka, 2011; Gendzier, 1973; Gilroy, 2010; Gibson, 1999, 2013), any instrumentalisation of children and childhood that subordinates the child to the adult (worker, slave labourer) that he will become is aligned with colonial exploitation. Fanon includes an extensive quotation from Aimé Césaire's *Les Armes miraculeuses*, where 'The Rebel' reports to the 'The Mother' that the master said: "'And all that man saw of my son's cradle was that it was a cradle of a chain-gang captain'" (quoted in *Wretched*: 68). This link between colonialism and capitalism not only highlights the mutual articulation between the categories of adult and child and racialisation as central to the elaboration of discourses of childhood in the US (Levander, 2006), and widespread current discussions of the schooling of children as active citizen workers (Ailwood, 2008; Fendler, 2001). It also anticipates more recent debates proposing that capitalism necessarily entailed colonialism (Buck-Morss, 2009; Mignolo, 2007).

Similarly, of a piece with his critique of colonial anthropology and psychiatry, Fanon repeatedly reversed or distanced himself from the equation of 'child' with 'primitive'. The only exception to this is when, in a rare criticism of modernity, Fanon equates it with its colonial, Western forms. In this example (from *Black Skin*), Fanon shifts narrative voice to mobilise the speaking position of the paternalist coloniser. He parodies how the colonised are seen as 'the childhood of the world', 'innocent', 'ingenuous', and 'spontaneous', portraying such representations as arising from the psychic violence of modern Western life, exemplified by life lived in 'big buildings' – evoking both cities and the factories on which city wealth is built. Fanon is here aligning cities with the colonial metropole, and with a corresponding model of development as alienation:

> Oh certainly I will be told, now and then when we are worn out by our lives in big buildings, we will turn to you as we do to our children – to the innocent, the ingenuous, the spontaneous. We will turn to you as to the childhood of the world. You are so real in your life – so funny, that is. Let us run away for a little while from ritualized, polite civilization and let us relax, bend to those heads, those adorably expressive faces. In a way, you reconcile us with ourselves.
> (Black Skin: 93)

Not only is Fanon here repudiating the dominant iconography of the colonised *as* children, 'those adorably expressive faces'. As with the discourse of nostalgia that inhabits dominant sentimentalised notions of childhood, he also analyses how this plays a key role in confirming – even apologising for – the power of the colonisers ('you reconcile us with yourselves') in offering a domesticated reminder to the coloniser of what they have lost.

So far, Fanon's subscription to Extemic child has worked as a frame to comment on the power relations elaborated within colonialism and the paradigm of development, where he mobilises and comments upon adult–child generational status to portray and ridicule the positions so elaborated. Child here is used as equivalence, as a substitution that imports new perspectives on colonial conditions. Yet, Fanon also discusses other kinds of children and childhoods. Within the framework used here, only some of these positions identified above qualify children as subjects. Fanon's adopted children are tropes within a critique of colonialism, nodes within a dystopian narrative of development rather than presented as actual descriptions of historical, embodied children as actional subjects. In this next section, however, I address a specific rendering of Extemic child as explicitly figured as subject within and as part of the social.

Extemic child as unmarked protagonist

Before we move on to discuss Fanon's well-known gendered depictions of prototypical anti-colonial subjects, it is worth noting that some such subjects are not specified as gendered, nor even specifically as children/young people. It has been suggested that queer theorists of childhood (such as Edelman, 2004) sometimes inadvertently reinstate the very naturalised developmental child, eliding individual and societal processes, they aim to critique by implying that a politics of futurity is maintained without contestation (Lesnik-Oberstein, 2010). In this regard, Fanon is aligned less with an Edelman-style 'no future' (the title of Edelman's 2004 book) since he draws attention to the partial ways in which specific children's futures are foreclosed, and in particular ways (as Pellegrini, 2008 notes, specifically in relation to educational programmes). Indeed, for Fanon, the status of being chronologically young is not necessarily a matter for topicalisation. Aside from its title, Fanon's 'Letter to the Youth of Africa', published in his posthumous book *Toward the African revolution: Political essays* (Fanon, 1964/1967) has no reference to any life-stage category; rather, the focus is on the political task and challenge of decolonisation at hand.

Where Fanon does discuss chronological, or historical, children and young people – that is, children as subjects, rather than only as narrative tropes expressing other developmental stories or affective attributes of colonial dynamics – these are often gender unmarked. For example, he expresses worries about what enforced idleness does to 'young people': 'The young people of an under-developed country are above all idle: occupations must be found for them' (*Wretched*: 158). Anticipating critiques of the ways that black bodies (especially young black bodies) are commodified and instrumentalised in capitalist sport, and also reflecting his perspective on racism as fetishism (Bhabha, 1983), Fanon comments: 'The youth of Africa ought not to be sent to sport stadiums but into the fields and into the schools' (*Wretched*: 158). He warns of young people as vulnerable to 'the various assaults made upon them by the very nature of Western culture' (157–158).

Elsewhere, children appear as unmarked actor in the anti-colonial struggle. A remarkably prescient piece, 'This is the Voice of Algeria' (Chapter 2 of *Dying Colonialism),* is put forward as a parable for modernisation and secularisation. This documents political vicissitudes structuring the reception and engagement with new technologies, specifically the radio (Painter, 2012). Initially, the radio was used as a key medium of colonial propaganda ('Before 1954, switching on the radio meant giving asylum to the occupiers' words', *Dying Colonialism*: 92), such that ownership signified collaboration ('Having a radio meant being besieged from within by the colonizer', ibid). However, over the course of the revolution a reversal took place such that the radio became a medium of anticolonial communication that was vital to revolutionary mobilisation ('Having a radio meant seriously going to war', 93). Curiously, here the focus is only on the abstracted (generalised as male) Algerian, without explicit gender or status differentiations. Extemic child, we may say here, is included, but not remarked upon. The now familiar current trope of the young as more readily adaptive and receptive to new technology does not appear at all. Instead, Fanon, via his undifferentiated address, speaks into being a *unified* national consciousness: *'The Voice of Algeria,* created out of nothing, brought the nation to life and endowed every citizen with a new status, *telling him so explicitly'* (*Dying Colonialism*: 96, emphasis in the original). Here Fanon emerges at his most democratically, if androcentrically, inclusive: by such an address he is arguing that the revolution is for everyone, the revolution changes, and will liberate and emancipate everyone, old as well as young.

Extemic child as generationally ordered gendered protagonist in the anticolonial struggle

Already, as an analytic approach to exploring shifting dynamics of inclusion, exclusion, and symbolisation of the social order, Extemic child has highlighted Fanon's mobilisation of gender and generational ordering. Next, we turn to a particularly contested arena of Fanon's theorising: the political role he accorded women and girls in the anticolonial struggle, alongside how gender also figures *as* a metaphor for this. Women and girls appear as political agents and revolutionaries in his rendering of the anticolonial struggle, rather than only as narrative figures for colonialism. But Fanon cannot quite escape some modernist tropes aligning women and national development. Here I draw on feminist engagements, especially from intersectionality theory and the 'affective turn' (Khanna, 2004; Rollock, 2012; Thompson, 2014), which have moved beyond critique of Fanon's (undoubted) androcentrism to offer more nuanced evaluations of his contribution. In addition, the focus from childhood studies on childhood as a positional, relational status (rather than a state or stage), draws particular attention to generational relationships (Alanen, 2005).

First, we can distinguish the girl as familial child within the generational order. Published in 1959 during the Algerian War, under the title *L'An Cinq, de la Révolution,* translated as *A Dying Colonialism*, hereafter *Dying Colonialism*, Fanon's second book assesses the pressures that the revolutionary struggle was putting on marital relations, including divorce and dispersal. In this he subscribes to a more positional analysis of children and childhood within family relationships, highlighting both the 'backwardness' imposed by the poverty and alienation and the transformative effects of revolutionary engagement. In Chapter 3 of *Dying Colonialism*, 'The Algerian Family', Fanon takes in turn the various gendered and generational positions ('the son and the father', 'the daughter and the father'). Perhaps as an expression of his secular modernist perspective, he places primacy on the younger party of each pair when discussing how political engagement and the modernising and empowering features of mobilisation transform 'the brothers', and 'the couple'. This includes mobilisation of the trope of the hungry child, now so familiar from charity and aid campaigns (for example, Black, 1992), through which he emphasises the disruption and violence done to 'the Algerian family', in particular the distortions and transformations of family and kinship relations: 'Children scattered to the winds, innumerable orphans who roam about, haggard and famished' (*Dying Colonialism*: 118), before concluding with stirring claims of how the struggle against tyranny will (re-)unite men and women as 'a dispersed people is realizing its unity and founding in suffering a spiritual community which constitutes the most solid bastion of the Algerian Revolution' (119).

Like age, gender is a relational status (also, of course, involving power relations). As already seen in this chapter, across Fanon's writings (like most others of that time), the child is ostensibly gender-free but presumed masculine, so that gender is marked or topicalised largely only in relation to girls. Hence, although (in 'The Algerian Family') there is no section on 'The sisters' to parallel that of 'The brothers', Fanon addresses in some detail the presumed or allotted lifecourse of girls in becoming women. Rather than claiming that Algerian girls and women are deprived of access to the category of childhood (which he would presumably critique as Eurocentric), he suggests that they have been traditionally denied adult status. Hence, he suggests that the graduation from girl to woman – unlike in the West that marks childhood as both a distinct period and as free from responsibility – is scarcely differentiated:

> The life of an Algerian woman does not develop according to the three periods known in the West – childhood, puberty and marriage. The Algerian girl knows only two stages: childhood-puberty, and marriage . . . Considered a minor indefinitely, the woman owes it to herself to find a husband as soon as possible.
>
> (Dying Colonialism: 107)

Significantly, the only reference to children as a reproductive and social burden *to* women (and girls) as mothers is, however, attributed to the colonisers: 'Colonial society blazes up vehemently against this inferior status of the Algerian woman. Its members worry and show concern for those unfortunate women, doomed "to produce brats;" kept behind walls, banned' (*Dying Colonialism*: 40).

Yet, Fanon also subscribes to the progressive nationalist, anticolonial, and socialist narrative of revolutionary change as equivalent to female emancipation: as 'restrictions . . . knocked over and challenged by the national liberation struggle . . . The freedom of the Algerian people from then on became identified with woman's liberation, with her entry into history' (*Dying Colonialism*: 107). Significantly, the example that Fanon provides here of the National Liberation Front (FLN) officers substituting for patriarchal fathers in giving permission for men and women in the Maquis (resistance) to marry or form relationships is an abstract version of the situation faced by 'B-' discussed in Chapter 4, of Fanon's patient trying to reconcile with the political imperative, mandated by the FLN, to 'take back' the wife he was estranged from, after she had been raped and tortured by French forces.

Extemic child in the anticolonial struggle – girl as prototypical protagonist

Critical debate of Fanon's treatment of women has in particular focused on the first chapter of *Dying Colonialism,* 'Algeria Unveiled'. This discusses shifts of meaning attending the adopting and shedding of the veil – as well as the motif of the violation and resistance strategies of the feminised body of the nation. Indeed Haddour (2010) situates Fanon's discussion in relation to the actual practice of veiling and unveiling as these figured in the Algerian revolution – both in terms of the use of veiling as a disguise to travel into French zones and also the strategy of forced unveilings – alongside beatings and rapes – used by the French in their brutal counterrevolutionary responses. In such a context it would be hard for Fanon not to reproduce the elision between woman and nation, even as he interrogates and in part explains it – especially in the chapter's title. To the European, 'This woman who sees without being seen frustrates the colonizer. There is no reciprocity. She does not yield herself, she does not give herself, does not offer herself' (*Dying Colonialism*: 44).

The veiled woman is perceived as resisting colonial gaze, and this excites particular resentment. As is ever the case, sexualised violence crucially includes unveiling, just as the metaphor of forced unveiling includes violence: 'Thus the rape of the Algerian woman in the dream of a European is always preceded by a rending of the veil. We witness here a double deflowering' (*Dying Colonialism*: 45).

Gender-specific references soon fall away in Fanon's account, however, making women and the veil function as a general metaphor for colonial oppression. In so doing Fanon is correctly criticised by feminists for both overlooking the specific dynamics and forms of colonised women's subjugation and its constitutive significance for colonisation (for example, Fraser, 2017), which Fuss (1994) extends also to a dubious gender incongruity in his account of colonial mimicry.

The only mention of the Algerian 'girl' in this chapter is in the context of 'the revolutionary character of the decision to involve all Algerian women' (*Dying Colonialism*: 51), unmarried as well as married. This last is warranted because of 'the more and more numerous volunteering of unmarried girls' (ibid.), that is, initiated by the young women themselves – an acknowledgement of their agency. Algerian women, especially the 'young Algerian women', are eulogised by Fanon. They are heralded as an index of the courage of new revolutionary subjects who literally go to new places – accessing spaces they were previously denied – for the cause. Maturity becomes depicted within a developmental trajectory that is political, as much as an individual – national rather than biographical. Fanon figures the transition from 'child' to 'Algerian woman, the young Algerian woman' (52) within a decolonising narrative of educational conscientisation that combines the intrapsychic with the political, as follows:

> Each time she ventures into the European city, the Algerian woman must achieve a victory over herself, over her *childish* fears. She must consider the image of the occupier lodged somewhere in her mind and in her body, remodel it, initiate the essential work of eroding it, make it inessential, remove something of the shame that is attached to it, devalidate it.
>
> *(ibid., emphasis added)*

Hence the young Algerian woman becomes the prototypical revolutionary subject who

> whenever she is called upon, establishes a link. Algiers is no longer the Arab city . . . From one area to another . . . the Revolution creates new links. More and more, it is the Algerian woman, the Algerian girl who will be assuming these tasks.
>
> *(53)*

The 'links' here are not only geographical, spatially distributed connections, but they are also interpersonal and intrapsychic, and within Fanon's narrative therefore polysemic.

In the context of the anticolonial struggle, the veil functioned politically in multiple ways. As is well known, the practice of veiling women was used to enable women (and sometimes men dressed as women) to smuggle arms and explosives into French colonial strongholds for actions. However, as already indicated, the staging of coerced unveiling public events by the French was carried out alongside the torture of men (and many women, too). In a move relevant to current debates on the veil (Haddour, 2010; Coloma, 2013), Fanon comments: 'What is in fact the assertion of a distinct identity, concern with keeping in fact a few shreds of national existence, is attributed to religious, magical, fanatical behaviour' (*Dying Colonialism*: 41), but '[t]he tenacity of the occupier in his endeavor to unveil the women, to make of them an ally in the work of cultural destruction, had the effect of strengthening traditional patterns of behaviour' (49). Alongside portraying gender roles in the traditional family as fulfilling a protective role against colonisation, then, Fanon also highlights women's mobilisation, and so transcendence, of those traditional roles – as central to the revolutionary struggle. Girls and women should not fulfil only the traditional gendered roles of nurse or home-maker, but are heralded as protagonists within armed struggle.

Considerable discussion has attended Fanon's final claim with which he ends 'Algeria Unveiled': 'Side by side with us, our sisters do their part in further breaking down the enemy system and in liquidating the old

mystifications once and for all' (67). This formulation positions the 'sisters'
as separate (from 'us'). While according a key place to women, if also
reworking it for a new national culture, Fanon risks mobilising the longstanding discourse of women's greater responsibility for the production
and reproduction of cultural identity (Yuval-Davis, 1997), now framed as
'liquidating the old mystifications'.

Much hinges on the interpretation of what doing 'their part' is understood
to be. Here Fanon can be seen as mobilising Extemic child within traditional
models of childhood and gendered adult–child relations. In illuminating the
dynamics of colonisation and how revolutionary struggle should challenge
these, he nevertheless consolidates some – especially gendered and familial –
representations even as he also reverses others.

Extemic child as gendered resistant/solidary other

Before we leave the discussion of gendered age and protagonism, let us consider one of Fanon's cases from Chapter 5 of *Wretched*, the only case in which
a (young) woman directly speaks. (Recall that in Chapter 4 I suggested that
in 'Series A, Case 1', 'B—'s' wife's voice functioned powerfully within the
case and its presentation, but this was only as indirectly inferred through
'B—'s' account.) In 'Series B, Case 3', Fanon reports on the '[n]eurotic
attitude of a young Frenchwoman whose father, a highly placed civil servant, was killed in an ambush'. As would be typical of a skilled psychoanalytic
practitioner, and as with his account of 'B—', Fanon dismisses the super-
ficial 'lucidity that touched on insensibility and later revealed, precisely by
its rationalism, this girl's uneasiness and the nature and origin of her
conflict' (222). He listens to the story, a story that provides a complemen-
tary perspective – in gender and generational terms, as well as in relation
to colonial privilege – to that of 'B—' discussed in Chapter 4. Like his, her
story is one of personal–political conflict, caught between her (political and
emotional) resistance to mourning a recently dead father she abhorred for his
active role in running interrogation centres that tortured and killed people,
and recognition of her inevitable cultural–colonial–racialised location (as her
father's daughter) within the colonial context.

Described as a 'girl' and a 'student', she presents with generalised anxiety
symptoms. Specifically, recalling the earlier discussion of 'shame' in Chapter 3,
'her hands were excessively moist and at times presented with, along with
palpitations and headaches, very worrying symptoms when sweat "flowed
all over her hands"' (223). The sweat that she reports as pouring over or out
of her hands is figured implicitly as equivalent to the money she has been
offered to support her after her father's death, money that she cannot bear as

"'the price of the blood spilt by my father'" (ibid.). She wants to finish her studies in order to support herself by earning a living, but she cannot. Indeed, her conflict is about who her real family is (she left her familial home to avoid witnessing the screams from the torture taking place in her father's house), while the relationships of affiliation are with the 'Algerian village' she grew up in: "'I knew almost all the families that lived there. The Algerian boys of my age and I had played together when we were small'" (222).

These were the boys who were being arrested, and in whose arrests she recognises she is perceived as being complicit: He quotes her as saying, "'In the end I didn't dare walk in the street any more. I was so sure of meeting hatred everywhere'" (223).

Unlike his account of 'B—', Fanon does not offer any resolution or therapeutic outcome. Rather, like the other case histories, this stands as testimony of the intractable psychic distress generated by the interpersonal (familial and cross-cultural) as well as political conflicts produced by colonial brutality and subjugation. Rather, it seems that Fanon's political and pedagogical message is to convey this young woman's views of justice and identification, and call to action: "'In my heart I knew that those Algerians were right'" (223).

So here Fanon, in the one place where he gives a direct voice to a woman, not only narrates an assertive, agentic speaking position; he also offers a pedagogical narrative of solidarity across difference, and against heteropatriarchal/familial limits of presumed 'natural' alliance. That is, the young woman's symptoms arose from her conflicted relationship with her murdered father whom she knew had been a torturer, while her sympathies lay with the oppressed Algerian people. Indeed, she comments: "'If I were an Algerian girl, I'd be in the Maquis'" (ibid.).

We will return to this 'case' when we come to discuss Fanon's pedagogy of solidarity. But, for now, let us recall the alignment of sweat and shame, for she is shamed by the actions of her father, who via his kinship or blood relationship with her, positioned her as having blood on her hands, alongside the mobilisation of youth also as a site of hope – a young French woman of 21. Yet Fanon here offers a narrative of cross-racialised hope. This 'girl' literally refuses the financial inheritance from her father, the torturer, and aligns herself with the Maquis.

Extemic child as therapeutic subject of 'the atmosphere of total war'

As illustration of Extemic child within the colonial war, I now address other 'Cases' where Fanon discusses children. This involves reports, unsurprisingly, of psychosomatic symptoms affecting younger children, as in 'Case 4'.

Behaviour disturbances in young Algerians of under ten' who have 'marked love for parental images, noise phobia, sleeplessness and sleep walking, enuresis, sadistic tendencies' (223–224). Here it is the adult–child *relation* and the impacts of its disturbance that is foregrounded (rather than privileging any particular depiction of children, or childhood, or subscribing to a model of what these should be).

In 'Series B', however, Fanon presents 'certain cases of groups of cases in which the event giving rise to the illness is in the first place the atmosphere of total war which reigns in Algeria' (217). Fanon's psychopolitical diagnosis (of 'the atmosphere of total war') should be read in itself as an intervention, since the French state failed to acknowledge the Algerian revolution as a war (both then, and scarcely even now, Thompson, 2014). Fanon's concern is with the psychic conflicts produced by the political repression, where the child as case is not singled out as a child, but as a case, that is, as a legitimate but not privileged political and therapeutic subject.

Most notably, 'Series B, Case 1' describes the murder of a European (that is, French *pied noir*) boy by two Algerian boys, of 13 and 14 years old respectively, in relation to which Fanon was asked to interview the boys (rather than conduct any therapeutic intervention). Fanon presents as apparently verbatim his cross-examination of these boys, including his efforts to establish whether they knew what they were doing, and to establish a motive. The boys admitted the crime, and claimed that there was no specific interpersonal precipitant, except their own desire to kill a European: 'We weren't a bit cross with him . . . He was a good friend of ours' (*Wretched*: 217). They are quoted as saying: 'One day we decided to kill him because the Europeans want to kill all the Arabs. We can't kill big people. But we could kill ones like him, because he was the same age as us' (217–218).

Mobilising the shock-value of this transgression of conventional iconographies of childhood innocence, Fanon can be read as presenting this case to graphically present psychological processes of depersonalisation and psychic splitting instigated by French repression. As Kuby (2015: 61) comments of this case: 'Their perpetration of violence was symptom, not cure.' Fanon here could be said to be 'using' these children to stand in not only for others, but for all Algerians. This mobilisation of part–whole relations, then, treats child as exemplar, as exemplary participant or protagonist, rather than as (with Idiotic child) securing the social order by their exclusion, or alternatively (as with Traumatogenic child, figured as transcendent or ventriloquised agent producing the traumatised racialised subject), or even as Therapeutic child in need of assimilation into a teleological narrative of development. Clearly there is no attempt to 'explain' these crimes, other than as an expression of the disorganised and distressing context of its occurrence. Gendzier (1973) acknowledges that 'no reader can be satisfied he has understood the psychological dynamics involved' (107). All that can be concluded is how: 'It is in the end, the few who commit such acts, although it may be the many who experience the degradation and despair of growing up in such a climate' (108).

Turning to other examples, alongside repudiating the 'criminal' or 'backward' mentality attributed by colonial psychiatry to Algerians, Fanon instead shows how this is a strategy of studied and assumed impenetrability or intransigence. Nevertheless, he does not romanticise this. As mentioned earlier, Fanon references children to highlight how colonial oppression turns people, even family and community members, against one another, where the evils of colonial oppression are further conveyed by the perversion of presumed natural relations of affection and care, including for children, such that they are 'a screen' for, or displaced projection of, the 'national enemy'. The child that infuriates the exhausted and exasperated native is not merely a child, but 'it so happens it is a little Algerian', alongside other adults who may equally elicit 'hatred and an overpowering desire to kill'. Here the child status of the 'little Algerian' works to emphasise that even a child has no special status under such conditions:

> [T]he natives fight among themselves. They tend to use each other as a screen, and each hides from his neighbour the national enemy. Then, tired out after a hard sixteen-hour day the native sinks down to rest on his mat, and a child on the other side of the canvas partition starts crying and prevents him from sleeping, it so happens that it is a little Algerian. When he goes to beg for a little semolina or a drop of oil from the grocer to whom he already owes some hundreds of francs, and when he sees that he is refused, an immense feeling of hatred and an overpowering desire to kill rises within him.
>
> *(Wretched: 248)*

Extemic child as continuing anticolonial protagonist

As seen earlier, discourses of childhood and youth often feature within conventional nationalist narratives of progress, or as its dystopian alternative. But there remains the question of how the suffering of chronological children is presented. This is a particularly tricky area given how, within the genre of aid and development campaigning, the suffering child so typically stands for more than itself, and figures to signify deservingness predicated on innocence. Yet agency remains prioritised over innocence and passivity in Fanon's documentation of the suffering of children, and the challenge posed *both to and by* brutalised and militarised young people. In the Preface to *A Dying Colonialism*, Fanon reproduces a report from a Swedish journalist visiting an Algerian refugee camp. The journalist, named as Mrs Christian Lilliestierna, describes a 7-year-old boy who was 'marked by deep wounds made by a steel wire with which he had been bound while French soldiers mistreated and killed his parents and sisters' (*Dying Colonialism*: 26). As a further torment, the soldiers had forced his eyes open to watch and remember this. Perhaps unsurprisingly, the child said: '[t]here is only one thing I want: to be able to cut a French soldier up into small pieces, tiny pieces!' (ibid.). Fanon comments:

> Does anyone think it is easy to make this child of seven forget both the murder of his family and his enormous vengeance? Is this orphaned child growing up in an apocalyptic atmosphere the sole message that French democracy will leave?
>
> *(ibid.)*

As also discussed in Chapters 3 and 4, this narrative of trauma links Fanon the psychiatrist/therapist with Fanon the anticolonial revolutionary and social pedagogue, here via the account of a child who has been specifically victimised *as a child* with affective – now severed – bonds to his family members. His 'growing up' – note how the developmental maturational descriptor is in the continuous present that connects present to future – is now situated in an 'apocalyptic atmosphere'. This atmosphere is imbibed by him, but not only him; this child is both specific and a token of many others, children and adults. Extemic child here is a token of itself but also more. What is left open is not only how possible, but also how desirable, it is to 'make this child of seven forget'.

This formulation – in both psychotherapeutic and political senses – offered by Fanon counters a reading of inciting or romanticising violence with which he is sometimes attributed, even as it also admits this as a likely reaction. As discussed in Chapter 4 in relation to one specific case, *Wretched* ends with Fanon, the psychiatrist, cataloguing psychological casualties and disturbances created by both chronic colonial repression and then the horrors of the massacres, battles, and torture with which the revolutionary struggle was met. Yet, following his comments on the 'orphaned child growing up in an apocalyptic atmosphere' (*Dying Colonialism*: 26), Fanon writes of the slow pace and unexpected scale of French resistance to Algerian independence (this was, after all, the fifth year of struggle). In a generalising move he shifts from the 'orphaned child' to talk of the position of the 'rising generations' – with 'rising' here appearing to qualify 'generation' as the next generation but also as the next generation of young insurgents:

> The rising generations are neither more flexible nor more tired than those who launched the struggle. There is, on the contrary, a hardening, a determination to be equal to the historical challenge, a determination too not to make light of the hundreds of thousands of victims. And there is also an exact appraisal of the dimensions of the conflict, of the friendships and solidarities, of the interests and the contradictions of the colonialist universe.
>
> *(Dying Colonialism: 26)*

The term 'rising' appears to qualify the generations to come, as well as to be brought up (so figuring into this the question of how they are to be brought up). It combines the notion of waking up (compare the Sleeping Beauty image discussed earlier) with a political dawn of consciousness. Significantly, these political nuances of 'rising' are commented upon by Batchelor (2017b), in relation to the translation choices made by Constance Farrington, who undertook the first English translation of *Wretched*. Since Batchelor's discussion is focused only on the translation of *Wretched*, rather than also *Dying Colonialism*, we cannot make direct connection across the texts. However, there are useful reminders. Batchelor notes both Farrington's Irish Republican sympathies, such that she saw the Algerian struggle as echoing that for Irish nationalism and therefore 'rising' held particular associations for her given contemporary events there, but also her commitment to retaining the revolutionary associations of the French '*Debout!*' ('Arise!') with the international revolutionary anthem ('Arise, ye wretched . . . '), which would have been immediately recognisable to the French public. Apparently, in line with her own interpretation of Fanon's writing as a call to action, she had argued that the title of the book should be 'The Rising of the Damned', which more clearly topicalises the activity to transform the subjective condition (of being 'wretched' or 'damned') rather than only depicting this as a state.

At any rate, what is being conveyed in the extract from *Dying Colonialism* above is not only a sense of threat, indicated by the 'hardening' of the (repeated and so doubled) 'determination', but also a sense of the next generation of activists as discriminating, informed, and deliberative – as aware of their historical responsibilities. The formulation of being 'neither more flexible nor more tired' works powerfully to render both the past and the future anticolonial fight (and fighters) as equally important. 'Neither more flexible nor more tired' is an understatement, a double negative that, in its form, explicitly counters any presumption that 'the rising generations' could be *more* 'flexible' (and so easily bought off or discouraged) or *more* 'tired' (and so led to terminate the revolution prematurely). It is mobilised to indicate a measured lack of impulsiveness that also includes clear-sighted judgement, the 'exact appraisal' both of structural questions of colonial interests and of the interpersonal possibilities of 'friendships and solidarities'. These (structural and interpersonal) 'dimensions of the conflict' can converge, but Fanon is also pointing here to key contradictions that enable alliances and joint mobilisations ('friendships and solidarities').

Extemic child as resisting the othering of children

Longstanding colonial dynamics link children with the colonised, as Fanon often topicalises. Fanon nevertheless disrupts some of these links in the service of his pedagogical project for both adults and children. Among many other critics, Fanon's political writings address how 'child' and 'primitive'/colonised have been figured as other to, but also as a true version of, the industrialised, Western self. As was noted when discussing its reinscription of the white mother and child's racialised hailings in Chapter 3, the articulation of these two tropes is far from accidental, since patriarchal domination of the family, which positioned women and children as ruled by the husband/father, was used as the naturalised model for colonial domination (McClintock, 1995). Levander (2006: 2–3) makes the point succinctly: 'The child works to establish race as a central shaping element of ostensibly raceless Western ideals. Excavating the child's importance to the development of white supremacy is urgently needed.'

We need to remember how dominant discourses of development originate in portraying white European middle-class men as their pinnacle, a dynamic that discourses and technologies of cross-national comparison always evoke (Burman, 2007), even as they may rework and reinterpret them. Moreover, these have been replayed 'at home' precisely in relation to child welfare agendas – as a key example we may recall how in its early days the UK National Society for the Prevention of Cruelty to Children (NSPCC) mobilised discourses of 'savagery' to apply to neglectful British working-class parents, while also drawing on Christian imagery of the Holy Family to figure child nurture and support (Flegel, 2009).

This common pedagogical motif has been mobilised by critiques applying postcolonial analyses to analyse and challenge the paternalism and incompetency accorded children, childhood, and the young (see Cannella, & Viruru, 2004). These have been inspired by analyses of colonialism and postcolonialism, in particular Said (1978), to indicate common dynamics of attributions of authenticity and unmediated access to nature, truth, and collective and individual corporeal well-being that arise as reverse tropes of the damaged subjectivities produced by modern Western capitalism – that is, of alienation from nature, from our bodies, and from one another. This is the disavowed colonial heritage of the originators of the child-centred pedagogies and the early education movement (Taylor, 2013). Attending to instabilities, destabilisations, and underspecifications surrounding (Fanon's and others') rhetorics and mobilisations of child is politically useful. Analysing Kipling's literary depictions of children, Sue Walsh suggests

> the concept of the 'child', especially as applied to the colonized subject, may have unlooked for and potentially destabilizing implications in the figurations of colonial ventures. What, for example, are the implications of the child/colonized analogy if the child's positioning as adult-in-waiting is allowed to feed through to the conception of the colonized?
>
> *(2010: 33)*

Concerning violence and its pedagogy

As discussed in Chapter 1, Fanon's final book, *Wretched of the Earth*, was both made famous and also infamous in part because Jean-Paul Sartre wrote its Preface. It was banned shortly after publication in France, and also across most of Latin American and South Africa. It is largely accepted that Sartre's Preface also has promoted key misunderstandings of Fanon's ideas, especially in relation to the role accorded violence (Macey, 2012: Hallward, 2011: Gibson, 2011b; Gordon, 2015; Kuby, 2015). Sartre's formulation of the subject as finding him/herself through violent resistance went beyond that of Fanon, including also in his depictions of childhood. Sartre, in his Preface, says: 'The child of violence, at every moment he draws from it his humanity. We were men at his expense, he makes himself man at ours: a different man; of higher quality' (20). 'Child' here is 'of violence', elided with it and made human by it. Sartre depicts a zero-sum relationship between this 'child of violence' and those at whose expense 'he' was denied humanity. By contrast, for Fanon, the question of violence is a matter for concern and for action, rather than uncritical celebration. The violence is already there, structured into the colonial context of inequality. Thus, any action on the part of the oppressed will be seen as violent in struggling to oppose or change this: 'It is understandable that the first action of the black man is a *reaction*' (*Black Skin*: 27, emphasis in the original).

Profoundly influenced as he was by Sartre's ideas, Fanon both used them for his own purposes and also marks key differences from them. For example, in *Black Skin*, he quotes Sartre's *Orphée Noir*, where Sartre adopts the voice of the black(ened), racialised subject to ask a series of questions: 'What did you expect when you unbound the gag that had muted those black mouths?

That they would chant your praises? Did you think that when those heads that our fathers had forcibly bowed down to the ground were raised again, you would find adoration in their eyes?' (22). Fanon's answer to these questions marks out a different project:

> I do not know; but I say that he who looks into my eyes for anything but a perpetual question will have to lose its sight; neither recognition nor hate. And if I cry out it will not be a black cry. No, from the point of view adopted here, there is no black problem. Or any rate if there is one it concerns the whites only accidentally.
>
> *(22)*

Perhaps anticipating his 'final prayer' that is the last sentence of *Black Skin* ('O my body, make of me always a man who questions!', 165), he refuses both to assume the adversarial position that Sartre later would attribute to him and also a wider project of closing off or knowing subjectivity. (Butler, 2015: 194, reads further possibilities in this 'perhaps the most insurrectionary of his speech acts' to find transformative gender ambiguities and possibilities in Fanon's reflexive address.) Fanon is refusing polarised racialised discourse and positionings; he claims that there is 'no black problem', rather than seeking to reverse the status of black and white. That the problem only concerns whites 'accidentally' indicates not only a rejection of a kind of essential, Manichean confrontation between black and white, but also a practical kind of decentring from white people and white knowledges. This perhaps anticipates perhaps how Chen (2010) will develop Fanon's ideas to form a postcolonial pedagogy of 'inter-referencing' between Asian countries rather than recapitulating the old orientation around Europe, maintained even via its repudiation, as discussed in Chapter 6. Instead, Fanon's address to the question of subjectivity, of enabling the (re)joining of reflection, affection, and action, was concerned with undoing the negative 'reactions' created by historical and current, everyday oppressive insults. That is, he understood that shedding the known discomfort of the position of being marginalised would require a subjective, decisive, agentic transformation, a necessary violence perhaps, to turn around and transform the psychic effects of alienation, dehumanisation, and desubjectification into something else. And where Sartre (1961/1963) appeals to a 'full-grown' or mature humanity ('And when one day our human kind becomes full-grown, it will not define itself as the sum total of the whole world's inhabitants, but as the infinite unity of their mutual need', 23), Butler (2015) reads possibilities of a less masculinist and prescriptive humanism but rather relational co-constitution that she attributes to Fanon's influence.

Fanon, then, joins other educational theorists in highlighting the violence of education, in its structural, symbolic, and colonial aspects – whether
in children's schooling or in models of professional practice (such as the
colonial psychiatry he devoted many pages to critiquing). The classed and
intergenerational violence that is done by the colonised in their emulation
of the coloniser: 'The middle class in the Antilles never speak Creole except
to their servants. In school the children of Martinique are taught to scorn
their dialect' (*Black Skin*: 15), while 'teachers keep a close watch over the
children to make sure they do not use Creole' (21). These are, of course,
not the only forms of violence at play within pedagogical processes. There is
the pedagogic violence necessarily structurally embodied by the position of
the 'teacher', of assuming one knows better, or of being institutionally positioned as such and so being rendered unable to support and respond to other
knowledges being formulated. Yet, the opposite of this can be just as problematic: abdicating on responsibility to teach and challenge, and so allow
prevailing modes and relations of power to continue uncontested. Such are
the dilemmas facing both 'radical' and 'liberal' educational models, including
those sometimes designated 'critical pedagogy' (Worsham, 1998).

From pedagogies of pathologisation to pedagogies of resistance

If we can characterise dominant ways of addressing and engaging with the
dispossessed as a pedagogy of pathologisation, as a recent account of the role
of schooling in the criminalisation of young black girls has put it (Annamana,
2018), various responses have been put forward to counter this (some of
which have already been indicated in previous chapters). Significantly, this
pedagogy functions precisely to deem some subjects as unworthy of, or inca-
pable of, education. We saw in Chapter 2 how the Brexit interviewees, and
especially the 'Brexit' 'kids' were configured in this way, as Idiotic child, a
manifestation of how the middle classes pathologise the British working class
in the service of their own exoneration.

We have already encountered 'pedagogies of shame', as one mode of (dis)
engagement. These may include other approaches that mobilise modes of
awareness-raising around dimensions of privilege and power (for example,
Yancy, 2012, 2017), but as we have seen (in Chapter 3) these threaten to
repeat rather than rectify traumatisation. Other accounts have argued for the
need to (re)claim 'guilt' as a mode of engagement that indicates alliance, without the aim of domination – of a mode of subjective engagement that is said to
precede analytical or cognitive approaches that arises from a form of listening
that does not try to know or understand (Todd, 2003). Sharon Todd's model

of guilt and listening arises from Kleinian psychoanalysis, and so understands guilt as necessary and reparative, rather than excoriating. This partakes of a therapeutic pedagogy that we also saw at work in Chapter 4, whose limitations Boler (1999) drew attention to. Boler's (1999) arguments are informed by a Foucaultian critique of confession. She argues against pedagogical efforts to promote (or 'school') 'empathy' as ushering in passivity through identification with the victimised rather than active transformation of the relations of oppression. This is a pedagogy of emotions that, even as it extends this, returns the focus to the therapeutic subjectivity of the oppressed rather than changing the relations of oppression. Instead, (like Bailey, 2017) she proposes a 'pedagogy of discomfort', whose discomfort arises not from being subjectively challenged by the victims (in the classroom or its texts) but rather by the challenge of undertaking the move from empathy to action, that will also necessarily extend outside the classroom or immediate pedagogical situation.

Fanon's pedagogy of resistance, then, was primarily addressed to those most psychically and materially affected and diminished by oppression, who demand justice and recognition of past injustices:

> [O]utside university circles there is an army of fools: what is important is not to educate them, but to teach the Negro not to be the slave of their stereotypes. That these imbeciles are the product of a psychological-economic system I will grant. But that does not get us much further along.
>
> *(Black Skin: 26)*

His focus was not on educating the 'army of fools' but on supporting psychic decolonisation, 'teaching the Negro not to be the slave of their [that is, the fools'] stereotypes'. He was far from castigating such 'fools' as either indicating all racists or colonialists, nor from denying that they were not also victims of psychic and material oppression. Hence, educational engagements with Fanon's writings address questions of alienation, normalisation, and the complex dynamics of multicultural teaching (see, for example, Bingham, 2006; Dei, & Simmons, 2010b; Huey-Li, 2003; Leonardo, & Porter 2010; Williams, 1976). Fanon's primary concern was the impacts of the violence and distortions *done to* the oppressed/colonised, and how this then constrained and disabled, repressed as well as oppressed them. As Dei and Simmons put it:

> Among the major problems that colonized, oppressed and marginalized peoples have to deal with are the negations of historical experiences and collective and cultural memories; negation of our subjectivities; the invalidation of the embodiment of our knowing; a continuing

struggle against our dehumanization and the 'spirit injury' of per-
petual resistance; and the oftentimes easy and seductive slippage into
the form, logic, and implicit assumptions of the very things we are
contesting. Fanon thus offers an opportunity to rethink transformative
pedagogy and education by pointing to the areas of focus. We need
to create a new humanity, and we must see the goal of education as
helping all learners 'become human'.

(2010a: xiii)

This 'human', however, is not the human of modern European discourse,
with all its exclusions. Rather a pedagogy of inclusive nurturance appears to
be at play, aiming to challenge internalised oppression and fostering climates
for countering exploitation and alienation. Inevitably, it has a therapeutic
project of integration in the service of individual and collective development:
'Decolonizing then becomes a process of healing and becoming healthy and
whole again through affective learning' (Dei, 2010a: 9). We may recall here
how, contrary to Octave Mannoni's (1969/2003) account, Don Talayesva,
the Hopi Sun Chief, who figured in Chapter 2, not only survived but also
critically re-worked his experiences in white government schools, returning
to become a leader of his community equipped to build new cultural-
political syntheses that could engage and negotiate more successfully with the
wider white settler institutions. That his autobiography was generated (and
sponsored) as a Yale University anthropology project (with the first edition
published under the name of the researcher and editor, Leo Simmons) makes
this text perhaps all the more remarkable for the tensions and struggles discernible therein, as a record not only of cultural practices in transition but
also of the interpersonal pressures of its production.

The problem here, though, is that we cannot exactly know how any
learner will experience any lesson or intervention, such that what could
be generative for one may be alienating to another. It is one matter, then,
to highlight how learning, being open to the new, necessarily involves
discomfort (whether learning of one's own history of oppression or that
of others'). It is another to know how to shape the conditions for that
learning so that the discomfort is tolerable, rather than so painful or
anxiety-inducing that – as also indicated in Chapter 3 – the subject retreats
or worse still rejects and attacks the material. On this point the debates
on feminist pedagogy in women's studies classrooms of the 1990s had
much to say, as also on the sometimes (at least in the short-term) inverse
relationships between politicisation in the classroom and academic success
(Burman, 2001b, 2001c, 2006).

Yet recognition of (one's own or others') past hurt is not the same as being transfixed by it, or of organising one's identity around it. All recognition is, as we have seen, misrecognition; so, lack or failure is intrinsic. But some misrecognitions are more noteworthy, and damaging, than others. Rather than seeking technical answers, then, in pedagogical staging of encounters aimed to be redistributive through the changing of awareness, or of relationship – that is, of (rather presumptuous practices of attempting to manipulate) recognition – we may be better off attending to their temporalities. As discussed by Bingham (2006), the temporality of the paradigm of recognition – both inside and outside educational arenas – has a before, during, and after. Britzman's (2003) attention to the 'after' focuses on how the learning happens as an individual subjective encounter, such that teachers cannot legislate for or specify whether or how it will take place. The project then becomes one of supporting a subjective development that can undertake such investigations independently (whether individually or collectively) – that is, after education. This attention to temporality, that is, to the before, during, and after, resonates with the narrative, temporally sensitive reading of Fanon and the disarticulation between individual learning process and externally imposed learning project (whether of a curriculum subject, or oppression/privilege awareness, or of developmentalism of a more neoliberal, state-imposed kind) that I have offered in this book.

Fanon's pedagogy of failure and solidarity

The various forms of 'child' discussed in this book have been generated from Fanon's corpus as resources to explore anti-colonial or revolutionary metaphorics of childhood, even as his diverse formulations do not allow for easy resolution. Attending to these various versions of 'child' highlights how Fanon neither offers an alternative metaphorics, which would then risk reinstating equivalent exclusions and normalisations, yet his depictions do not merely repeat old oppressive models. Fanon's playful use of familial, relational, generational discourses reverses, as well as recapitulates, prevailing understandings of age and chronological as well as sexed, gendered, and other power relations.

Earlier (in Chapters 2 and 4) I discussed Fanon's pedagogy of failure as informing his therapeutic approach, as well as methodological or philosophical position. The warding off of teleology and presumption to know better than his interlocutors was clearly built from a therapeutic sensitivity (and indeed there is now a large psychotherapeutic literature that critiques 'knowing' from the perspective of appropriating or colonising the client's/patient's lifeworld, for example, Hoffman, 1991; Rober, & Seltzer, 2010). Such refusals of certainty have typically been associated with feminist, postmodern, and posthuman approaches, as ways to avoid reproducing patriarchal and colonial dynamics of mastery in research as also therapeutic relationships. In his insistence on the limits of 'bur[ying] himself in the vast black abyss . . . of a mystical past' (*Black Skin*: 12) in particular as thereby 'renouncing the present and the future' (ibid.), Fanon committed himself to an 'architecture . . . rooted in the temporal . . . Ideally the present will always contribute to the building of the future' (11), that is, much like second-wave feminist interventions of the 1970s and 1980s, as also within psychotherapeutic discourse, working to prefigure the kind of relations in the present that could help envisage and build a different future.

As noted in Chapter 1, such formulations have resonance with Rancière's (1991) 'ignorant schoolmaster' while the reflexive and tentative character of the claims being made, and Fanon's acknowledgement of his own inscription within them, echo aspects of feminist theorising, notably Judith Butler's (2005) discussion of accountability. More recently debates in social and educational theory have been concerned with questions of solidarity, perhaps precisely because of the ways our current times seem so devoid of this amid rising xenophobias and attacks on those positioned as marginal and non-normative (whether on the basis of gender, class, migration status, sexuality, unemployment, disability, or other economic status, or indeed various combinations of or intersections between these). Laments of loss of solidarity concern the erosion of social bonds, and analysis has focused on why and how this has come about. Balibar's (2012) post-Foucaultian analysis of the ways neoliberal governmentality has fostered a 'post-democratic' relation to the state, such that the only available position for the subject is one of compliance rather than contestation, comes to mind.

The notion of solidarity is less concerned with identity than activity. That is, it is not who you are but what you do that matters. Moreover (as with feminist debates about coalitions or affinity groups), it is not organised around prescriptions of or for similarity. It does not specify programmatic preconditions, but is built through joint action. Notwithstanding Fanon's many professions of not being primarily interested in (changing) white people's subjectivities in *Black Skin*, by the time of his revolutionary participation he is able to offer examples of practical modes of mutually supportive engagement. Of particular significance in relation to Fanon's political project is that his pedagogical address crosses prevailing racialised (and gendered) boundaries and enlists all into the revolutionary struggle.

I discussed above Fanon's example (from *Wretched*) of the French young woman who identified with the anti-colonial struggle. Fanon narrated this as an unresolved clinical case, so underscoring the ways that political conflicts are played out within intra-familial and intra-psychical relations – for those positioned as colonisers as well as colonised. However, Chapter 5 of *Dying Colonialism*, entitled 'Algeria's European minority', merits attention as offering an account that completely refutes any conception of Fanon as proposing irreconcilable differences across historical racialised or colonial positions. In this chapter he outlines the multiple ways the various 'minority' communities, 'Jews', 'city dwellers', even 'settlers' have supported the liberation struggle, even as some from the same communities also opposed them. The pedagogical mode that Fanon adopts here is one of documentation, of highlighting what has happened, to demonstrate that such solidarity is not only possible but is actually already occurring. While he acknowledges the contradictions and barriers to building such alliances, Fanon is here indicating how trust across historically opposed positions can be built, and that support may emerge from the most surprising quarters, and Gendzier (1973) offers some historical corroboration of this. His examples even include police giving advance warnings to insurgents of planned – police and army – actions. Plainly the narrative, pedagogical project here is to emphasise how (the Algerian) emancipation is open to all who are willing to join its project. Whatever the seeming smoothing over of possible political differences or 'mistakes' that sometimes occurred, Fanon is here clearly favouring collaboration between differently positioned actors, indeed highlighting how they can achieve more precisely through those different positionings, rather than closing down the possibility of communication and engagement. (In generating this reading I am, incidentally, fundamentally opposing Kuby's, 2015: 65, interpretation of Fanon as envisaging that decolonial struggle would give rise to national homogeneity.) Moreover, as if to demonstrate this point, this chapter is not only composed of his own narrative but rather he hands it over to two others, presenting testimonies of two non-Algerian men who joined the FLN liberation struggle, and these two Appendices in fact equal Fanon's main text in length (both are fifteen pages long). (The longer of these is in fact identified by the translator as Charles Geronimi, Fanon's colleague at Blida-Joinville.) His account, then, is both a passionate plea for and an example of an account of, the possibilities of solidarity, practically performed through different voices telling of individual engagements and contributions to a shared struggle.

What Extemic child brings to antiracist pedagogies and pedagogies of solidarity is the Fanonian analysis of the project of 'disalienation', in both in its negative and positive forms. Fanon offers a catalogue of psychic and material injury arising from racialised oppression that threatens to erupt from resentment into revenge. His model to address this insists on the need for changed political as well as interpersonal conditions. A starting point has to be a common commitment to challenging injustice, seen not merely as psychologised grudge or fantasised insult. A pedagogy of solidarity engages Extemic child as joint partner in a project of transformation that is personal, societal, and political. Solidarity here is not identity; that is, it does not erase difference. However, it does allow for (shifting, relational) moments of identification, whether historically generated (in fantasy or reality) or forged through current projects of joint action. As Fanon shows, from both his psychotherapeutic and philosophical analyses, this requires the psychic as well as socio-political capacity to tolerate uncertainty, lack of closure, and difference that extends from managing the anxiety of insecure and unstable coalitions or alliances to warding off a commitment to a fixed developmental endpoint in favour of enabling and celebrating the nurturing of more imminent creative capacities. As also more recently formulated within feminist pedagogical project of transnational solidarity (Mohanty, 2003), emotions and learning, feelings and politics, the personal and the political, are all conjoined aspects of projects of change.

Child as method and Fanon's pedagogy of determined hope

We saw (in Chapter 3) that in *Black Skin* Fanon invoked shame as a pedagogy to unite black and white to oppose racism together. As his contribution to the flurry of articles assessing Fanon and *Wretched* 50 years after its initial publication, Fanon's biographer David Macey subtitled his 'Frantz Fanon as a source of continued political embarrassment'. He discusses the various ways Fanon did not fit into available categorisations, and so – notwithstanding the cycle of revivals of interest in his work across the world – he has been misread or overlooked often especially in the national contexts within which he was most active, that is, Martinique and Algeria. He was a Martinican who died as an Algerian (in exile), an antipsychiatrist psychiatrist, an internationalist nationalist, a philosophical revolutionary who opposed the prevailing black intellectuals 'negritude' movement of his time, an unorthodox socialist who was also aligned with some Marxist ideas, even a Marxist psychoanalytic psychotherapist. Fanon just did not 'fit', and, hence, Macey identifies the challenges he posed, and continues to pose, as 'a source of continued political embarrassment'. Initially, I puzzled over this title, as an assessment of Fanon's contribution. Yet, it can be interpreted positively. As the current theorists of shame note (Johnson, & Moran, 2013), embarrassment is more transitory than shame and closer to the kind of discomfort that draws attention to something that needs to be changed, and can be changed (Bailey, 2017).

Macey, then, considers the 'embarrassment' attending Fanon's writing as a positive assessment of the continuing challenge posed by it.

I would claim that child as method, as practised across this book, works similarly. The various modes of child thematising its substantive chapters offer some intransigence and opacity to conventional modes of categorising children and childhoods. Taking up Laplanche's (1999) discussion of the ways that enigmatic signifiers traverse and so compose the subjectivity of the young child (that Butler, 2005, discusses in her account of the dynamics of moral accountability), we may rather say that child as method reverses Laplanche's account instead to treat the child as enigmatic signifier, whose opacities produce surfaces of both under- and over-determination of the social. Hence, through the enigmatic, ambiguous positioning of child, the relationships that hold between economic, material, interpersonal, and intrapsychic arenas can be interrogated – including whether they are constitutive or contingent. (Remember, for Fanon in *Black Skin* they were so contingent that the child was 'drowned' in it.) Correlatively, such relationships demand reconsideration of the positions and roles accorded children and childhoods.

Hence, in this chapter I have mobilised the term Extemic to show how what appears as being on the inside from one vantage point turns out at another to be outside. This reflects something of the mobility and looping effects achieved by configurations of child. Child as method, like Fanon, is suspicious of origin stories; rather, its focus is on current relations, and inter-relations. What child as method brings to this project, through both its psychoanalytic and anti-colonial engagements, is a warding off of any progressivist or developmental pretensions to those temporal attunements. The pedagogical challenge may well be 'when' to do something, as well as 'what' to do. But (and this is precisely what advocates of 'early intervention' policies miss) the 'after' is already in the 'before', in the retroactive re-imagining that occurs in the minds of students, teachers, and (especially) policymakers: the what I understood before is always being reconfigured by and through the perception of what I now (think I) understand, as well as the who (individually and collectively) I want to be, and be with. Even if some such alienation is socially and relationally inevitable, and is even in part productive, Fanon topicalises what needs to happen for the 'during' of (mis)recognition to occur in meaningful and 'positive', rather than only alienating, ways.

In terms of analytical or methodological frameworks, such unsettlings could be read as deconstructionist – denaturalising assumed positions and arrangements, and so revealing more about their precise and contingent configurations. (Let us recall that Jacques Derrida, the theorist of deconstruction, was an Algerian émigré, from the community of Jewish Algerians, some of whom Fanon describes as crucially involved in supporting the revolutionary struggle.) Yet, as we have seen, Fanon is also a modern developmentalist, formulating policies to turn the young of the nation into 'mature' ('conscious', 'responsible') adults, albeit that sometimes the 'Youth' are addressed less as deficient and vulnerable but as the future national subjects and agents. In both his clinical psychiatric writings and his cultural, psychopolitical analysis evoking racialised subjectivities, Fanon draws on a psychodynamic understanding of childhood experience as formative – and he uses this for the depiction of dystopian ('apocalyptic') future social-political relations. Fanon's children, therefore, not only include the child of '"Look, a Negro!"', that is, a child tainted by racism, whose ventriloquism (Macherey, 2012) works to emphasise the violence done to the agents and heirs of racist rule as well as its victims. As with in his other depictions of dangerous and damaged children and childhoods, Fanon portrays children as extemic: as societal participants, and as products and agents within the social relation, whether as morally responsible or culpable, inviting (as Dei, & Simmons, 2010, and Maldonado, et al., 2005 note) questions of practical engagement.

I suggest that Fanon's rhetorics of childhood and development pressurise the child–other relation arguably as much as, and as a reflection of, his analysis of the self–other relation as produced through structures of racialised symbolic and structural violence (Hage, 2010). His depictions provoke re-evaluation of whether and how what happens after decolonisation departs from, or reproduces, dominant models of development. Moving from the designation 'underdeveloped' to 'developed', or to something else, opens up space for discussion about the role for education (or indeed 'counter education', Brenneman, & Margonis, 2012), as recent assessments of the educational relevance of Fanon's psychoaffective account appreciate (De Lissovoy, 2010, 2012; Zembylas, 2015a, 2015b).

The various forms of Extemic child differentiated in this chapter both arise from, and promote, different pedagogical modes of address and engagement. As we have seen, some of Fanon's depictions could be categorised within a modern, nationalist frame, since he readily mobilises the young as the future of the nation, also including particular gender chauvinisms and heterosexed norms. Yet, his hostility to models of Western development on which, arguably, many models of child as well as economic development rely (Burman, 2008a), allows for further possibilities. Without forcing or overstating Fanon's radical imaginary of children and childhood, readings can be retrieved that remain open or uncommitted about children, childhood, and the relationship between childhood and political and economic development. At such times as these, where education is increasingly tied to fixed and instrumental agendas, I suggest such readings are politically and pedagogically important. One clearly significant feature is Fanon's opposition to origin narratives, whether of lost childhoods or lost national developments; another is his open pedagogy of solidarity.

I have come to think of this pedagogy as being one of determined hope. That is, that Fanon recognised the many ways subjects are indeed determined, but also was committed to elaborating practical and political strategies for resisting those determinations, as also transforming the conditions giving rise to them. Fanon's radical humanism was an expression of that hope, that belief in change. From reflective analyses of white supremacist discourse following Trump's electoral victory (Sullivan, 2017) to #Black Lives Matter, social and educational movements are similarly going beyond these polarised positions.

It remains unclear whether and, if so, how the conditions of children's lives and the political-economic level accorded the countries they live in should be connected. Some critics of development(al) discourse (including myself) have called for their disaggregation, as one of the many ways children's subjectivities and current (social and educational) conditions are instrumentalised and subordinated to economic-national priorities, as indicated in particular ways by neoliberalism (Ailwood, 2008; Fendler, 2001). Yet, as is reflected in Fanon's case histories, composed almost entirely of distressed people less than 30 years old, and most under 20, those countries that in Fanon's time were achieving independence from colonial rule are now precisely those whose populations are chronologically young. The relation between the West and its former colonial others remains one of old world–new world in the sense that over-developed rich countries face the crisis of caring for an ageing (and presumed economically less productive) population.

Fanon's discussion of conditions for revolutionary subjectivity resonate in both inspiring and disturbing ways with current contexts of global wars, both acute and devastating but also of the chronic low-intensity kind that generate other kinds of subjective conditions of alienation and resignation. In particular, his accounts address the conditions of children caught up in securitisation regimes of surveillance and self-surveillance, and other kinds of neocolonial occupation. Children abound within current discourses of political radicalisation, reflecting a particular, and particularly racialised, modality of current geopolitical dynamics. Explanatory frameworks emphasise either moral corruption or psychological vulnerability and so fail to engage adequately with the interpretive and affectively responsive sense-making capacities of those it surveys.

While social and educational theorists are taking up perhaps equivalent resources within readings of Deleuzian, posthuman, or new materialist approaches, this book places Fanon alongside these. A full treatment of their mutual compatibilities and tensions lies beyond the scope of this work, but clearly such is possible. For example, Washick and Wingrove (2015) highlight the ways that such approaches risk subordinating politics to epistemology, re-instate a voluntaristic humanism by focusing on ethical choices and responsibilities and correspondingly depict a 'narrowing of collective action' (77). Fanon, instead, offers a corrective specificity and collective engagement. Further, Gerrard, et al. (2016) mobilise Fanon in their postcolonial critique of so-called 'post-qualitative' educational research. Fanon's radical humanism aligns with the reading of posthumanism that, for example, Braidotti (2013) puts forward, as surpassing the exclusionary and discretionary limits of European enlightenment humanism without ceding its democratic and technical achievements. Fanon may be read as a proto-Deleuzian in his thwarting of teleology and attention to temporality, and his concrete political engagements perhaps can be read alongside those of Deleuze and Guattari. (Indeed, given Fanon's mobilisations of Lacanian ideas, it is relevant to note that Deleuze participated in Lacanian debates, and Guattari remained a practising psychoanalyst alongside his theoretical contributions.) Each resource has its specific focus and differences, and certainly Fanon's political projects came to be much more specified and directed towards different, arguably urgent, arenas of pedagogical and political intervention. Yet, as elaborated in earlier chapters, the specificity of his geopolitical analyses are increasingly being recognised as offering more helpful philosophical as well as political insights than some theorists of the Western canon. In this era of the resurgence of the pathologisation of young black men (in particular) (Yancy, 2017; Bhattacharrya, 2008), whether addressing post-conflict militarised youth, or envisaging post-racist societies (after all, Fanon points out, 'let us remember that our purpose is to make possible a healthy encounter between black and white', *Black Skin*: 57), Fanon's narrative strategies for traversing the child–colony relation continue to offer significant conceptual-political resources for educational theory and practice.

6

CHILD AS METHOD

Throughout this book I have named child as method as the analytical framework informing analysis of the various forms of child inhabiting Fanon's writings, as a significant and indicative corpus. In this final chapter I outline what child as method is, as a developing approach. I identify its conceptual underpinnings and claims, as well as situating this approach in relation to others. As indicated by the previous chapters in this book, child as method is an analytical approach that reads socio-political practices through the positioning accorded the child/childhood/children, where child is understood as a figure or trope (Burman, 2008a; Castañeda, 2002), childhood as a social condition or category, and children the living, embodied entities inhabiting these. It formulates a set of problems and agendas for, but also beyond, childhood studies that founds an interdisciplinary and cross-disciplinary political project via the analysis of childhood. Crucially, child as method counters the dominant cultural practice of abstracting concern about (and for) children from other cultural-political dynamics, as has been evident in aid and development charity campaigning (for example, Burman, 1994, 2013a; Wells, 2013; Zarzycka, 2016) and enters into wider social policy and practices (Meiners, 2016). The aim, instead, is to attend to the ways that these dynamics produce and interact with meanings accorded to childhood.

Second, as a consequence of this, while focused on the child, children, and childhoods, this approach is oriented as much to situating these in relation to wider socio-political relations as vice versa. Child as method is therefore allied to a strongly culturalist-materialist reading of childhood, which goes beyond 'lighter' (Danziger, 1997) constructionist claims (that suffer from voluntarism) to understand what childhood is, and correspondingly how children inhabit this category, as formulated and organised within specific and contingent socio-historical and political conditions. This enables a crossing of the structure–agency binary that has traditionally preoccupied childhood and educational studies, and – mobilising especially a more activist reading of Foucault, evident from his own writings (Foucault, 1977b, 1980, plus see Allen, & Goddard, 2014) alongside Butler (1997) – understands classificatory, regulatory, and normalising practices to produce subjectivities that are effects of these practices and that also, by such interactions and re-enactments, transform as well as reproduce them.

The multiple indexing of 'child/childhood/children' highlights how constructions of childhood, including those attending the figure of child, produce and constrain the forms of childhood that individual children live and practice. The absence of article (either definite – 'the', or indefinite – 'a') qualifying 'child' gestures to the problem either qualification would pose of normalisation or, alternatively, differentiation: which child? Whose? Similarly, 'childhood' may now be understood as a life stage that is legally defined (through the United Nations Convention on the Rights of the Child (UNCRC)) in relation to a chronological age threshold (with 'minority'/ child status as less than 18 years), yet the discipline of childhood studies speaks to and of the other many meanings childhood carries, that reflect distinct cultural histories and corresponding philosophical positions, and that function far beyond (albeit also impacting very significantly) on the lives of specific historical and embodied children. Even the pluralising of child to children risks subordinating specificities and diversities to the presumed generality or commonality of the collective noun.

Child as method is therefore concerned with the (structural and subjectively occupied) positions produced for and about children, and how children engage with these positions. But it is also as much about the consequences of such constructions for the others mobilised and organised by and through childhood, including adults, and the other roles and identities with which children and childhood are interwoven and enmeshed. This also necessarily includes critical reflexivity/diffraction (see Barad, 2014; Thiele, 2014) as part of the ethical-political framing of the project. While the status of 'method' will be considered below, for now what should also be noted is the work done by the preposition 'as', indicating a relationship between surrounding terms but not identification (Burman, 2013b). Inevitably, questions of recognition, misrecognition, and the symbolic violence of what is included and excluded in the implied alignments come to the fore, alongside topicalising the necessarily involved, implicated, or entangled viewing position from which such alignments are made.

Third, acknowledging this socio-political basis should not be read as meaning that such constructions directly or completely determine those childhoods. Far from disallowing children's agentic activity, this attention to modes of childhood available within specific cultural-political contexts enables attention to how children navigate and negotiate these, and acknowledges their necessary engagement with these. Hence, its agenda is to invite deeper analysis of how forms of childhood practices (including those as practiced by children) reflect and inform wider socio-political dynamics, rather than attempting to resolve or adjudicate on debates about the ontological status of children. Questions around the status of children's perspectives or 'experiences' – alongside how these may be accessed, generated, co-produced, listened to, or interpreted – while clearly important, are, therefore, temporarily displaced in favour of an analytic focus addressing how these connect with and are constituted in relation to specific material and relational conditions. However, as will be further discussed below, child as method, is not a meta-theory, but a research analytic to formulate innovative enquiries for, about, and with children, including also the study of cultural artefacts of and about childhood.

Specific antecedents

In this section I outline three related paradigms or frameworks that inform and have shaped the formulation of child as method: *Asia as Method, Border as Method*, and intersectionality theory.

Asia as Method

Child as method is a creative transformation of Kuan-Hsing Chen's (2010) influential text *Asia as Method*. This book reviews and evaluates the current state of postcolonial cultural studies, in particular the problem of the continuing orientation towards colonial centres that, whether favourable or hostile, still maintains their structuring influence. It both analyses 'Asia' as an imaginary space but also the historical and current relations between different countries comprising contemporary Asia (he focuses primarily on Taiwan, Japan, and China) so warding off essentialised readings of either colonial or pre-colonial (or what may be called 'indigenous') cultural practices. *Asia as Method, developing earlier analyses* (see Chen, 2012) engages discussions about the status of modernity, challenging its alignment with Westernisation or the Euro-US, in ways that correspond with recent calls for connected sociologies (Bhambra, 2007, 2014).

Child as method is not only an application of that text, as Chen's project and agendas are different. Rather, child as method arises out of a resonant reading of *Asia as Method*, to envisage convergent preoccupations with decol-onisation and materialist approaches. Chen sets out an agenda for decoupling cultural studies from orientalist and colonial imaginaries and practices. Tracing intellectual and political contributions from Frantz Fanon, Albert Memmi, Edward Said, Stuart Hall, and others, Chen argues for a geo-materialist analy-sis that not only includes decolonisation (as a political event or process), but also de-imperialisation (so engaging affective investments and desires on the part of both the coloniser and the colonised) (see also Chen, 2017). Notably, he also motivates for focusing on the continuing legacies of the Cold War (as a key global dynamic that has configured, and continues to configure, local and regional transnational relations). Arising from these three frames is an approach that emphasises the connections between material conditions and the psychosocial. Indeed, questions of subjectivity as well as structural positioning, and specific geopolitical relations arise as central to this project.

Chen's postcolonial project resonates with key debates about how con-ceptions of childhood, and also children, relate in complicated ways with but also complicate the history of colonialism. Writing of Anglo and French colonial policies in Africa, Jennifer Beinart (1992) discusses temporal shifts in colonial interest in children, as reflected in photographic records, so reflect-ing changing colonial strategies – from children as equated with nature, the flora and fauna of the colonial scene, to being key objects of intervention and manipulation in the service of modernisation and Westernisation agen-das. Ann Laura Stoler's (2002) key text, *Carnal Knowledge and Imperial Power*, indicates how children were both objects of colonial policy in the (former) Dutch East Indies but also the site through which this colonial policy was resisted and reformulated (including through the actions of children them-selves). As indicated by the (sub)title of her book, *Race and the intimate in colonial rule*, everyday domestic practices – specifically questions of affective engagement with and by children – are very much political matters, whose political valences reverberate in multiple directions.

These historical studies testify to the longstanding, as well as current, ways that children and childhood figure within (neo-colonial) development projects – both national and transnational. They help to de-naturalise the 'social investment' and human capital models that now inform interna-tional development policies (whether of the World Bank, the International Monetary Fund (IMF), the World Health Organization, or indeed of the United Nations Children's Fund (UNICEF) and the United Nations Development Programme (UNDP)), whereby children as well as women are focused upon as the primary material for social and economic development (Lister, 2006), so exhibiting what childhood studies theorists have described as a 'children as becomings' approach (rather than 'children as beings')

(Qvortrup, 1994). It is this elision – or, at best, imposed homology – between child, national, and international development projects that is in need of disruption (Burman, 2008a). What Stoler's and Beinart's studies (as merely two indicative examples) also fruitfully highlight is the importance of attending to specific cultural-historical moments, and the diverse interests, relationships, and affective investments of the various actors and agents involved.

Three key points arising from Chen's treatment include, first, how questions of subjectivity as well as structural positioning and specific geopolitical relations also come to the fore. (Fanon, of course, is a key critical source here, grounding debates about subjectivity and change within political conditions, specifically racialised and colonial conditions in relation to political transformation (and, I would add, gender and generational orders). Second, how the trope equating childhood with colonisation (mobilised across many arenas) is problematic, notwithstanding some alignment of positioning of colonised peoples with children through common practices of disempowerment and minority status (for example, Cannella, & Viruru, 2004) (as indicated by my efforts to trace the multiple and mutually contesting models of childhood within Fanon's own models of childhood). Third, countering the methodological nationalism of many current analyses in social theory and cultural studies, Chen highlights longstanding mutual and mutually constitutive influences between national contexts (as I highlight also in relation to the varying history and interpretations of Fanon's work in different moments and contexts).

It is important to clarify that child as method does not simply transpose Chen's analysis of (post)colonial conditions onto children/childhood, as either an 'application' or assumed equivalence. Clearly, equation of childhood and colonisation is problematic, notwithstanding some alignment of the position of colonised peoples with children through common practices of naturalised ideological regimes of disempowerment, exploitation, and minority status. While this is the starting point for Cannella and Viruru's (2004) influential text on this topic, the primary concern of these authors is to import postcolonial analyses to help inform understandings of children and childhood, rather than to elide colonisation and childhood. It is useful to maintain the distinction between these two domains in order to better interrogate the complex ways they have formed, and continue to inform, each other. In this sense, the project can be understood as equivalent to that of decolonial de-linking, as discussed by Mignolo (2007), albeit that discussions of 'decoloniality' have tended to be associated with critical theory emerging from Latin America, while 'postcolonial' debates have typically emerged from and in relation to South East Asia (Shahhajan, 2011).

Chen moves from critique to advocate specific interventions, including 'inter-referencing', or re-orienting focus away from traditional sources of power/knowledge (originating from Europe or North America) to attend to local and regional relations, and noticing new 'syncretic' practices combining the old and new, or traditional/indigenous and modern/'Western'. This avoids both spurious dichotomisation of indigenous versus 'Western'/northern colonial knowledges, and also wards off incipient essentialisms attending claims to pre-colonial or indigenous knowledges. Rather, Chen advocates attending to the complex ways these diverse resources are mobilised and become interwoven into new syntheses and performances (including performances of narrations of imagined historical pasts) within specific local contexts.

Three further points are crucial to note here. First, while the dis-investment from the primary colonial relation frees up engagement with cultural and geographical neighbours, these relations have also been colonial and often hostile. Addressing historical grievances and building regional alliances is therefore a significant and challenging political project, even if some such divisions were precisely those manufactured by European colonial powers. (Fanon's practical activity in building alliances for the Algerian National Liberation Front (FLN) with other decolonising African states comes to mind.) Second, the attention to 'syncretism' arises from a historical understanding that is resolutely anti-essentialist – that is, hybrids, blends, and reformulations of cultural and political practices, between and across states, have always and will always take place. Fanon exemplified this not only via his philosophical commitments to both psychoanalysis and existentialism (so acknowledging individual histories as formative but also not inevitably determining) but also in his critique of 'negritude' and invocations of common African or pre-colonial pasts as the basis for political unity and mobilisation. Drawing on these ideas, third, Chen instead invites attention to how cultural practices are forged through and as responses to current conditions and become recognised through prevailing histories of the present.

The implications of these strategies for approaches to 'child as method' will be addressed below (in the section on 'method').

Border as Method

A second, related, inspirational resource for child as method is Mezzadra and Neilson's (2013) *Border as Method*, an intervention from geography and development studies focused on migration and labour that also explicitly references Chen's *Asia as Method*. Their key guiding assumption is that borders *include* as well as *exclude* and so demand study of the specific and active forms of inclusion/exclusion they produce, the relations between these, and for whom. Building from Hardt and Negri's (2009) influential account, their mode of argument, therefore, analyses the complex relations and mutual impacts between apparently diverse forms of labour and production occurring across the world. By focusing on the figure of the migrant, the authors claim to deepen Marxist analysis of current forms of dispossession and exploitation beyond 'neoliberalism' and 'globalisation' to, in particular, recompose debates about sovereignty and citizenship as well as permit attention to (what they call) the multiplication, as well as recent divisions (including global redistributions), of labour. Notwithstanding the different disciplinary orientation, with *Border as Method* clearly engaged with social and political science paradigms rather than *Asia as Method*'s address to cultural studies, there is considerable overlap in conceptual project and approach. Both aim towards connecting with, and so also enriching the reading of, political economy – as also does child as method.

There are resonances here with Nieuwenhuys' (2007) identification of the 'global womb' to describe how women and children's labour functions as a nexus for (what she calls) 'superexploitation' by capital. This marginal labour – informal, insecure, unregulated, and low paid, precisely because it traverses the production/reproduction binary – is what capital increasingly relies upon for its extraction of surplus value.

Mezzadra and Neilson's attention to the various forms of *differential,* or relative, inclusion produced through borders (seen as not only national, and indeed not only physical but also cultural and affective) is clearly relevant to considerations of childhood. (This recalls Fanon's analysis of the marginalisation and exclusion of the cultural and racialised outsider.) For, like migrants, children are not only 'excluded' from practices that shape their lives. Not only is this exclusion productive in various ways, but it also produces particular forms of participation (for some actors, if not for the excluded) such that by such exclusion the excluded become 'central protagonists in the drama of composing the space, time and materiality of the social itself' (Mezzadra, & Neilson, 2013: 159). Developing this argument in relation to children and childhood studies, we may explore not merely how, for example, children produce work for adults (as teachers, carers, social workers, and so forth), but also how the divisions and distinctions between adult and child, specifically those which exclude children from this, thereby configure the construction of what the social is and does. Similar to Chen on syncretism, Mezzadra and Neilson's discussion of differential inclusion also draws attention to its distributed and locally navigated, and so variable, practice. Under globalised and multi-national capitalism, governmental powers are devolved across and between nation states such that local non-governmental organisations may be delegated to assume governmental activities and even authority, so complicating how national international policies are enacted (whether as enforcing or resisting these). This analysis of contradictions and divisions in action helps to disrupt any easy or unambiguous designations occurring in relation to adult–child binaries, instead inviting close attention to where, when, and how such inclusions, exclusions, and migrations between categories occur. (Clearly, this can be read as aligned with Fanon's anticolonial and decolonial analyses of both the economic conditions of colonial exploitation and the orientation to the subjectivity of the colonised.)

The dominant developmental lexicon of individual and child development is replete with quasi-geographical metaphors (of journey, migration, transition across borders, and so on), the naturalisation and corresponding abstraction from socio-political conditions of which has recast these as norms – and thence into standards (Coons, 2014). Restoring the geographical reading of these terms enables a more situated, relational, and embodied analysis that can resist individualisation and psychologisation. As Foucaultian analyses have highlighted (Rose, 1985; Gordo López, & De Vos, 2010; De Vos, 2015), these two important and related dynamics work to strip away the socio-political from the interpretation of inequalities, both to concentrate focus on individuals, families, and communities as the site for intervention and change and also thereby occluding the role of state and wider agencies in producing those inequalities (Foucault, 1970, 1977, 1980, 1981; Foucault, et al., 2008). Individualisation and psychologisation are, therefore, key aspects of the practice of late capitalism, sometimes called neoliberalism (Foucault, & Ewald, 2003; Burman, 2012a; Fraser, 2003; Ball, & Olmedo, 2013). Hence, close attention to particular spaces and contexts in which such norms and practices have emerged and are practised, enables the socio-political configuring of the conditions of and for certain activities to be available for documentation.

Attending to the journey, rather than the destination, is of course a key strategy to resist the teleological reading of childhood as mere preparation for adulthood, while also indicating multiple and non-progressive trajectories that become evident when attending to larger spatio-temporal scales (O'Dell, et al., 2017), including enabling more agentic as well as interdependent readings of these (Holt, 2013; Benjamin, 1969). However, the relevance of *Border as Method* to child as method is not simply one of transposing the standpoint and trajectory of the figure of the migrant to the embodied chronological developmental journeying of children. This would be to miss the point of both ventures, which rather seek to show how these (in some respects equivalent, but distinct) marginal subjects of economic and social development in fact constitute those very norms to which they are so – in some cases devastatingly – subject.

The 'turn to space' in social theory supposedly marking the shift to late capitalism (Jameson, 1984) also accompanied an interpretive move from depth to surface, and from history to geography, that can be seen to correspond with the rise of sociological, anthropological, and geographical studies of childhood and education to displace the previous predominance of developmental psychology and also inspired new methodological approaches. Reprising the 'spatial turn', Mezzadra and Neilson call for reconsideration of the temporal as well as spatial features as necessary to understanding complex and shifting subjectivities at play. This, too, speaks to the transitional and complex embodied historical continuities and discontinuities inhabited by children (as also adults who were once children). Child as method instantiates some of the spatio-temporal intensities and diversities discussed in *Border as Method,* but interrogates and develops further the critical attention to the complex interplay between biographical trajectories, environments, and relationships, and subjectivities – that is, how these specific contexts and relationships enable the emergence of particular forms of (childhood) practice. Hanson's (2017) recent call to attend to the 'been' as well as the 'becoming' of childhood suggests some moves in this direction. Further, while clearly relevant, Mezzadra and Neilson's focus on practices of differential inclusion may not only deepen, but also be deepened by, attending to (what they call) 'borderscapes' as well as border crossings as multiply and intergenerationally encountered (including as 'subjects in transit', Mezzadra, & Neilson, 2013: 6). Hence, in this book I have engaged with such complex transitions by attending not only to the subjectivity attributed to the various children in Fanon's accounts but also by evaluating their social status (as included or excluded in the social order), especially focusing on their often borderline status and the productive role this status plays – both for child/ren and for other people and processes.

Intersectionality

A third resource informing the above, as also child as method, is intersectionality theory. This distinctive contribution from feminist theory arises from Black, Indigenous, Latina, and Asian feminist activism from the 1970s onwards (c.f. the Combahee River Collective's, 1981, 'interlocking systems of oppression' and Collins', 2002, 'matrix of domination'). Such formulations emerged as a way of acknowledging the mutually constitutive but spatio-temporally (cultural-historical and politically) complex relations between key statuses or positions that produce and diversify one another, such that gender (for example) cannot be considered except in its mutually constitutive relation to 'race', class, (dis)ability, or sexuality (to take some notable characteristics). While intersectionality theory arises out of black feminist scholarship and activism, the term is often attributed specifically to discussion of a legal case (by Kimberlé Crenshaw in mounting a landmark pay claim), that was successful in arguing that the combination of being black and a woman amounted to more than occupying each of those positions alone, proving that the black women workers were discriminated against in terms of pay on the basis of both their 'race' and gendered positions (Crenshaw, 1991). In a recent treatment, Collins and Bilge (2016) identify the following as central ideas foregrounded by intersectionality as an analytical tool: inequality, relationality, power, social context, complexity, and social justice.

Debates continue to rage over whether intersectionality is a theory or an approach to other theories; whether it works as a methodology (Nash, 2008), and if so, how (McCall, 2005; Winker, & Degele, 2011); whether it can be used only to challenge inequalities; and whether it escapes – and even should escape – the trappings of identity politics (focused on black women) whose philosophical and political limitations (solipsism and hierarchies of oppression, respectively) had in part generated the need for it in the first place (Puar, 2012; Cho, et al., 2013). Further discussions concern whether the approach – through its origins in a standpoint epistemology – favours structure over experience (or felt identifications), or vice versa. Valuable as these discussions have been to clarify the status and uses of intersectionality approaches, they largely miss the key point that what makes an analysis intersectional is a matter of how it is used, or put to work, rather than secured by some a priori theoretical precepts. It is both a critical enquiry and a critical praxis (Collins, & Bilge, 2016: chapter 2); that is, it combines both theory and action.

Nevertheless, alongside a common concern with questions of power, inequality, and social justice, what intersectionality theory brings to childhood and educational studies, and so also child as method, is not only an attention to the mutually interwoven, relational, and socio-structurally situated character of children's diverse sexed, gendered, classed, racialised, and geographical positionings (to name just a few relevant possible axes). Its incorporation into institutions, across disciplines, and within transnational discourse offers an example of how a civil rights issue (as posed by Crenshaw) has been taken up within human rights policies. A further insight is that, depending on the specific context or encounter, these intersecting positions may become salient in determining children's actions, interactions, and indeed treatment by others beyond (but also in relation to) their childhood status. Just as Collins and Bilge (2016) claim that '[w]ithin intersectional frameworks there is no pure racism or sexism. Rather, power relations of sexism and racism gain meaning in relation to one another' (27), so the (often, but not exclusively, diminished) status of being a child does not operate independently of, for example, gendered, racialised, or classed positioning, but is rather modulated (whether intensified, mitigated, or complexified) by these (see also Konstantoni, et al., 2017; Rosen, & Twamley, 2017).

Intersectionality theory has clearly figured throughout this book in the sustained attention to the ways that racialisation and childhood status are constituted by other significant social structural axes, dynamics, positions, and experiences. Just as there are longstanding feminist critiques of Fanon, and also specific feminist engagements with colonial histories and practices, so also recent educational treatments of Fanon (which focus on the position and subjectivity of children as learners and political actors), acknowledge the challenge posed by intersectionality theory (for example, Dei, & Simmons, 2010). Within the educational field, there is now a substantial feminist literature highlighting how gendered positionings intersect with racialisation to produce quite specific trajectories through schooling (for example, Mirza, 1992, 2009). In this book I have mobilised feminist theory, bringing it into dialogue with psychoanalytic, social, political, and educational theory to (re)consider the status of child in Fanon, such that gender and generational relations as well as class, sexuality, and racialisation have to be seen to operate constitutively at some moments even if at others these features appear to be less important. As Spyrou (2017) recently noted, the question of centring or decentring around childhood status demands rigorous analysis, and feminist and intersectionality theory plays a key role in this.

Intersectionality, then, is a key resource for child as method for four reasons. First, because it is specifically identified as a feminist intervention in social (and human) science discourse, given that feminist contributions are too often relegated as derivative or subsidiary to other, 'grander' narratives. (On this point, relevant reference could also be made to recent calls for modest or immature theory, both in relation to childhood studies, Gallacher, & Gallagher, 2008, and elsewhere, Haraway, 1997.). Second, intersectionality is explicitly referenced and mobilised in both *Asia as Method* and *Border as Method* (perhaps as one way of marking alignment with feminist approaches generally). Third, intersectionality theory's focus on relationality, interdependency, and the necessary and constitutive relationships between structural positioning and subjectivity (however configured) bridge appropriations of Marxist theories of praxis and consciousness with more recent feminist engagements with performance and performativity (Butler, 1990). Fourth, there is a clear focus on how power relations constitute and constrain how and which axes of subjectivity and positioning acquire their salience.

Finally, the explicit marking of intersectionality theory as arising from black feminisms (notwithstanding some efforts to generalise from this, such as, Winker, & Degele (2011), even while others critique its cultural-national limits to the US (Erel, et al. (2010)), usefully foregrounds questions of racialisation and colonialism in ways that preceded the preoccupations with differential claims and entitlements to citizenship, rights, and mobility of *Asia as Method* and *Border as Method*. Not only does such feminist theory pre-figure the wider attention to border theory and theory from the margins, it also carries implications for knowledge claims. Specifically, along with other feminist theories, what is highlighted here is how knowledge – including that of the researcher – is necessarily situated and perspectival, which carries implications for the conduct as well as interpretation of research (see also Haraway, 1988, 1991; Hekman, 1997). As Collins and Bilge (2016) put it: 'Using intersectionality as an analytic tool means contextualizing one's arguments, primarily by being aware that particular historical, intellectual and political contexts shape what we think and do' (28). As they point out, this is particularly important in the consideration of power relations underlying which perspectives get to be heard (and which are not).

There is now an accumulating literature that acknowledges and starts to explore the relevance of intersectionality theory for childhood studies (Alanen, 2016; Konstantoni, et al., 2017; Gutierrez, & Hopkins, 2015). Overall, intersectionality theory contributes a useful analytic attention to diversities of positioning that de-homogenises the categories of child/children/childhoods, to indicate how these are created through power relations. But, once again, this is not only a question of application. There are areas of mutual tension, as well as potential mutual learning between these paradigms or domains. Elsewhere (Burman, 2013b) I have suggested that the necessary attention to questions of temporality, including psychological, social, and embodied change, that are central to childhood and education, pose some challenges to intersectionality theory, in ways that are also shared with critical disability studies' focus on ability/disability statuses as tempo-rary as well as situationally and relationally defined (Burman, 2017c). In this book, an intersectional analysis informs the attention to Fanon's narra-tive staging of subjectivity as related to the mobilisations of childhood he describes (whether as expressed by him or others).

A method?

Like *Asia as Method,* and *Border as Method*, child as method owes a great deal to so-called 'post-structuralist', specifically Foucaultian frameworks, and social psychoanalytic perspectives as well as feminist debates on intersectionality (discussed above). Since these first two resources are common to all three 'antecedents' indicated above, I will not go into further detail. However, like these, the notion of 'method' at play is not a question of technical specification or approach but rather an 'epistemic angle' (Mezzadra, & Neilson, 2013: 6), or 'narrative tool' (as Park, 2016: 213, puts it), even 'an attitude and epistemological orientation' (214).

Such conjoint perspectives clearly subscribe to a critique of prevailing models of research, and corresponding techniques and practices, as complicit (at least) with colonialism, imperialism, and patriarchy. Beyond acknowledging and tracing through the consequences of such historical knowledge/power relations within current regimes of testing, assessment, and measurement (Rose, 1985), feminist and decolonisation research approaches refuse the separation between theory and method, as also between methodology and method, to advocate for an activist ethical-political responsibility and engagement that transcends particular research technologies or paradigms (Smith, 2013; Takayama, et al., 2015; Gaztambide-Fernández, & Thiessen, 2012). Feminist researchers have long argued that what counts as knowledge, and how it is received and interpreted, reflects how, where, when, and by whom it was generated (Stanley, & Wise, 1983; Haraway, 1991). Thus, ontological (and correspondingly ethical-political) questions about the perspective and status of the knowledge-generator enter into the epistemological status of what is generated in ways that are embraced and actively harnessed rather than obscured.

Child as method draws on these discussions as a conceptual intervention to enable the posing of more interesting questions that better engage with the cultural-political complexities, diversities, and fluidities of children's positions and lives. Like 'southern theory' (Connell, 2014), it is less a 'method', then, than a set of epistemological commitments, or even a manifesto, to generate new research agendas. It is 'not a fixed set of propositions but a challenge to develop new knowledge projects and new ways of learning with globally expanded resources' (210). Or as Mezzadra and Neilson (2013) put it, 'provid[ing] productive insights on the tensions and conflicts that blur the line between inclusion and exclusion, as well as on the profoundly changing code of social inclusion in the present' (6).

Child as method, therefore, takes 'child' as a nodal point in a set of practices, social relationships, and institutional arrangements as a way of reading cultural-political practices, including academic practices. In this sense, while not being committed to any specific model or theory of childhood, child as method is nevertheless committed to the generation of ethically-politically engaged and theory-developing, as well as theory-driven, empirical research. While maintaining a role for the empirical, then, the model of research being formulated here is far from traditional scientific and even social science approaches, whether experimental ones concerned with prediction, manipulation of variables and refutation of hypotheses, or even ethnographic stances that merely describe and do not seek to alter or change what they record. As with *Asia as Method,* and *Border as Method*, child as method is allied to activist approaches to research, that understand research as a set of socially negotiated and co-enacted practices conducted in solidarity with, and often co-produced with, marginalised and oppressed groups. The aim would be to make possible some change, even if this change is – in the first instance – at the level of conceptualisation, alongside an epistemological commitment to attend closely to lived experiences and perspectives of those most affected. Clearly how such documents (whether of experience or of other kinds) are generated and interpreted would depend on the specific topic and focus.

So, as would be expected from a specific epistemological stance, some methodological considerations follow. Chen's (2010) 'inter-referencing' could be applied to decouple forms of childhood away from the normalising teleology of (rich, northern, advanced capitalist) models of development, to focus instead on the local relations (both crossovers and frictions) between various (spatially or temporally distinct) competing and consecutive practices of childhood and education. This would be consistent with Mezzadra and Neilson's (2013) call (drawing on Sakai, 2010) to move research agendas away from comparative studies or what used to be called 'area studies', to do transnational analysis that instead, as they put it, attend to 'resonances and dissonances produced by the encounters and clashes between concepts and a materiality that can be very distant from the one within which they were originally formulated' (8). This is similar to the methodological argument also put forward by Katz (2004) in relation to conceptualising changing childhoods in different geographical contexts across similar political-historical and economic conditions that nevertheless affect these contexts and subjects differently. Recent sociology of education literature has mobilised equivalent arguments to motivate for a move away from comparative educational studies towards transnational studies (Takayama, et al., 2017), in particular highlighting the covert nationalist and statist politics presumed by the 'methodological nationalism' (Chernilo, 2008) of prevailing cross-national educational comparison instruments, and illustrating how this suppresses attention to global processes maintaining and reproducing local and regional inequalities, and environmental pressures (Shahjahan, & Kezar, 2013; Shahjahan, et al., 2017). On the other hand, a recent fruitful line of critical childhood and educational research is precisely exploring the ways that nation states have historically produced, and still currently produce, specific narratives of childhood (Millei, & Imre, 2016).

Similarly, as already indicated, Chen's strategy of 'syncretism' aligns with, and is indeed perhaps intensified by, Mezzadra and Neilson's (more Deleuzian-influenced) focus on crossing points and borderscapes. Together these resources clearly displace concern with origins in favour of encounters, meetings, crossings, and crossovers, which offer helpful concepts for framing critical childhood enquiries. As a research analytic, then, far from 'method' not being a concern of child as method, the aim is to foster and bring into dialogue diverse, innovative, and creative research approaches in the service of documenting how child/childhood/children are understood, and the institutional practices that surround them, across a range of geopolitical and disciplinary arenas. Importantly, though, the process of documenting goes beyond one of description to bring under critical scrutiny the ethical-political practices involved in the crafting, interpretation, and application and reception of the material.

Perhaps these questions have already been, or would anyway be, posed by childhood researchers. But the overall project to highlight the necessary intersections between the political economy of childhood and geopolitical dynamics, alongside their local and global relations, must figure as part of the postcolonial, antipatriarchal, anti-capitalist project, in which children figure as more than policy or theory tropes. In this sense, child as method is compatible with current moves in educational studies towards 'southern theory' (Takayama, et al., 2016), as also recent feminist interrogations of the mutually constitutive, if thereby asymmetrical and sometimes conflictual, positioning of women and children (Burman, & Stacey, 2010; Rosen, & Twarmley, 2017; Baird, 2008).

Notwithstanding the almost total absence of children and childhood in both *Asia as Method* and *Border as Method* (the latter especially striking considering its focus on labour), child as method therefore mobilises these critical frameworks but this is not simply in the service of cross-disciplinary conversation. Cultural studies, postcolonial studies, or migration studies are all key contributors to, as well as interlocutors with, childhood and educational studies. However, the mutual engagement with childhood studies is envisaged not as direct equivalence, nor – as indicated above – of intersectionality theory, but rather as a syncretic emergence from common problems and resources that resonate with these other visionary texts and so aims for mutual engagement, rather than mere application. Clearly, different disciplines – from education to economics to colonial studies to the law, to take just a few examples – generate interesting and distinct constructions of child/childhood/children, which are themselves worthy of study, as also are the various histories of efforts to connect and contrast these disciplinary approaches. Indeed, rather than becoming entangled in the debates about the disciplinary status of childhood studies (as interdisciplinary, multidisciplinary, transdisciplinary, or indeed post-disciplinary, c.f. Pain, 2010), it may be better to consider child as method as 'off-disciplinary'. This formulation would perhaps better capture its status as less aligned with or concerned to privilege any specific disciplinary orientation. Fanon's 'methodology of failure' here has been an important influence for such disciplinary 'derelictions' and border crossings, alongside his diverse philosophical and political commitments.

There is now a considerable literature from educational and early childhood studies exploring the implications of *Asia as Method*, although (as Park, 2016, 2017, also notes) much of this oversimplifies Chen's text to apply it merely as the study of the practice of education/childhood within Asian contexts, or in intercultural educational encounters that include Asian (origin, migrant, or heritage) teachers or children. Such readings risk insufficiently analysing the wider political transnational dynamics at play. Currently, there appear to be no explicit applications of *Border as Method* to childhood or educational studies, although much current work on child migrants and borders could be read through this frame (as Palmary, & Mahati's, 2015, analysis certainly indicates). This book elaborates child as method through a set of critical readings of the writings of Frantz Fanon, while elsewhere (Burman, 2018a) I indicate its use in reading sociocultural theory, another critical resource heralded by Thorne (2007) for childhood studies. Silova et al. (2017) have used it as an analytical frame for interpreting ethnographic (including autobiographical) memories of (post)socialist childhoods, while Nizami (2017) has applied it to policies on preventing child sexual exploitation. As a postcolonial and intersectional framework, it has been extended to other contexts – such as Siddiqui's (2017, 2018) elaboration of 'ghost as method'.

Related concepts and approaches

There are three other frameworks or conceptualisations that child as method should be distinguished from.

Childism

A key concept both to relate to and distinguish 'child as method' from is 'childism'. This concept is sometimes used as a contrast with 'adultism' (the shaping of structures and practices arising from the assumption of being an adult). It was largely popularised by Young-Bruehl (2012), who used it to describe a systematic form of prejudice against children, analogous to (in her examples) sexism, racism, or anti-semitism. She emphasises how, like these, 'children are a target group' (19) for systematically different and discriminatory treatment, while – also like these – highlighting the question of standpoint (or the need to privilege the perspective of those who suffer such oppression). That is, children know about childism from the ways adults treat them, and so we need to learn from children about the oppressions and injustices this involves. Notwithstanding this social justice frame, however, and perhaps owing to her reliance on the concept of prejudice, Young-Bruehl is focused on the psychological and interpersonal domains, defining 'childism' as '[t]he prevailing images of children that adults use to rationalise their feelings towards them' (19) or

> legitimation of an adult's or a society's failure to prioritise or make paramount the needs of children over those of adults and the needs of the future adults over the needs of the present adults. It is role reversal at the level of a principle.
>
> *(280)*

Young-Bruehl appears to build on an earlier analysis by Pierce and Allen (1975: 15) who also highlighted the domain of fantasy and the psychoaffective to argue: 'Childism is the automatic presumption of superiority of any adult over any child; it results in the adult's needs, desires, hopes, and fears taking unquestioned precedence over those of the child.'

A difficulty here is that the domain of both conceptualisation and intervention envisaged stays at the level of the psychological (unsurprising since she is primarily oriented to therapeutic practices). This clearly not only limits the focus of interventions but also the scale and model of the nature of the problem. Unsurprisingly perhaps (since her analysis is addressed to US readers, and so focuses on a national level debate), Young-Bruehl's analysis is cast within a human rights framework. While not sharing the same psychological commitments, more recent formulations of childism nevertheless retain a similar rights-based politics, albeit that Wall (2013) heralds it as leading a 'third wave' in childhood studies. By contrast, child as method, like *Border as Method*, treats rights discourses as also in need of critical analysis. This is not only because of the discretionary status of who is included or excluded in being 'human' (which are currently undergoing much critical attention from both postcolonial and also ecological/posthuman debates), but also because the normativities inscribing legal systems, both national and transnational, have undergone fragmentation so that as 'a multiplicity of societal constitutions emerge outside of institutionalized politics and normative orders [they] can no longer be firmly anchored to systems of law, either national or international' (Mezzadra, & Neilson, 2013: 255). Reservations about the limits of rights discourse are no stranger to childhood studies, and indeed that rights may limit as much as enable children's agentic engagements has long been discussed (consider, for example, Hanson, 2016's recent editorial commentary). Earlier critiques, as formulated by Evans (2005) and taken up by Tarulli and Skott-Myhre (2006) highlight the possessive individualism as well as presumption of adversariality attending rights (in which model rights have to be claimed rather than bestowed). Such critiques highlight the need for relational and transformative approaches to rights, including to children's rights. Similarly, Mezzadra and Neilson argue:

> To analyze the nexus of human rights and migration [or – we might say – child] management means recognizing that human rights play just as much a role in establishing the conditions under which border crossing can be blocked or slowed as those under which it is facilitated.
> *(2013: 174–5)*

Hence, rights models are complicit within existing exclusionary systems rather than external to them, and 'increasingly becoming internal to the exercise of power insofar as processes of governmentalization of power are underway' (245).

Nevertheless, like child as method, Young-Bruehl's (and other advocates of childism such as Wall's) agenda is less concerned to launch advocacy work for and with children (since thankfully that work is underway), but rather to 'help researchers connect a lot of dots' (8). Or in Wall's (re)formulation, to import philosophies of difference, especially as formulated from feminist theory, to reconsider the status and practice of childhood. Hence, taken more generally, the project of 'childism' has been understood as one of 'studying the social through the prism of childhood) [which] challenges fundamental epistemological and ontological presumptions in the social sciences and allow us to rethink social theories and gain new or deeper insights to decisive issues of current society' (as a 2017 conference at Roskilde University put it in their call for papers). The 'prism' (of childhood) is the device through which other features (about children but also the study of the social) can be investigated and re-interpreted, through the new alignments and perspectives generated. The portrayal of childhood as a 'prism' suggests it is an entity through whose refractions other features become visible. The term 'prism' comes from optics and, significantly, prisms can be both naturally occurring (found or extracted) or manufactured, such that – as with child as method – the use of the term does not presume any specific model or history of origins, but rather opens up these questions again. Child as method certainly converges with this broader frame. The splitting, or refractions, of light disclosing other perspectives also invite connections with feminist new materialist analysis that advocate for diffraction as a better metaphor to attend to the production and relationships with difference (for example, Barad, 2014). These are both spatial and temporal and indeed undo or at least trouble prevailing binaries and dichotomies, such as those between animate/inanimate, or organic/inorganic that (as part of the nature/culture ideological binary) inform images of and claims about child/childhood/children. Alongside this, so-called 'affirmative' ethico-political orientation are emerging (Theile, 2014). (It is perhaps worth recalling that Prism is the name for the US national security programme, so highlighting important textual-political alignments between the project of seeing, surveillance, and securitisation that are very much concerned with what children and childhood currently are and do.)

Becoming-child/adult

Deleuze (1994, 2007) and Deleuze and Guattari's (2004) critiques of the normalisation of childhood, sexuality, and familial relations (and composition) have been influential in childhood and educational studies. In particular, commentators have taken up their rejection of so-called oedipal psychoanalysis as complicit with capitalism and the installation of (what we would now call, after Butler (1990)) heteronormativity. Child as method shares some of the assumptions that have led to the take up of their ideas into childhood studies. With its lexicon of 'bodies without organs', 'flows' and 'assemblages', this has prompted further developments in the conceptualisation of children and childhoods, particularly relational and posthuman approaches. Specifically, they focus on 'becoming' (*devenir*), defined in the 'glossary of Schizo-analysis' (Guattari, 2006: 415–416), as follows: 'This term relates to the economy of desire. Desire flows proceed by affects and becomings, independently of the fact that they can fold over onto [*se rebattre sur*] persons, images, identifications or not.'

The entry continues (by way of explanation): 'So an individual, anthropologically labelled masculine, can be traversed by multiple, and apparently contradictory, becomings: becoming feminine [*devenir féminin*], can co-exist with becoming a child, becoming an animal, becoming invisible, etc.' (416). Here we see how affects or desires shift across and between entities and persons in ways that change the understanding of the stability or distinctness of those entities.

Hence, the evocative claim, 'The girl and the child does not become; it is becoming itself that is a child or a girl' (Deleuze, & Guattari, 2004: 306) has been widely discussed. (It is worth noting that the gendered qualification or characterisation of the child here is accorded varying attention by theorists, some making this central while others generalising this to all children, or indeed to the childhood of everyone.) This is followed closely by the claim that 'the child is the becoming-young of every age' (ibid.), which extends not only to questioning dominant notions of age and ageing, but also to under- standings of speed and movement involved. These phrases can be seen to have been taken up in discussions of childhood and education in five ways.

First, Deleuze and Guattari's subscription to a non-linear, non-evolutionary, and non-developmental model of time (in their terms, 'lines of flight') has been important. This dismantles what they call 'adultomorphism', that is, the adult–child binary that subordinates childhood practices to the impera- tive of 'growing up' in normative ways towards a normalised destination (for example, Corbett, 2009). (Hence their ideas have also been taken up in queer theory, as discussed below.) The project becomes one of drawing attention to processes of divergence and deviation from prescribed pathways. As Tarulli and Skott-Mhyre (2006: 191, emphasis in the original) highlight: 'Becoming, in other words, is always a becoming-*other* (that is, other than the norm or ideal inscribed in moral binaries). It is movement without advance destina- tion, process without endpoint.'

This gives rise, second, as Jones (2013: 292) puts it, to: 'a further move in destabilising and unsettling stable subjectivities that are codified, given substance and made rock-like by common sense and by reiterative practices'. This means that identities are no longer stable, or even (only) individual. Instead, there is a focus on the relational and embodiment (with the body seen as an assemblage of forces creating a temporarily partially stable system) and, as a corollary of this, a further convergence is the focus on affect, desire, and their material consequences.

Third, the distinction between 'molar' and 'molecular' works to dismantle the human/non-human binary, such that, 'the animal, flower, or stone one becomes are molecular collectivities, not molar subjects, objects, or form that we know from the outside and recognize from experience, through science, or by habit' (Deleuze, & Guattari, 2004: 303).

A fourth convergence of interest is the attention to the ways macropo- litical power relations inscribe and constrain specific possibilities. Tarulli and Skott-Mhyre (2006) continue: 'Such a process of aging, as becoming, is a distillation of the thoroughly material conditions of a given historical moment, comprised of its geography, temporality and force' (191).

Significantly, fifth, like child as method, this Deleuzian model of child- hood does not necessarily qualify (molar) embodied, chronological children, as this would return the model to precisely the kinds of metaphysical claims about what it is to be a child that it seeks to disrupt. Indeed, 'the child is the becoming-young of every age' (Deleuze, & Guattari, 2004: 277). As Hickey-Moody (2012: 282) notes: 'becoming-child is a set of affects and capacities to be affected which can be activated at any stage of life'. Here 'becoming child' risks becoming yet another cultural trope that merely reproduces prevailing romanticised understandings of childhood (as, for example, is evident in current fashion or reading books that mobilise the genre of children's clothes and literature as a way of evoking a sense of guiltless transgression and freedom from social constraint, as well as generating a new market niche). Yet, as Gill-Peterson (2013) concludes, becoming-child is not without proposals for how children could mobilise it:

> [I]t is a capacity that can be activated by actual children under the right conditions. An analysis of the generation of the child, then, that worked through affects to dispense with adultomorphism, and attended both to how the body is 'stolen' from children by normalization, while simultaneously engaging in becomings that would otherwise pass under our radar: *that* is the proposal I find in Deleuze and Guattari's *oeuvre*.
>
> *(fn2, emphasis in the original)*

Indeed, Skott-Myhre, et al. (2016), among others, address this in terms of youth work practice.

Various childhood and educational researchers have engaged this approach to promote new ways of conceiving of children and childhood, claiming that it 'allows movement away from those theoretical frames which seek to first "know" children and second to tie or nail them into particular identities ... see[ing] beyond usual or familiar scripts that circumscribe and represent children' (Jones, 2013: 294; Ringrose, 2011; Coleman, 2009). Highlighting these 'scripts', in this case constellated around play in a make-believe castle, also enables attention to practices of 'con(script)ing', whereby 'both children's selves and their bodies are con(script)ed, codified and pressed into being where binary logic, common sense and habitual practices leave little choice but to be either [one of the gendered positions of] a jester or a princess' (Jones, 2013: 294).

Yet notwithstanding these seeming alignments, and fruitful empirical possibilities, child as method should be differentiated from these Deleuzian perspectives in two grounds. First, notwithstanding the repudiation of metaphysical claims (about essences or intrinsic qualities), the key concepts nevertheless are vulnerable to being reconstructed as reconstituting these. As Hickey-Moody (2012) notes, Deleuze's children function as figures, standing for 'vectors of affect' that 'are romanticised sites of political freedom' (278). This is aside from the ways the (boy)child, rather than the girl, appears to work in this way (with a whole other, especially queer, discussion focusing on

Deleuze and Guattari's comments about girl(s), Driscoll, 1997). Indeed, child-hood becomes 'an object, it is the assemblage of new frontiers: a surface. It is not the same thing as the lived experience of youth' (Hickey-Moody, 2012: 283). A second matter of further 'concern' noted by Hickey-Moody, although she does not develop this further, is how their model 'uses the political poten-tial of childhood subjectivity without acknowledging the lived difficulties to which children have to respond' (281). Clearly in doing this, Deleuze and Guattari are in a long line of philosophers who have mobilised the trope or figure of the child to evoke a romanticised sense of possibilities or potential unfettered by ideology or institutional constraints (see also Burman, 1998). Such romanticisations would also risk re-inscribing longstanding colonial and cultural dynamics of precisely the kind of Fanon's arguments – and the forms of postcolonial and decolonising theories they have inspired, including 'southern theory', as also indicated by Garrard, et al. (2016) and Washick and Wingrove (2015).

Here it may be worth distinguishing Guattari's contribution from his joint work with Deleuze. This is because Guattari remained involved with psychoanalytic practice as well as being a significant critic of, as well as innovator in, psychoanalytic theory (Guattari, 1984). The sociological insights of schizo-analysis were directly related to his transformation of 'institutional psychotherapy' (a term that he does not relate to the work of Fanon's mentor Tosquelles), which Guattari also calls 'institutional thera-peutics', into a form of 'group-analysis' (a term he uses without referencing the work of the Foulkes, the British settled founder of an approach of this name, for example, Foulkes, 1975). Guattari's continuing commitment to mental health practice aligns with the practical-political project of child as method in attending to questions of subjectivity and subjectification, as also with the ways Fanon's psychoaffective analyses combined individual with socio-political transformation.

At any rate, Deleuze and Guattari's writings resonate with the emphasis placed on affect, emotion, and subjectivity as critical political topics. Indeed, as a further connection with the resources informing 'child as method', it should be noted that Naoki Sakai, whose theory of language and translation figures prominently within *Border as Method,* argues for the importance of emotions, rather than historical events, in understanding the continuing impacts of colo-nialism, saying: 'postcoloniality is primarily the problem of shame . . . the crucial issue is that of shame rather than of guilt in decolonization' (2010: 271). He continues:

> Postcoloniality, therefore, has little to do with what comes after the demise of colonial reign. It indicates how decisively and irredeem-ably the fantasy of the colonial relationship is etched in our identities.

Regardless of whether that fantasy adequately summarizes the collective experience of the past or not. This is to say, the post of postcoloniality means the irredeemability of the colonial experience due to which it is impossible to posit some original identity prior to a colonial reign, namely, a collective and essential identity not yet contaminated by the colonial relationship.

(Sakai, 2010: 271)

In relation to child as method, the same point could be made about the desire for, but impossibility of, an originary state of childhood that, as Chapter 5 in particular indicated, is a claim that Fanon rigorously and critically interrogated.

Queering child

Given Deleuze and Guattari's critiques of the oedipal family and its relationship to capitalism, as well as their destabilisation of sexed/gendered positions and identities (also after Butler, although the differences between the two positions should not be overlooked, Hickey-Moody, & Rasmussen, 2009), it is perhaps unsurprising that they have been widely taken up in queer theory. One clear intervention in the discourse of teleology in favour of diversity was Stockton's (2009) notion of growing sideways (rather than growing up). Perhaps even more influential than Deleuze and Guattari here, however, is Edelman's (2004) critique of the ways the child signifies reproductive (and so heteronormative) futurity. While this account has in turn been critiqued for both conceptual incoherence and political limitations (Lesnik-Oberstein, 2010; Gill-Peterson, 2013), this analysis has also been taken up in discussions of 'race', labour and neoliberalism (Gill-Peterson, 2015). If these earlier queer theory critiques of dominant models of the child as subject to delay (Stockton, 2009) and reproductive futurity (Edelman, 2004) were insufficiently attentive to classed and racialised dynamics inflecting and producing this (consider, for example, Stockton's problematically named 'child queered by color'), more recent engagements have attended to their specific disaggregations and stratifications (Gill-Peterson, et al., 2016).

Here, too (perhaps inviting a critical reading alongside Mezzadra and Neilson, 2013), labour becomes consequential. Gill-Peterson (2015) highlights how under neoliberalism, parents as well as nation states invest (economically as well as affectively) in children as human capital that can be understood as a form of financial futures trading. He makes an important point about how this convergence works paradoxically not only to intensify the privatisation of structurally produced inequalities into personal concerns, but also to transform interventions to address these into (financialised) labour as well (consider student loans, for example). He argues that the theory of human capital deploys the child to recalculate the value of the future in terms of private investment . . . Human capital hence turns childhood into futures training for parents, who have to speculate on the effect on endowments like race and gender on their investments . . . Given that human capital rationalises investment as a private practice, even though race and gender are understood as coefficients their value remains private, so that the conversion of education and other forms of care into labor becomes the only way to address endemic inequality.'

(Gill-Peterson, 2015: 186–189)

As well as disregarding the ways majority world children, families, and communities are excluded from the dominant modes of childhood, Edelman's (2004) influential critique positioning the child as guarantor of reproductive (and so heterosexed) futurity even overlooks the labour of even feminised heterosexed white girls. Gill-Peterson (2015) discusses the latter's 'digital labour', for example, in making 'haul videos' as also futures trading since 'even investment in the ideologically valuable child cannot wait until adulthood to begin demanding returns' (190). This is because it produces value through turning consumption into production through the rehearsal of gendered modes of consumption, as well as, second, through the generation of advertising revenue. This, Gill-Peterson suggests, draws attention to how a form of digital child labour 'passes under the radar because it is fully *socialised:* it happens without calling itself work' (ibid., emphasis in the original).

What emerges from such analyses is how discourses of childhood, even the powerful ones about play as the work of childhood, can be instrumentalised – financialised in the service not only of capital but also in rendering (what can be understood as) children's labour invisible (alongside instrumentalising women's, Roy, 2014; Roberts, 2014; Rankin, 2013). At the very least the binary between work and play, always tricky if also heavily ideologised in relation to children and childhood, emerges as more complex once these wider political dynamics are admitted. Such close readings documenting the exploitative incursions of capital into the subjectivities, desires, and aspirations, of children and parents – happening in different ways across axes of class, gender, and racialisation, but happening to all – indicate what child as method can offer.

Fanon and child as method

Child as method, as a critical practice of deconstructive reading and of teaching, is oriented to the elaboration of a pedagogy of, and for, decolonisation and redistribution. My reading of Fanon through the motifs of Idiotic child, Trauamatogenic child, Therapeutic child, and Extemic child in this book exemplify this approach. A key starting point for child as method is resisting the abstraction of the child from sociopolitical relations that position it as 'other' (Burman, 2017a, 2008a). Four wider methodological, analytical, and political implications for decolonising pedagogies are also exemplified by this analysis, as also indicated by the analysis in this book. First, the attention to the particular. As Hudis (2015) also emphasises, Fanon both confines his claims to the Antilles but simultaneously also generalises them to any colonial situation, insisting therefore that colonialism is racism. Therefore, second, the link to the general does not rely on invoking psychological universals. This differentiates Fanon from Mannoni in his earlier 1950/1964 text, *Prospero and Caliban*. Instead what is needed is to attend to specific socioeconomic material conditions. Doing this, third, offers a route between psychological reductionism and social determinism – forging a psychopolitical (after Fanon) but not psychologising account that acknowledges the psychic within the political but does not reduce the political to the personal. Fourth, (generated in particular from Fanon's psychoanalytic sensibility) child as method engages a pedagogy of failure, rather than omnipotence or completion, that opens up new relational and transformational possibilities. Moreover, as a bridge between childhood studies and educational theory, child as method can be seen to contribute to the wider project of decolonisation in three ways. First, by advancing the conceptualisation of childhood within educational theory and practice; second, by helping situate educational processes within cultural-political practices; while, finally, child as method indicates what can be achieved by mobilising child as an anticolonial lens through which to read educational and wider social pedagogical practices.

REFERENCES

Abane. B. (2011). Frantz Fanon and Abane Ramdan: Brief encounter in the Algerian revolution. In N. C. Gibson (Ed.) *Living Fanon: Global perspectives* (pp. 27–43). New York: Palgrave.

Adorno, T. (1951/2005). *Minima Moralia: Reflections on damaged life*, London: Verso. www.marxists.org/reference/archive/adorno/1951/mm/ch01.htm

Ahmed, A. (2009). Embodying diversity: Problems and paradoxes for black feminists. *Race, Ethnicity & Education*, 12(1), 41–52.

Ahmed, S. (2004a). Declarations of whiteness: The non-performativity of anti-racism, borderlands e-journal, 3(2). www.borderlands.net.au/vol3no2_2004/ahmed_decla rations.htm

Ahmed, S. (2004b). *The Cultural Politics of Emotion*. Edinburgh: Edinburgh University Press.

Ailwood, J. (2008). Learning or earning in the "smart state'. *Childhood: A global journal of child research*, 15(4), 535–551.

Alanen, L. (2005). Childhood as generational condition. In C. Jenks (Ed.) *Childhood: Critical concepts in sociology*, Vol. 3 (pp. 286–298). London: Routledge.

Alanen, L. (2009). Generational order. In J. Qvortrup, W. A. Corsaro, & M. S. Honig (Eds) *The Palgrave Handbook of Childhood Studies* (pp. 159–174). Basingstoke: Palgrave Macmillan.

Alanen, L. (2016). 'Intersectionality' and other challenges to theorizing childhood. *Childhood*, 23(2), 157–161.

Alessandrini, A. (1997). Whose Fanon? *Minnesota Review*, 48(9), 235–242.

Alessandrini, A. C. (2000). Humanism in question: Fanon and Said. In H. Schwarz and S. Ray (Eds) *A Companion to Postcolonial Studies* (pp. 431–450). Malden, MA: Blackwell.

Alessandrini, A. C. (Ed.). (2005). *Frantz Fanon: Critical Perspectives*. New York: Routledge.

Alessandrini, A. C. (2009). The humanism effect: Fanon, Foucault, and ethics without subjects. *Foucault Studies*, (7), 64–80.

Allen, A., & Goddard, R. (2014). The domestication of Foucault: Government, critique, war. *History of the Human Sciences*, 27(5), 26–53.

Allen, K., & Taylor, Y. (2012). Placed parenting, locating unrest: Failed femininities, troubled mothers and rioting subjects. *Studies in the Maternal*, 4(2). www.mamsie.bbk.ac.uk

Allen, R. L. (2005). Whiteness and critical pedagogy. In Z. Leonardo (Ed.) *Critical Pedagogy and Race* (pp. 53–68). Malden, MA: Blackwell.

Althusser, L. (1971). *Lenin and Philosophy, and Other Essays* (trans., B. Brewster). London: New Left Books.

Andreotti, V. (2011). *Actionable Postcolonial Theory in Education*. Basingstoke: Palgrave.

Annamma, S. A. (2018). *The Pedagogy of Pathologization: Dis/abled girls of color in the school-prison nexus*. New York: Routledge.

Applebaum, B. (2012). Stay! Refusing forms of evasion. *Philosophy of Education Archive*, 55–59.

Bailey, A. (2017). Tracking privilege – preserving epistemic pushback in feminist and critical race philosophy classes. *Hypatia*, 32(4), 876–892.

Baird, B. (2008). Child politics, feminist analyses. *Australian Feminist Studies*, 23(57), 291–305.

Baldwin, J. (1955). *Notes of a Native Son*. New York: Beacon Press.

Balibar, E. (2012). The 'impossible' community of the citizens: Past and present problems. *Environment and Planning D: Society and space*, 30, 437–449.

Barad, K. (2014). Diffracting diffraction: Cutting together-apart. *Parallax*, 20(3), 168-187.

Barthes, R. (1981). *Camera Lucida: Reflections on photography*. New York: Hill & Wang.

Bartky, S. L. (1996). The pedagogy of shame. In C. Luke (Ed.) *Feminisms and Pedagogies of Everyday Life* (pp. 225–241). Albany: State University of New York Press.

Batchelor, K. (2017a). Introduction: Histoire croisée, microhistory and translation history. In K. Batchelor & S. Harding (Eds) *Translating Frantz Fanon across Continents and Languages* (pp. 1–17). New York: Routledge.

Batchelor, K. (2017b). The translation of *Les Damnés* into English: Exploring Irish connections. In K. Batchelor & S. Harding (Eds) *Translating Frantz Fanon across Continents and Languages* (pp. 40–75). New York: Routledge.

BBC Radio Four (2016a). Brexit Street. www.bbc.com/news/uk-37306646, 20 July, archived at www.bbc.com/news/uk-37306646

BBC Radio Four (2016b). PM, Brexit Street. www.bbc.com/news/uk-37306646, 10 September.

Beinart, J. (1992). Darkly through a lens: Changing perceptions of the African child in sickness and health, 1900–1945. In R. Cooter (Ed.) *In the Name of the Child: Health and welfare, 1880–1940* (pp. 220–243). London: Routledge.

Benedict, R. (1935). *Patterns of Culture*. London: Routledge and Kegan Paul.

Benedict, R. (1967). *The Chrysanthemum and the Sword: Patterns of Japanese culture*. New York: Houghton Mifflin.

Benjamin, W. (1969). Theses on history. *Illuminations*. New York: Schocken.

Bergner, G. (1995). Who is that masked woman? Or, the role of gender in Fanon's *Black Skin, White Masks*', *PMLA*, 110(1), 75–88.

Bergner, G. (1999). Politics and pathologies: On the subject of race in psychoanalysis. In A. Alessandrini (Ed.) *Frantz Fanon: Critical perspectives* (pp. 219–236). London: Routledge.

Bhabha, H. K. (1983). The other question: The stereotype and colonial discourse. *Screen* 24(6), 18–36.

Bhabha, H. K. (1986). Foreword: remembering Fanon: Self, psyche and the colonial condition. In *Black Skin, White Masks*. London and Sydney: Pluto.

Bhabha, H. K. (1994a). Interrogating identity: Frantz Fanon and the postcolonial prerogative. In H. Bhabha *The Location of Culture* (pp.40–65). New York: Routledge.

Bhabha, H. (1994b). *The Location of Culture..* New York: Routledge.

Bhambra, G. K. (2007). Multiple modernities or global interconnections: Understanding the global post the colonial. In N. Karagiannis, & P. Wagner (Eds) *Varieties of World-making: Beyond globalization* (pp. 59–73). Liverpool: Liverpool University Press.

Bhambra, G. K. (2014). Postcolonial and decolonial dialogues. *Postcolonial Studies*, 17(2), 115–121.

Bhattacharrya, G. (2008). *Dangerous Brown Men*. London: Zed.

Bhopal, K., & Preston, J. (Eds) (2012). *Intersectionality and 'Race' in Education*. Abingdon: Routledge.

Bingham, C. (2006). Before recognition and after: The educational critique. *Educational Theory*, 56(3), 325–344.

Birmingham Centre for Contemporary Cultural Studies (1982). *The Empire Strikes Back: Race and racism in 70s Britain*. London: Hutchinson.

Black, M. (1992). *A Cause for Our Times: Oxfam – the first fifty years*. Oxford: Oxfam.

Boler, M. (1997). Disciplined emotions: Philosophies of educated feelings. *Educational Theory*, 47(2): 203–237.

Boler, M. (1999). *Feeling Power: Emotions and education*. New York: Routledge.

Bourdieu, P. (2004). Algerian landing. *Ethnography*, 5, 415–442.

Bourke, J. (2007). *Rape: A cultural history*. London: Virago.

Boyden, J. (1990). Childhood and the policymakers: A comparative perspective on the globalization of childhood, In A. James and A. Prout (Eds) *Constructing and Reconstructing Childhood* (pp. 196–210). Lewes: Falmer Press.

Braidotti, R. (2013). *The Posthuman*. Cambridge: Polity.

Brenneman M., & Margonis, F. (2012). Degrees of disenchantment: A review essay. *Educational Theory*, 62(2), 225–247.

Breuer, J., & Freud, S. (1893–1895/1955). Studies on hysteria. In J. Strachey (Ed. and Trans.) *The Standard Edition of the Complete Psychological Works of Sigmund Freud*, II (pp. 1–305). London: The Hogarth Press.

Britzman, D. (2003). *After-education: Anna Freud, Melanie Klein, and psycho-analytic histories of learning*. Albany: SUNY Press.

Britzman, D. P. (2010). *Freud and Education*. New York: Routledge.

Brooks, J. G. (2011). Bearing the weight: Discomfort as a necessary condition for 'less violent' and more equitable dialogic Learning. *The Journal of Educational Foundations*, 25(1/2), 43.

Brown, D., & Zinkin, L. (Eds) (1994). *The Psyche and the Social World*. London: Routledge.

Brown, S. A., & Lock, R. (2018). Enhancing intergenerational communication around climate change. In *Handbook of Climate Change Communication: Vol. 3* (pp. 385–398). Cham: Springer.

Brown, T., Atkinson, D., & England, J. (2006). *Regulatory Discourses in Education: A Lacanian perspective*. New York: Peter Lang.

Buck-Morss, S. (2009). *Hegel, Haiti and Universal History*. Pittsburgh: University of Pittsburgh Press.

Burman, E. (1992). Identification and power in feminist psychotherapy: A reflexive history of a discourse analysis. *Women's Studies International Forum*, 15(4), 487–498.

Burman, E. (1994). Innocents abroad: Projecting Western fantasies of childhood onto the iconography of emergencies. *Disasters: Journal of disaster studies and management*, 18(3), 238–253.

Burman, E. (1995). Discourses of feminist psychotherapy: Identification, subjectivity and power. In J. Siegfried (Ed.) *Therapeutic and Everyday Discourse as Behavior Change* (pp. 469–490). New York: Ablex.

Burman, E. (1998). Pedagogics of post/modernity: The address to the child in Walter Benjamin and Jean-Francois Lyotard. In K. Lesnik-Oberstein (Ed.) *Children in Culture: Approaches to childhood* (pp. 55–88). New York and London: Macmillan.

Burman, E. (2001a). Engendering authority in the group. *Psychodynamic Counselling*, 7(3), 347–369.

Burman, E. (2001b). Emotions in the classroom: And the institutional politics of knowledge. *Psychoanalytic Studies*, 3(4), 313–324.

Burman, E. (2001c). Fictioning authority. *Psychodynamic Counselling*, 7(2), 187–205.

Burman, E. (2006). Emotions, reflexivity and feminised action research. *Educational Action Research*, 14(3), 315–332.

Burman, E. (2007). Between orientalism and normalisation: Cross-cultural lessons from Japan for a critical history of psychology. *History of Psychology*, 10(2), 179–198.

Burman, E. (2008a). *Developments: Child, image, nation*. London: Routledge.

Burman, E. (2008b). Resisting the deradicalization of psychosocial analyses. *Psychoanalysis, Culture & Society*, 13(4), 374–378.

Burman, E. (2008c). Beyond 'women vs. children' or 'womenandchildren': engendering childhood and reformulating motherhood. *International Journal of Children's Rights*, 16(2), 177–194.

Burman, E. (2011). Environ-mentalizing the matrix. *Group Analysis*, 44(4), 374–384.

Burman, E. (2012a). Deconstructing neoliberal childhood: Towards a feminist antipsychological approach. *Childhood*, 19(4), 423–438.

Burman, E. (2012b). Group acts and missed encounters: Lacan and Foulkes. *Lacunae*, 1(2), 23–42.

Burman, E. (2013a). Desiring development? Psychoanalytic contributions to anti-developmental psychology. *International Journal of Qualitative Studies in Education*, 26(1), 56–74.

Burman, E. (2013b). Conceptual resources for questioning 'Child as Educator'. *Studies in Philosophy and Education*, 32(3), 229–243.

Burman, E. (2015). Educational intimacies: Writing bodily relations in early childhood and education. In A. B. Reinertsen, & A. M. Otterstad (Eds) *Metodefestival og Øyeblikksrealisme [Method-celebration/Party and Moments of Realism]* (pp. 180–197). Bergen: Fagbokforlaget.

Burman, E. (2016a). Fanon and the child: Pedagogies of subjectification and transformation. *Curriculum Inquiry*, 46(3), 265–285.

Burman, E. (2016b). Fanon, Foucault, feminisms: Psychoeducation, theoretical psychology, and political change. *Theory & Psychology*, 26(6), 706–730.

Burman, E. (2016c). Fanon's Lacan and the traumatogenic child: Psychoanalytic reflections on the dynamics of colonialism and racism. *Theory, Culture & Society*, 33(4), 77–101.

Burman, E. (2017a). *Deconstructing Developmental Psychology*. London: Routledge.

Burman, E. (2017b). Fanon's other children: Psychopolitical and pedagogical implications. *Race Ethnicity & Education*, 20(1), 42–56.

Burman, E. (2017c). A necessary struggle-in-relation? In R. Rosen, K. Twarmley, & A. Varley (Eds) *Feminism and the Politics of Childhood: Friends or foes?* (pp. 23–39). London: University College London Press.

Burman, E. (2018a). Child as method: Anticolonial implications for educational research. *International Studies in the Sociology of Education* DOI – http://dx.doi.org/ 10.1080/09620214.2017.1412266

Burman, E. (2018b). Child as method. In D. Cook (Ed.) *Encyclopedia of Children's and Childhood Studies*. Thousand Oaks: Sage.

Burman, E., Gowrisunkur, J., & Sangha, K. (1998). Conceptualising cultural and gendered identities in psychological therapies: Models and practices. *European Journal of Psychotherapy, Health and Counselling*, 1(2), 231–256.

Burman, E., Greenstein, A., Bragg, J., Hanley, T., Kalambouka, A., Lupton, R., McCoy, L., Sapin, K., & Winter, L. (2017). Discoursing educational impacts of welfare cuts: From regulation to resistance? *Education Policy Analysis Archives*. http://epaa.asu.edu/ojs/article/view/2320/1889

Burman, E., & Stacey, J. (2010). The child and childhood in feminist theory. *Feminist Theory*, 11(3), 227–240.

Burnett, J. (2016). *Racial Violence and the Brexit State*. London: Institute of Race Relations. www.irr.org.uk/publications/issues/racial-violence-and-the-brexit-state/

Butler, J. (1990). *Gender Trouble: Feminism and the subversion of identity*. New York: Routledge.

Butler, J. (1997). *The Psychic Life of Power: Theories in subjection*. Stanford, California: Stanford University Press.

Butler, J. (2000). Competing universalities. In J. Butler, E. Laclau, & S. Žižek, *Contingency, Hegemony, Universality: Contemporary dialogues on the left* (pp. 136–181). London: Verso.

Butler, J. (2005). *Giving an Account of Oneself*. New York: Fordham University Press.

Butler, J. (2015). *Senses of the Subject*. New York: Fordham University Press.

Butler, J. (2017). Interview. In G. Yancy (Ed.) *On Race: 34 conversations in a time of crisis* (pp. 53–60). New York: Oxford University Press.

Calhoun, C. (2006). Pierre Bourdieu and social transformation: Lessons from Algeria. *Development and Change*, 37(6), 1403–1415.

Cannella, G. S., & Viruru, R. (2004). *Childhood and Postcolonization: Power, education, and contemporary practice*. New York: Psychology Press.

Caplan, P. J., & Hall-McCorquodale, I. (1985). Mother-blaming in major clinical journals. *American Journal of Orthopsychiatry*, 55(3), 345–353.

Carby, H. (1996). White women listen! Black women and the boundaries of sisterhood. In H. A. Baker, Jr, M. Diawara, & R. H. Lindeborg (Eds) *Black British Cultural Studies: A reader* (pp. 163–172). Chicago: University of Chicago Press.

Caselli, D. (2016) Attack of the Easter bunnies: Walter Benjamin's *Youth Hour*. *Parallax*, 22(4), 459–479.

Castañeda, C. (2002). *Figurations: Child, bodies, worlds*. Durham and London: Duke University Press.

Chamberlain, K. (2000). Methodolatry and qualitative health research. *Journal of Health Psychology*, 5(3), 285–296.

Chase, E., & Walker, R. (2013). The co-construction of shame in the context of poverty: Beyond a threat to the social bond. *Sociology*, 47(4), 739–754.

Chen, K. H. (2010). *Asia as method: Towards deimperialization*. Durham: Duke University Press.

Chen, K. H. (2012). Takeuchi Yoshimi's 1960 'Asia as method' lecture. *Inter-Asia Cultural Studies*, 13(2), 317–324.

Chen, K. H. (2017). Review essay: On Mamdani's mode of thought. *Cultural Studies*, 31(4), 580–601.

Cherki, A. (2006). *Frantz Fanon: A Portrait* (trans., Nadia Benabid). Ithaca: Cornell University Press.

Cherki, A. (2011). Fanon, fifty years later: Resisting the air of our present time. In N.C. Gibson (Ed.) *Living Fanon: Global perspectives* (pp. 131–138). New York: Palgrave.

Chernilo, D. (2008). *A Social Theory of the Nation-state: The political forms of modernity beyond methodological nationalism*. London: Routledge.

Cho, S., Crenshaw, K. W., & McCall, L. (2013). Toward a field of intersectionality studies: Theory, applications, and praxis. *Signs: Journal of women in culture and society*, 38(4), 785–810.

Chow, R. (1999). The politics of admission: Female sexual agency, miscegenation and the formation of community in Frantz Fanon. In A. Alessandrini (Ed.) *Frantz Fanon: Critical perspectives* (pp. 35–58). London: Routledge.

Cockburn, C. (2013). War and security, women and gender: An overview of the issues. *Gender & Development*, 21(3), 433–452.

Coleman, R. (2009). *The Becoming of Bodies: Girls, images, experience*. Manchester: Manchester University Press.

Collins, P. H. (2002). *Black feminist thought: Knowledge, consciousness, and the politics of empowerment*. New York: Routledge.

Collins, P. H., & Bilge, S. (2016). *Intersectionality*. Cambridge: Polity Press.

Coloma, R. S. (2013). Empire: Analytical category for educational research. *Educational Theory*, 63(6), 639–658.

Combahee River Collective (1981). This Bridge Called My Back: Writings by radical women of color. New York: Kitchen Table Press.

Combres, L. (2016). Critique et discours sur le colonialisme: Fanon vs Mannoni. *Research in Psychoanalysis* (2), 218a–226a.

Connell, R. (2014). Using southern theory: Decolonizing social thought in theory, research and application. *Planning Theory*, 13(2), 210–223.

Coons, G. (2014). The replacement of geography by standards and what to do about it. *Journal of Science and Technology of the Arts*, 6(1), 31–40.

Cooper, A. (1997). Thinking the unthinkable: "White liberal' 'defences against understanding in anti-racist training. *Journal of Social Work Practice*, 11(2), 127–137.

Copjec, J. (1994). *Read my Desire: Lacan against the historicists*. London: Verso Books.

Corbett, K. (2009). *Boyhoods: Rethinking masculinities*. New Haven: Yale University Press.

Cornwall, A. (2016). Towards a pedagogy for the powerful. *IDS Bulletin*, 47(5). http://bulletin.ids.ac.uk/idsbo/article/view/2801/ONLINE%20ARTICLE DOI: 10.19088/1968-2016.168.

Crenshaw, K. (1991). Mapping the margins: Intersectionality, identity politics, and violence against women of color. *Stanford Law Review*, 43(6), 1241–1299.

Crowe, K. (2015). Sexual assault and testimony: Articulation of/as violence. *Law, Culture and the Humanities*. https://doi.org/10.1177/1743872115577917.

Dalal, F. (2002). *Race, Colour and the Process of Racialization: New perspectives from group analysis, psychoanalysis, and sociology*. London: Psychology Press.

Dalal, F. (2009). Skirts, sarees and sarongs: The rhetoric and reality behind the celebration of diversity in organisational life. *International Journal of Learning and Change*, 3(3), 308–328.

Dale, R., & Robertson, S. (2009). Beyond methodological 'ISMS'in comparative education in an era of globalisation. In R. Cowen, & A. M. Kazamias (Eds) *International Handbook of Comparative Education* (pp. 1113–1127). New York: Springer.

Danto, E. A. (2005). *Freud's Free Clinics: Psychoanalysis & social justice, 1918–1938*. New York: Columbia University Press.

Danziger, K. (1997). The varieties of social construction. *Theory & Psychology*, 7(3), 399–416.

De Benedictis, S. (2012). Feral parents: Austerity parenting under neoliberalism. *Studies in the Maternal*, 4(2). www.mamsie.bbk.ac.uk

De Lissovoy, N. (2010). Staging the crisis: Teaching, capital, and the politics of the subject. *Curriculum Inquiry*, 40(3), 418–435.

De Lissovoy, N. (2012). Education and violation: Conceptualizing power, domination and agency in the hidden curriculum. *Race, Ethnicity & Education*, 15(4), 463–484.

De Oliveira, A. V. (2011). (Towards) decoloniality and diversality in global citizenship education. *Globalisation, Societies and Education*, 9(3–4), 381–397.

De Vos, J. (2013). *Psychologization and the Subject of Late Modernity*. Basingstroke: Palgrave Macmillan.

De Vos, J. (2015). Deneurologizing education? From psychologisation to neurologisation and back. *Studies in Philosophy and Education*, 34(3), 279–295.

Dei, G. J. S. (2010a). Rereading Fanon for his pedagogy and implications for schooling and education. In G. J. S. Dei, & M. Simmons (Eds), *Fanon & Education: Thinking through pedagogical possibilities* (pp. 1–28). New York: Peter Lang.

Dei, G. J. S. (2010b). An Introduction. In George J. Sefa Dei, & Marlon Simmons (Eds) *Fanon & Education: Thinking through pedagogical possibilities* (pi–xviii). New York: Peter Lang.

Dei, G. J. S., & Simmons, M. (2010a). The pedagogy of Fanon: An introduction. In G. J. S. Dei, & M. Simmons (Eds) *Fanon & Education: Thinking through pedagogical possibilities* (pp. xiii–xxv). New York: Peter Lang.

Dei, G. J. S., & Simmons, M. (Eds) (2010b). *Fanon & Education: Thinking through pedagogical possibilities*. New York: Peter Lang.

Deleuze, G. (1994). *Difference and Repetition*. London: Continuum.

Deleuze, G. (1997). *Essays Critical and Clinical* (trans, Daniel W. Smith, & Michael A. Greco). Minneapolis: University of Minnesota Press.

Deleuze, G., & Guattari, F. (2004). *A Thousand Plateaus: Capitalism and schizophrenia.* London: Continuum.

Desai, M. U. (2014). Psychology, the psychological, and critical praxis: A phenomenologist reads Frantz Fanon. *Theory & Psychology*, 24(1), 58–75.

Doane, M. A. (1999). Dark continents: Epistemologies of racial and sexual difference in psychoanalysis and the cinema. In J. Evans, & S. Hall (Eds) *Visual Culture: The reader* (pp. 448–456). London: Sage.

Driscoll, C. (1997). The little girl, Deleuze and Guattari. In G. Genosko (Ed.) *Critical Assessment of Leading Philosophers*, Vol. 3 (pp. 1462–1479). London: Routledge.

Dutro, E., & Bien, A. (2014). Listening to the speaking wound: A trauma studies perspective on student positioning in schools. *American Educational Research Journal*, 51(1), 7–35.

Edelman, L. (2004). *No Future: Queer theory and the death drive.* Durham: Duke University Press.

Eichenbaum, L., & Orbach. S. (1983). *What Do Women Want?* Harmondsworth: Penguin.

Ellison, R. (1995). *Invisible Man.* New York: Vintage/Ramdom House.

Enloe, C. H. (2010). *Nimo's War, Emma's War: Making feminist sense of the Iraq war.* Berkeley: University of California Press.

Erel, U., Haritaworn, J., Rodríguez, E. G., and Klesse, C. (2010). On the depoliticisation of intersectionality talk: Conceptualising multiple oppressions in critical sexuality studies. In *Theorizing intersectionality and sexuality* (pp. 56–77). London: Palgrave Macmillan.

Escobar, A. (2000). Beyond the search for a paradigm? Post-development and beyond. *Development*, 43(4), 11–14.

Evans, J., & Hall, S. (Eds) (1999) *Visual Culture: The reader.* London: Sage.

Evans, T. (2005). International human rights law as power/knowledge. *Human Rights Quarterly*, 27(3), 1046–1068.

Fanon, F. (1952/1970). *Black Skin, White Masks* (trans., C. L. Markmann). London: Paladin.

Fanon, F. (1959/1965). *A Dying Colonialism* (trans., H. Chevalier). New York: Grove Press.

Fanon, F. (1961/1963). *The Wretched of the Earth* (trans., C. Farrington). London: Penguin.

Fanon, F. (1964/1967). *Toward the African Revolution: Political essays* (trans. H. Chevalier). New York: Grove Press.

Fanon, F. (2018). *Alienation and Freedom* (eds, Jean Khalfa and Robert J. C. Young, trans., Steven Corcoran). London: Bloomsbury.

Farred, G. (2011). Wretchedness. In N. C. Gibson (Ed.) *Living Fanon: Global perspectives* (pp. 159–172). New York: Palgrave.

Fendler, L. (2001). Educating flexible souls: The construction of subjectivity through developmentality and interaction. In K. Hultqvist, & G. Dahlberg (Eds) *Governing the Child in the New Millenium* (pp. 119–142). New York and London: RoutledgeFalmer.

Ferguson, K. E. (1991). Interpretation and genealogy in feminism. *Signs: Journal of women in culture and society*, 16(2), 322–339.

Fernando, S. (2010). *Mental Health, Race and Culture*. Abingdon: Palgrave Macmillan.

Ficek, D. (2011). Reflections on Fanon and petrification. In N. C. Gibson (Ed.) *Living Fanon: Global perspectives* (pp. 75–84). New York: Palgrave.

Fine, M. E., Weis, L. E., Powell, L. C., & Wong, L. (1997). *Off White: Readings on race, power, and society*. New York: Routledge.

Flegel, M. (2009). *Conceptualizing Cruelty to Children in Nineteenth-Century England*. London: Ashgate.

Foucault, M. (1970). The order of discourse. Reprinted in I. Parker (Ed.) (2011) *Critical Psychology: Critical concepts in psychology, volume 4, dominant models of psychology and their limits* (pp. 190–220). London and New York: Routledge.

Foucault, M. (1977a). *Discipline and Punish* (trans., A. Sheridan). New York: Pantheon.

Foucault, M. (1977b). *Language, Counter-memory, Practice: Selected essays and interviews* (ed. D. Bouchard) Ithaca, New York: Cornell University Press.

Foucault. M. (1981). *History of Sexuality, Vol 1: An introduction*: Harmondsworth: Pelican.

Foucault, M. (1988). Technologies of the self. In L. Martin, H. Gutman, & P. Hutton (Eds) *Technologies of the Self: A seminar with Michel Foucault* (pp. 16–49). London: Tavistock.

Foucault, M., Davidson, A. I., & Burchell, G. (2008). *The Birth of Biopolitics: Lectures at the Collège de France, 1978–1979*. New York: Springer.

Foucault, M., & Ewald, F. (2003). *'Society Must Be Defended': Lectures at the Collège de France, 1975–1976* (Vol. 1). Basingstoke: Macmillan.

Foulkes, S. H. (1975). *Group-Analytic Psychotherapy*. London: Maresfield Press.

Foulkes, S. H., & Anthony, E. (1957). *Group Psychotherapy: The psychoanalytic approach*. Harmondsworth: Pelican.

Fournier, S., & Crey, E. (1997). *Stolen from Our Embrace: The abduction of first nations children and the restoration of Aboriginal communities*. Vancouver, British Columbia: Douglas & McIntyre Ltd.

Frankenberg, R. (1993). *White Women, Race Matters: The social construction of whiteness*. Minneapolis, Minnesota: University of Minnesota Press.

Frankenberg, R. (2001). The mirage of an unmarked whiteness. In B. Brander Rasmussen, E, Kinenberg, I. J. Nexica, & M. Wray (Eds) *The Making and Unmaking of Whiteness* (pp. 72–98). Durham: Duke University Press.

Fraser, N. (2003). From discipline to flexibilization? Rereading Foucault in the shadow of globalization. *Constellations*, 10(2), 160–171.

Fraser, N. (2017) Interview. In G. Yancy (Ed.) *On Race: 34 conversations in a time of crisis* (pp. 155–166). New York: Oxford University Press.

Freire, P. (1972). *Pedagogy of the Oppressed* (trans., Myra Bergman Ramos). New York: Herder and Herder.

Freud, S. (1901/2003). *The Psychopathology of Everyday Life* (trans., Alan Tyson). Harmondsworth: Penguin.

Freud, S. (1914). On narcissism: An introduction. In J. Strachey (Ed. and Trans.) *The Standard Edition of the Complete Psychological Works of Sigmund Freud, XIV(67)*. London: The Hogarth Press.

Freud, S. (1916/2003). *The Joke and its Relation to the Unconscious*. Harmondsworth: Penguin.

Freud, S. (1921). Group Psychology and the Analysis of the Ego. In J. Strachey (Ed. and Trans.) *The Standard Edition of the Complete Psychological Works of Sigmund Freud*, XVIII (pp.73–104). London: The Hogarth Press.

Freud, S. (1927). Splitting of the ego in the process of defence. In J. Strachey (Ed. and Trans.) *The Standard Edition of the Complete Psychological Works of Sigmund Freud*, XXIII (pp. 275–278). London: The Hogarth Press.

Frosh, S. (2003). Psychosocial studies and psychology: Is a critical approach emerging? *Human Relations*, 56(12), 1545–1567.

Frosh, S. (2010). *Psychoanalysis Outside the Clinic: Interventions in psychosocial studies.* Basingstoke: Palgrave Macmillan.

Frosh, S., & Baraitser, L. (2008). Psychoanalysis and psychosocial studies. *Psychoanalysis, Culture & Society*, 13(4), 346–365.

Fuss, D. (1994). Interior colonies: Frantz Fanon and the politics of identification. *Diacritics*, 24(2), 20–42.

Gallacher, L. A., & Gallagher, M. (2008). Methodological immaturity in childhood research? Thinking through participatory methods. *Childhood*, 15(4), 499–516.

Galloway, S. (2015). What's missing when empowerment is a purpose for adult literacies education? Bourdieu, Gee and the problem of accounting for power. *Studies in the Education of Adults*, 47(1), 49–63.

Gates, H. L. (1991). Critical Fanonism. *Critical Inquiry*, 17(3), 457–470.

Gaztambide-Fernández, R. (2010). Interruption and imagination in curriculum and pedagogy, or how to get caught inside a strange loop. *Curriculum Inquiry*, 40(3), 409–417.

Gaztambide-Fernández, R. A. (2012). Decolonization and the pedagogy of solidarity. *Decolonization: Indigeneity, Education & Society*, 1(1), 41–67.

Gendzier, I. (1966). Frantz Fanon: In search of justice. *Middle East Journal*, 20(4), 534–544.

Gendzier, I. (1973) *Frantz Fanon: A critical study*. New York: Pantheon Books.

Gerrard, J., Rudolph, S., & Sriprakash, A. (2017). The politics of post-qualitative inquiry: History and power. *Qualitative Inquiry*, 23(5), 384–394.

Gibson, N. C. (2013). A wholly other time? Fanon, the revolutionary, and the question of organization. *South Atlantic Quarterly*, 112(1), 39–55.

Gibson, N. C. (1999). Thoughts about doing Fanonism in the 1990s. *College Literature*, 26(2), 96–117.

Gibson, N.C. (2011a). *Fanonian Practices in South Africa: From Steve Biko to Abahlali base Mjondolo*. Scottsville: UKZN Press.

Gibson, N. C. (Ed.) (2011b) Living Fanon? In N.C. Gibson (Ed.) *Living Fanon: Global perspectives* (pp. 1–10). New York: Palgrave.

Gibson, N. C. (Ed.) (2011c) *Living Fanon: Global perspectives*. New York: Palgrave.

Gibson, N. C. (2013) Finding Fanon, looking for second liberations. Presentation at the Algiers conference on Fanon and Africa, June.

Gill-Peterson J. (2013). Childhood blocks: Deleuze and Guattari's infant affects. https://juliangillpeterson.wordpress.com/2013/04/29/childhood-blocks-deleuze-and-guattaris-infant-affects/#_ftn2

Gill-Peterson, J. (2015). The value of the future: The child as human capital and the neoliberal labor of race. *WSQ: Women's studies Quarterly*, 43(1), 181–196.

Gill-Peterson, J., Sheldon, R., & Stockton, K. B. (2016). What is the now, even of then? *GLQ: A journal of lesbian and gay studies*, 22(4), 495–503.

Gilroy, P. (2010). Fanon and Améry: Theory, torture and the prospect of humanism. *Theory, Culture & Society*, 27(7–8), 16–32.

Giordano, C. (2011). Translating Fanon in the Italian context: Re-thinking the ethics of treatment in psychiatry. *Transcultural Psychiatry*, 48(3), 228–256.

Giraldo, M. (2012). *Dialogues in and of the Group*. London: Karnac.

Go, J. (2013). Decolonizing Bourdieu: Colonial and postcolonial theory in Pierre Bourdieu's early work. *Sociological Theory*, 31(1), 49–74.

Gordo López, A., & De Vos, J. (2010). Psychologism, psychologising and de-psychologisation. *Annual Review of Critical Psychology*, 8, 3–7.

Gordon, L. R. (2011). Requiem on a life well lived: In memory of Frantz Fanon. In N. Gibson (Ed.) *Living Fanon: Global perspectives* (pp. 12–26). New York: Palgrave.

Gordon, L. R. (2015). *What Fanon Said: A philosophical introduction to his life and thought*. New York: Fordham University Press.

Grinberg, J., & Saavedra, E. (2000). The constitution of bilingual/ESL education as a disciplinary practice: Genealogical explorations. *Review of Educational Research*, 70, 419–441.

Grosz, E. (1990). *Jacques Lacan: A feminist introduction*. London: Routledge.

Guattari, F. (1984). *Molecular Revolution: Psychiatry and politics*. Harmondsworth: Peregine Books.

Guattari, F. (2006). *The Anti-Oedipus Papers*. New York: Semiotext(e).

Gutierrez, C. O. N., & Hopkins, P. (2015). Introduction: Young people, gender and intersectionality. *Gender, Place & Culture*, 22(3), 383–389.

Haddour, A. (2010). Torture unveiled: Rereading Fanon and Bourdieu in the context of May 1958. *Theory, Culture & Society*, 27(7–8), 66–90.

Hage, G. (2010). The affective politics of racial mis-interpellation. *Theory, Culture & Society*, 27(7–8), 112–129.

Hallward, P. (2011). Fanon and political will. *Cosmos and History: The Journal of Natural and Social Philosophy*, 7(1), 104–127.

Hanson, K. (2016). Children's participation and agency when they don't 'do the right thing'. *Childhood*, 23(4), 471–475.

Hanson, K. (2017). Embracing the past: 'Been', 'being' and 'becoming'children. *Childhood*, 24(3), 281–285.

Haraway, D. (1988). Situated knowledges: The science question in feminism and the privilege of partial perspective. *Feminist studies*, 14(3), 575–599.

Haraway, D. J. (1991). *Simians, Cyborgs and Women: The reinvention of nature*. London: Verso.

Haraway, D. J. (1997). *Modest_Witness@ Second_Millennium. FemaleMan_Meets_OncoMouse: Feminism and technoscience*. New York: Psychology Press.

Harding, S. (Ed.). (2004). *The Feminist Standpoint Theory Reader: Intellectual and political controversies*. London: Psychology Press.

Harding, S. (Ed.) (2006). *Feminism & Methodology*. Buckingham: Open University Press.

Harding, S. G. (2017). Fanon in Arabic: Tracks and traces. In K. Batchelor, & S. Harding (Eds) *Translating Frantz Fanon across Continents and Languages* (pp. 207–268). New York: Routledge.

Hardt, M., & Negri, A. (2009). *Commonwealth*. Cambridge, MA: Belknap Press of Harvard University Press.

Harrison, T. (2000). *Bion, Rickman, Foulkes and the Northfield experiments: Advancing on a different front*. London: Jessica Kingsley.

Hartsock, N. (1990). Foucault on power: A theory for women? In L. Nicholson (Ed.) *Feminism/Postmodernism* (pp. 157–175). New York and London: Routledge.

Hekman, S. (1997). Truth and method: Feminist standpoint theory revisited. *Signs*, 22(2), 341–365.

Hekman, S. (2010). *The Material of Knowledge: Feminist disclosures*. Bloomington and Indianapolis: Indiana University Press.

Hekman, S. J. (Ed.) (1996). *Feminist Interpretations of Michel Foucault*. University Park, PA: Pennsylvania State University Press.

Henriques, J., Hollway, W., Venn, C. Walkerdine, V. and Urwin, C. (1984). *Changing the Subject: Psychology, social regulation, and subjectivity*. London: Routledge.

Hickey-Moody, A. (2012). Deleuze's children. *Educational Philosophy and Theory*, 45(3), 272–286.

Hickey-Moody, A., & Rasmussen, M. L. (2009). The sexed subject in between Deleuze and Butler. In C. Nigianni, & M. Storr (Eds) *Deleuze and Queer Theory* (pp. 37–53). Edinburgh: Edinburgh University Press.

Higgins, C. (2009). Open-mindedness in three dimensions. *Philosophical Inquiry in Education*, 18(1), 44–59.

Higgins, C. (2010). Introduction: Why we need a virtue ethics of teaching. *Journal of the Philosophy of Education*, 44(2–3), 189–208.

Hoffman, L. (1991). A reflexive stance for family therapy. *Journal of Strategic and Systemic Therapies*, 10(3–4), 4–17.

Holmstrom, L. L., & Burgess, A. W. (1979). Rape: The husband's and boyfriend's initial reactions. *Family Coordinator*, 28(2), 321–330.

Holt, L. (2013). Exploring the emergence of the subject in power: Infant geographies. *Environment and Planning D: Society and space*, 31(4), 645–663.

Hook, D. (2005). A critical psychology of the postcolonial. *Theory & Psychology*, 15(4), 475–503.

Hook, D. (2012). *A Critical Psychology of the Postcolonial: The mind of apartheid*. New York: Routledge.

Hopper, E. (2003). *The Social Unconscious: Selected papers*. London: Jessica Kingsley.

Hudis, P. (2015). *Frantz Fanon: Philosopher of the barricades*. London: Pluto Press.

Huey-Li, L. (2003). Bioregionalism and global education. *Educational Theory*, 53(1), 55–73.

Jacobs, M. D. (2006). Indian boarding schools in comparative perspective: The removal of Indigenous children in the United States and Australia, 1880–1940. *Faculty Publications, Department of History*, 20. Lincoln: University of Nebraska. http://digitalcommons.unl.edu/historyfacpub

Jameson, F. (1984). Postmodernism, or the cultural logic of late capitalism. *New Left Review*, 146, July/August, 71–72.

Jardine, A. (1981). Introduction to Julia Kristeva's 'Women's Time'. *Signs*, 7(1), 5–12.

Johnson, E., & Moran, P. (Eds) (2013). *The Female Face of Shame*. Bloomington: Indiana University Press.

Jones, K., & Appignanesi, J. (2012) *Rufus Stone*. https://microsites.bournemouth.ac.uk/rufus-stone/

Jones, L. (2013). Becoming child/becoming dress. *Global Studies of Childhood*, 3(3), 289–296.

Jones, R., Pykett, J., & Whitehead, M. (2013). *Changing Behaviours: On the rise of the psychological state*. Cheltenham, UK, and Northampton, MA: Edward Elgar.

Katz, C. (1996). Towards minor theory. *Environment and Planning D: Society and Space*, 14(4), 487–499.

Katz, C. (2004). *Growing up Global*. New Jersey: Minnesota University Press.

Keller, R. (2007). Clinician and revolutionary: Frantz Fanon, biography, and the history of colonial medicine. *Bulletin of the History of Medicine*, 81(4), 823–841.

Khalfa, J. (2015). Fanon and psychiatry. *Nottingham French Studies*, 54(1), 52–71.

Khanna, R. (2004). *Dark Continents: Psychoanalysis and colonialism*. Durham: Duke University Press.

Khanna, R. (2013). The lumpenproletariat, the subaltern, the mental asylum. *The South Atlantic Quarterly*, 112(1), 129–143.

Kipfer, S. (2011). The times and spaces of (de-)colonisation: Fanon's countercolonialism then and now. In N. C. Gibson (Ed.) *Living Fanon: Global perspectives* (pp. 93–104). New York: Palgrave.

Kitzinger, J. (1988). Defending innocence: Ideologies of childhood. *Feminist Review*, 28(1), 77–87.

Konstantoni, K., Kustatscher, M., & Emejulu, A. (2017). Travelling with intersectionality across time, place and space. *Children's Geographies*, 15(1), 1–5.

Kovel, J. (1970). *White Racism: A psychohistory*. New York: Pantheon.

Krieken, R. (1999). The barbarism of civilization: Cultural genocide and the 'stolen generations'. *The British Journal of Sociology*, 50(2), 297–315.

Kristeva, J., Jardine, A., & Blake, H. (1981). Women's time. *Signs*, 7(1), 13–35.

Kuby, E. (2015). Our actions never cease to haunt us: Frantz Fanon, Jean-Paul Sartre, and the violence of the Algerian war. *Historical Reflections/Reflexions Historiques*, 41(3), 59–78.

Lacan, J. (2006a). *Ecrits* (trans., B. Fink). New York: WW Norton & Company.

Lacan, J. (2006b). The mirror stage as formative of the *I* function as revealed in psychoanalytic experience. In J. Lacan *Ecrits* (trans., B. Fink) (pp. 75–81). New York and London: Norton.

Lacan, J. (2006c). Logical time and the assertion of anticipated certainty. In J. Lacan *Ecrits* (trans., B. Fink) (pp. 161–175). New York and London: Norton.

Laplanche, J. (1999). *Essays on Otherness*. London: Routledge.

Larrier, R. (2010). A tradition of literacy: Césaire in and out of the classroom. *Research in African Literature*, 41(1), 33–45.

Lather, P. (1992). Critical frames in educational research: Feminist and post-structural perspectives. *Theory into Practice*, 31(2), 87–99.

Lather, P. (2007). *Getting Lost: Feminist efforts toward a double(d) science*. New York: Suny Press.

Lave, J., & Wenger, E. (1991). *Situated Learning: Legitimate peripheral participation*. New York: Cambridge University Press.

Lazali, K. (2011). The emergence of the subject in politics: Some reflections on the Algerian context and the work of Frantz Fanon. In N. C. Gibson (Ed.) *Living Fanon: Global perspectives* (pp. 149–158). New York: Palgrave.

Lazarus, N. (1993). Disavowing decolonization: Fanon, nationalism, and the problematic of representation in current theories of colonial discourse. *Research in African Literatures*, 24(4), 69–98.

Lebeau, V. (2005). Children of violence. In M. Silverman (Ed.) *Frantz Fanon's* Black Skin White Masks: *Interdisciplinary essays* (pp. 128–135). Manchester: Manchester University Press.

Lee, N. (2001). *Childhood and Society: Growing up in an age of uncertainty.* Basingstoke: McGraw-Hill Education.

Leonardo, Z. (2009). *Race, Whiteness, and Education.* New York: Routledge.

Leonardo, Z. (2011). After the glow: Race ambivalence and other educational prognoses. *Educational Philosophy and Theory*, 43(6), 675–698.

Leonardo, Z., & Porter, R. K. (2010). Pedagogy of fear: Toward a Fanonian theory of 'safety' in race dialogue. *Race, Ethnicity and Education*, 13(2), 139–157.

Lesnik-Oberstein, K. (2010). Childhood, queer theory, and feminism. *Feminist Theory*, 11 (3), 309–321.

Levander, C. (2006). *Cradle of Liberty: Race, the child, and national belonging from Thomas Jefferson to WEB Du Bois.* Durham: Duke University Press.

Lewis, H. B. (1980). 'Narcissistic personality,' or 'shame-prone' superego mode. *Comprehensive Psychotherapy*, 1, 59–80.

Lewis, H.B. (1987). Introduction. Shame, the 'sleeper' in psychopathology. In H. B. Lewis (Ed.) *The Role of Shame in Symptom Formation* (pp. 1–28). New Jersey: Lawrence Erlbaum.

Lindo, K. (2013). Interrogating the place of *Lajja* (Shame) in contemporary Mauritius. In E. Johnson and P. Moran (Eds) (2013) *The Female Face of Shame* (pp. 212–228). Bloomington: Indiana University Press.

Lister, R. (2006). Children (but not women) first: New Labour, child welfare and gender. *Critical Social Policy*, 26(2), 315–335.

Litwack, S. D., Beck, J. G., & Sloan, D. M. (2015). Group treatment for trauma-related psychological disorders. In U. Schnyder and M. Cloitre (Eds) *Evidence Based Treatments for Trauma-Related Psychological Disorders* (pp. 433–448). New York: Springer International Publishing.

Locke, J. (2016). *Democracy and the Death of Shame: Political equality and social disturbance.* New York: Cambridge University Press.

Lorde, A. (1982). *Zami: A new spelling of my name.* New York: Persephone Press.

Lorde, A. (1984). *Sister Outsider.* New York: Crossing Press.

Macey, D. (2010). I am my own foundation: Franz Fanon as a source of continued political embarrassment. *Theory, Culture & Society*, 27 (7–8), 33–51.

Macey, D. (2012). *Frantz Fanon: A biography.* London: Verso.

Macherey, P. (2012). Figures of interpellation in Althusser and Fanon. *Radical Philosophy*, 173, 9–20.

Maher, M. J. (2012). *Racism and Cultural Diversity: Cultivating racial harmony through counselling, group analysis and psychotherapy.* London: Karnac.

Maldonado, D. E. Z., Rhoads, R. and Buenavista, T. L. (2005). The student-initiated retention project: Theoretical contributions and the role of Self-empowerment. *American Educational Research Journal*, 42(4), 605–638.

Mannoni, M. (1963/1973). *The Retarded Child and the Mother*. London: Tavistock Publications.

Mannoni, M. (1970/1987). *The Child, His illness and the Others*. London: Karnac Books.

Mannoni, O. (1950/1964). *Prospero and Caliban: The psychology of colonization* (trans., Pamela Powesland). New York: Praegar University Press.

Mannoni, O. (1966). The decolonisation of myself. *Race*, 7(4), 327–335.

Mannoni, O. (1969/2003). *Clefs pour l'imaginaire ou l'Autre Scène*. Paris: Seuil.

Mannoni, O. (2003). I know well, but all the same. In M. A. Rothenberg, D. A. Foster, & S. Žižek (Eds) *Perversion and the Social Relation* (pp. 68–92) (trans., G. M. Goshgarian). Durham, NC: Duke University Press. First published as pp. 9–33 of Mannoni, O. (1969). *Clefs pour l'imaginaire ou l'Autre Scène*. Paris: Seuil.

Marginson, S., & Rhoades, G. (2002). Beyond national states, markets, and systems of higher education: A glonacal agency heuristic. *Higher Education*, 43, 281–309.

Massey, I. (1976). *The Gaping Pig: Literature and metamorphosis*. Berkeley: University of California Press.

McCall, L. (2005). The complexity of intersectionality. *Signs: Journal of women in culture and society*, 30(3), 1771–1800.

McClintock, A. (1995). *Imperial Leather: Race, gender, and sexuality in the colonial contest*. New York: Routledge.

McCulloch, J. (1983). *Black Soul White Artifact: Fanon's clinical psychology and social theory*. Cambridge: Cambridge University Press.

Meek, J. (2016). How to grow a weetabix. *London Review of Books*, 38(12) (June), 7–16. www.lrb.co.uk/v38/n12/james-meek/how-to-grow-a-weetabix

Meek, J. (2017). Somerdale to Skarbimierz. *London Review of Books*, 39(8) (April), 3–15.

Meiners, E. R. (2016). *For the Children?: Protecting innocence in a carceral state*. Minneapolis: University of Minnesota Press.

Menozzi, F. (2015). Fanon's letter: Between psychiatry and anticolonial commitment. *Interventions*, 17(3), 360–377.

Mercer, K. (1996). Decolonisation and disappointment: Reading Fanon's sexual politics. In A. Read, H. K. Bhabha (Eds) *The Fact of Blackness: Frantz Fanon and visual representation* (pp. 114–131). London and Seattle [Wash.]: Bay Press, Institute of Contemporary Arts, Institute of International Arts.

Mezzadra, S., & Neilson, B. (2013). *Border as Method*. Durham, NC: Duke University Press.

Mignolo, W. D. (2007). Delinking: The rhetoric of modernity, the logic of coloniality and the grammar of de-coloniality. *Cultural Studies*, 21 (2–3), 449–514.

Millei, Z., & Imre, R. (Eds) (2016). *Childhood and Nation: Interdisciplinary engagements*. Basingstoke: Palgrave.

Miller, J.-A. (1994). Extimité. In M. Bracher, M. W. Alcorn Jr., R. J. Corthell, and F. Massardier-Kenney (Eds), *Lacanian Theory of Discourse: Subject, structure and society* (pp. 74–87). New York: NYU Press.

Mirza, H. S. (1992). *Young, Female and Black*. London: Routledge.

Mirza, H. S. (2009). *Race, Gender and Educational Desire: Why black women succeed and fail.* Abingdon: Routledge.

Mitchell, J. (1974) *Psychoanalysis and Feminism.* Harmondsworth: Penguin.

Mohanty, C. T. (2003). 'Under western eyes' revisited: Feminist solidarity through anticapitalist struggles. *Signs: Journal of women in culture and Society,* 28(2), 499–535.

Mojab, S. (2009). Imperialism, 'post-war reconstruction' and Kurdish women's NGOs. In N. Al-Ali, & N. Pratt (Eds) *Women and War in the Middle East: Transnational perspectives* (pp. 99–128). London: Zed Press.

Motzkau, J. F. (2009). The semiotic of accusation: Thinking about deconstruction, development, the critique of practice, and the practice of critique. *Qualitative Research in Psychology,* 6(1–2), 129–152.

Murard, N. (2008). Psychothérapie institutionnelle à Blida. *Tumultes,* 31(2), 31–45. www.cairn.info/revue-tumultes-2008-2-page-31.htm

Musser, A. J. (2012). Anti-Oedipus, kinship, and the subject of affect: Reading Fanon with Deleuze and Guattari. *Social Text,* 30(3 112), 77–95.

Naimou, A. (2013). Masking Fanon. *College Literature: A Journal of Critical Literary Studies,* 40(3), 38–59.

Nandy, A. (1984). Reconstructing childhood: A critique of the ideology of adult-hood. *Alternatives,* 10(3), 359–375.

Nash, J. C. (2008). Re-thinking intersectionality. *Feminist Review,* 89(1), 1–15.

Nayak, S. (2014). *Race, Gender and the Activism of Black Feminist Theory: Working with Audre Lorde.* Abingdon: Routledge.

Nieuwenhuys, O. (2007). Embedding the global womb: Global child labour and the new policy agenda. *Children's Geographies,* 5(1–2), 149–163.

Nizami, N. (2017). Intersectionality and Changing the Culture of Denial in Child Sexual Exploitation Policy. Paper presented at the International Society for Theoretical Psychology, Tokyo, August.

O'Dell, L., Brownlow, C., & Bertilsdotter-Rosqvist, H. (Eds) (2017). *Different Childhoods: Non/Normative Development and Transgressive Trajectories.* Abingdon, Oxon: Routledge.

Oliver, K. (2001). *Witnessing: Beyond recognition.* Minneapolis: University of Minnesota Press.

Oliver, K. (2004). *The Colonization of Psychic Space: A psychoanalytic social theory of oppression.* Minnesota: University of Minnesota Press.

Oliver, K. (2005). The good infection. *Parallax,* 11(3), 87–98.

Oswell, D. (2013). *The Agency of Children: From family to global human rights.* Cambridge: Cambridge University Press.

Pablo, M. (1959). The permanent revolution in Algeria (December 1959).' *Fourth International,* 8(58). www.marxists.org/archive/Pablo/1959/12/algeria.htm

Pablo, M. (1962). 'Colonials' and 'Europeans': A review of Frantz Fanon's *Les Damnés de la Terre.' Fourth International,* (May–June), 30–34.

Padel, R. (1981). Madness in fifth-century (BC) Athenian tragedy. In P. Heelas, & A. Lock (Eds) *Indigenous Psychologies: The anthropology of the self* (pp. 105–132). London: Academic Press.

Pain, R. (2010). Ways beyond disciplinarity. *Children's Geographies,* 8(2), 223–225.

Painter, D. (2012). Occupy words: Language, commodification, and the (re)-appropriation of voice. The second Marxism and psychology conference, Morelia, Mexico, August.

Palmary, I., & Mahati, S. (2015). Using deconstructing developmental psychology to read child migrants to South Africa. *Feminism & Psychology*, 25(3), 347–362.

Park, J. (2016). Asian education and Asia as method. In C-M. Lam, & J. Park (Eds) *Sociological and Philosophical Perspectives on Education in the Asia-Pacific Region* (pp. 205–225). Singapore: Springer.

Park, J. (2017). Knowledge production with Asia-centric research methodology. *Comparative Education Review*, 61(4), 760–779.

Parker, I. (2005). Lacanian discourse analysis in psychology: Seven theoretical elements. *Theory and Psychology*, 15(2), 163–182.

Parker, I. (2010). *Lacanian Psychoanalysis: Revolutions in subjectivity*. London: Routledge.

Parker, I. (2012). Postcolonial psychology. *Postcolonial Studies*, 15(4), 499–505.

Parker, I., Georgaca, E., Harper, D., McLaughlin, T., & Stowell-Smith, M. (1995). *Deconstructing Psychopathology*. London: Sage.

Parry, B. (1994). Signs of our times: Discussion of Homi Bhabha's *The Location of Culture*. *Third Text*, 8(28–29), 5–24.

Pavón-Cuéllar, D. (2014) Extimacy. In T. Teo (Ed.) *Encyclopedia of Critical Psychology* (pp. 661–664). New York: Springer.

Pellegrini, A. (2008). What do children learn at school? Necropedagogy and the future of the dead child. *Social Text*, 26(4), 97–105.

Phoenix, A. (2009). De-colonising practices: Negotiating narratives from racialised and gendered experiences of education. *Race, Ethnicity & Education*, 12(1), 101–114.

Phoenix, A., & Pattynama, P. (2006). Intersectionality. *European Journal of Women's Studies*, 13(3), 187–192.

Pickett, B. L. (1996). Foucault and the politics of resistance. *Polity*, XX VIII(4), 445–466.

Pierce, C. M., & Allen, G. B. (1975). Childism. *Psychiatric Annals*, 5(7), 15–24.

Pinar, W. (2011). *The Character of Curriculum Studies: Bildung, Currere & recurring questions of the subject*. New York: Palgrave Macmillan.

Plastow, M. G. (2014). *What is a Child?: Childhood, Psychoanalysis, and Discourse*. London: Karnac Books.

Preston, J., & Bhopal, J. (2012). Conclusion: Intersectionality theory and 'race': From 'tool-kit' to 'mash-up'. In K. Bhopal, & J. Preston (Eds) *Intersectionality and 'Race' in Education* (pp. 213–220). Abingdon: Routledge.

Price Tangney, J., & Dearing, R. (2002). *Shame and Guilt*. New York: The Guilford Press.

Probyn, E. (2005). *Blush: Faces of shame*. New Jersey: University of Minnesota Press.

Puar, J. K. (2012). 'I would rather be a cyborg than a goddess': Becoming-intersectional in assemblage theory. *PhiloSOPHIA*, 2(1), 49–66.

Pykett, J. (2012). The new maternal state: The gendered politics of governing through behaviour change. *Antipode*, 44(1), 217–238.

Qvortrup, J. (1994). Childhood matters: An introduction. In J. Qvortrup, M. Bardy, G. Sgritta, & H. Wintersberger (Eds) *Childhood Matters: Social theory, practice and politics* (pp. 1–24). Aldershot: Avebury.

Qvortrup, J. (2005). Varieties of childhood. In J. Qvortrup (Ed.) *Studies in Modern Childhood* (pp. 1–20). Basingstoke: Palgrave.

Rabaka, R. (2011). Revolutionary Fanonism: On Frantz Fanon's modification of Marxism and decolonization of democratic socialism. *Socialism and Democracy*, 25(1), 126–145.

Rack, P. (1982). *Race, Culture, and Mental Health*. London: Tavistock.

Raiford, L. (2009). Photography and the practices of critical black memory. *History and Theory*, 48(4), 112–129.

Rancière, J. (1991). *The Ignorant Schoolmaster*. Stanford, CA: Stanford University Press.

Rancière, J. (2011). *Althusser's Lesson*. London: Bloomsbury Publishing.

Rankin, K. (2013). A critical geography of poverty finance. *Third World Quarterly*, 34(4), 547–568.

Razanajao, C. L. Postel, J., & Allen, D. F. (1996). The life and psychiatric work of Frantz Fanon. *History of Psychiatry*, 7, 499–524.

Renault, M. (2011). Rupture and new beginning in Fanon: Elements for a genealogy of postcolonial critique. In N. C. Gibson (Ed.) *Living Fanon: Global perspectives* (pp. 105–116). New York: Palgrave.

Richards, G. (1997). *'Race,' Racism and Psychology: Towards a reflexive history*. London: Routledge.

Richardson, T. (2012). Disrupting the coloniality of being. Towards de-colonial ontologies in the philosophy of education. *Studies in the Philosophy of Education*, 31(5), 539–551.

Ringrose, J. (2011). Beyond discourse? Using Deleuze and Guattari's schizoanalysis to explore affective assemblages, heterosexually striated space, and lines of flight online and at school. *Educational Philosophy and Theory*, 43(6), 598–618.

Rober, P., & Seltzer, M. (2010). Avoiding colonizer positions in the therapy room: Some ideas about the challenges of dealing with the dialectic of misery and resources in families. *Family Process*, 49(1), 123–137.

Roberts, A. (2014). Gender, financial deepening and the production of embodied finance: Towards a critical feminist analysis.' *Global Society*. DOI: 10.1080/13600826.975189

Roberts, R. (Ed.) (2007). *Just War: Psychology and terrorism*. Ross-on-Wye: PCCS Books.

Robinson, C. (1993). The appropriation of Frantz Fanon. *Race & Class*, 5(1), 79–91.

Rogers, A., & Pilgrim, D. (2014). *A Sociology of Mental Health and Illness*. Buckingham: McGraw-Hill Education.

Rojas-Sosa, D. (2016). The denial of racism in Latina/o students' narratives about discrimination in the classroom. *Discourse & Society*, 27(1), 69–94.

Rollo, T. (2018). The color of childhood: The role of the child/human binary in the production of anti-black racism. *Journal of Black Studies*. https://doi.org/10.1177/0021934718760769

Rollock, N. (2012). The invisibility of race: Intersectional reflections on the liminal space of alterity. *Race, Ethnicity & Education*, 15(1), 65–84.

Rose, J. (1984). *The Case of Peter Pan, or, The Impossibility of Children's Fiction*. Pennsylvania: University of Pennsylvania Press.

Rose, N. (1985). *The Psychological Complex*. London: Routledge & Kegan Paul.

Rosen, R., & Twarmley, K. (Eds) (2017). *Feminism and the Politics of Childhood: Friends or foes?* London: UCL Press.

Roth, M. (1981). Foucault's 'history of the present'. *History and Theory*, 20(1), 32–46.

Roskilde University (2017). Call for papers for 'Capturing the social through the prism of childhood: Bridging childhood research and the social sciences', Symposium, 16–17 November.

Rowbotham, S., Segal, L., & Wainwright, H. (2013). *Beyond the Fragments: Feminism and the making of socialism*. London: Merlin Press.

Roy, A. (2014). Subjects of risk: Technologies of gender in the making of millenial modernity. *Public Culture*, 24(1), 131–155.

Sachs, W. (1937/1996). *Black Hamlet: The mind of an African Negro revealed by psychoanalysis*. Baltimore: Johns Hopkins University Press.

Sachs, W. (Ed.) (1992). *The Development Dictionary: A guide to knowledge as power*. London: Zed.

Said, E. (1978). *Orientalism*. New York: Vintage.

Sakai, N. (2010). From area studies towards transnational studies. *Inter-Asia Cultural Studies*, 11(2), 265–274.

Sánchez-Eppler, K. (2005). *Dependent States: The child's part in nineteenth-century American culture*. Chicago: University of Chicago Press.

Sartre, J. P. (1944). *Huis Clos/No Exit* first performed at the Théâtre du Vieux-Colombier, May.

Sartre, J. P. (1961/1963). Preface. In F. Fanon, *The Wretched of the Earth* (trans., C. Farrington) (pp. 7–26). London: Penguin.

Saskiestewa Gilbert, M. (2013). Foreword to the second edition. In D. C. Talayevsa *Sun Chief: The autobiography of a Hopi Indian*, 2nd edn (pp. ix–xvi). New Haven: Yale University Press.

Scheidlinger, S. (1994). An overview of nine decades of group psychotherapy. *Psychiatric Services*, 45(3), 217–225.

Scheidlinger, S. (2000). The group psychotherapy movement at the millennium: Some historical perspectives. *International Journal of Group Psychotherapy*, 50(3), 315–339.

Scheurich, J., & K. McKenzie (2005). Foucault's methodologies: Archaeology and genealogy. In N. Denzin, & Y. Lincoln (Eds) *The SAGE Handbook of Qualitative Research* (pp. 141–169). Thousand Oaks: Sage.

Schostak, J. (2016). Leaders, leadership and democracy – are they compatible? *Management in Education*, 30(1), 4–9.

Scott, C. (1999). *Spoken Image: Photography and language*. London: Reaktion Books.

Scourfield, J., & Drakeford, M. (2002). New Labour and the problem of men. *Critical Social Policy*, 22(4), 619–640.

Sekyi-Otu, A. (2011). Fanon and the possibility of postcolonial critical imagination. In N. C. Gibson (Ed.) *Living Fanon* (pp. 45–59). New York: Palgrave.

Seshadri-Crooks, K. (2002). *Desiring Whiteness: A Lacanian analysis of race*. New York: Routledge.

Seu, I. B., & Heenan, M. C. (Eds). (1998). *Feminism & Psychotherapy*. London: Sage.

Seymour, R. (2017) Racism and child sexual abuse. www.leninology.co.uk/2017/08/racism-and-child-sexual-abuse.html, accessed 21 December.

Shahjahan, R. A. (2011). Decolonising the evidence-based education and policy movement: Revealing the colonial vestiges in educational policy, research, and neoliberal reform. *Journal of Educational Policy*, 26(2), 181–206.

Shahjahan, R. A., Blanco Ramirez, G., & Andreotti, V. D. O. (2017). Attempting to imagine the unimaginable: A decolonial reading of global university rankings. *Comparative Education Review*, 61(S1), S51–S73.

Shahjahan, R. A., & Kezar, A. J. (2013). Beyond the 'National Container': Addressing methodological nationalism in higher education research. *Educational Researcher*, 42(1), 20–29.

Shepherd, L. J. (2008). *Gender, Violence and Security: Discourse as practice*. London: Zed Books.

Shildrick, T., & MacDonald, R. (2013). Poverty talk: How people experiencing poverty deny their poverty and why they blame 'the poor'. *The Sociological Review*, 61(2), 285–303.

Siddiqui, S. (2017). A turn to ghost in social science theorizing. Presentation at the International Society for Theoretical Psychology Conference, Rikkyo University, Tokyo, 21–25 August.

Siddiqui, S. (2018). Pathologising psychoanalytic narrative in ethnographic research. Invited lecture to Manchester Psychoanalytic Matrix event, 'Pathology inside and outside the clinic', Manchester Institute of Education, University of Manchester, 5 February.

Sikuade, A. (2012). Fifty years after Frantz Fanon: Beyond diversity. *Advances in Psychiatric Treatment*, 18(1), 25–31. http://apt.rcpsych.org/content/18/1/25.full, accessed 3 July 2015.

Silova, I., Millei, Z., & Piattoeva, N. (2017). Interrupting the coloniality of knowledge production in comparative education: Postsocialist and postcolonial dialogues after the Cold War. *Comparative Education Review*, 61, S74–S102.

Silverman, M. (Ed.) (2005). *Frantz Fanon's Black Skin White Masks: Interdisciplinary essays*. Manchester: Manchester University Press.

Singh, G. (2016). Post-racial pedagogy – challenges and possibilities. *Race, Ethnicity and Education*. 1–9. doi.org/10.1080/13613324.2016.1248830

Skott-Myhre, H., Pacini-Ketchabaw, V., & Skott-Myhre, K. (Eds) (2016). *Youth Work, Early Education, and Psychology: Liminal encounters*. New York: Palgrave Macmillan US.

Smith, L. T. (2013). *Decolonizing Methodologies: Research and indigenous peoples*. London: Zed.

Spyrou, S. (2017). Time to decenter childhood? *Childhood*, 24(4), 433–437.

Stainton Rogers, R., & Stainton Rogers, W. (1992). *Stories of Childhood: Shifting agendas of child concern*. Lewes: Harvester Wheatsheaf.

Stanley, L., & Wise, S. (1983). *Breaking out: Feminist consciousness and feminist research*. London: Routledge & Kegan Paul.

Staudt, K. (2010). Globalization and gender at border sites. In M. Marchant and A. Sisson Runyan (Eds) *Gender and Global Restructuring: Sightings, sites and resistances*, 2nd edn (pp. 187–200). Abingdon: Routledge.

Steedman, C. (1995). *Strange Dislocations: Childhood and the idea of human interiority, 1780–1930*. London: Virago.

Stockton, K. B. (2009). *The Queer Child, or Growing Sideways in the Twentieth Century.* Durham: Duke University Press.

Stoler, A. L. (2002). *Carnal Knowledge and Imperial Power: Race and the intimate in colonial rule.* Berkeley: University of California Press.

Sullivan, S. (2017). White priority. *Critical Philosophy of Race.* 5(2), 171–182.

Sutton Smith, B. (2001). *The Ambiguity of Play.* Cambridge, MA: Harvard University Press.

Swan, E. (2017). What are white people to do? Listening, challenging ignorance, generous encounters and the 'not yet' as diversity research praxis. *Gender, Work & Organization,* 24(5), 547–563.

Takayama, K, Heimans, S., Amazan, R., & Maniam, V. (2016). Doing southern theory: Towards alternate knowledges and knowledge practices in/for education. *Postcolonial Directions in Education,* 5(1), 1–25.

Takayama, K., Sriprakash, A., & Connell, R. (2015). Rethinking knowledge production and circulation in comparative and international education: Southern theory, postcolonial perspectives, and alternative epistemologies. *Comparative Education Review,* 59(1), v–viii.

Takayama, K., Sriprakash, A., & Connell, R. (2017). Toward a postcolonial comparative and international education. *Comparative Education Review,* 61(S1), S1–S24.

Talayevsa, D. C. (1942) *Sun Chief: The autobiography of a Hopi Indian* (ed., L. Simmons). New Haven: Yale University Press. (Published in French in 1959 as *Soleil Hopi,* trans. G. Mayoux, Paris: Plon.).

Talayevsa, D. C. (2013) *Sun Chief: The autobiography of a Hopi Indian,* 2nd edn. New Haven: Yale University Press.

Tarulli, D., & Skott-Myhre, H. (2006). The immanent rights of the multitude: An ontological framework for conceptualizing the issue of child and youth rights. *International Journal of Children's Rights,* 14(2), 187–201.

Taylor, A. (2013). *Reconfiguring the Natures of Childhood.* London: Routledge.

Thiele, K. (2014). Ethos of diffraction: new paradigms for a (post)humanist ethics. *Parallax,* 20(3), 202–216.

Thompson, V. (2014). The master's tools will never dismantle the master's house: Reading France's recognition politics through Fanon's critique of whiteness and coloniality. In V. Watson, D. Howard-Wagner, & L. Spanierman (Eds) *Unveiling Whiteness in the Twenty-First Century: Global manifestations, transdisciplinary interventions* (pp. 171–192). British Columbia: Lexington Books.

Thompson, V. (2015). Using intersectionality? Using Marxism-Feminism?. Discussant comments to 'The Strength of Critique' Panel, Rosa Luxemburg Stiftung, Berlin, March.

Thorne, B. (2007). Crafting the interdisciplinary field of childhood studies. *Childhood,* 14(2), 147–152.

Todd, S. (2003) *Learning from the Other: Levinas, psychoanalysis, and ethical possibilities in education.* Albany: SUNY Press.

Tosquelles, F. (2017a). Frantz Fanon en Saint-Alban (1975). *Teoría y Crítica de la Psicología,* 9, 223–229.

Tosquelles, F. (2017b). Frantz Fanon y la psicoterapia institucional (1991). *Teoría y Crítica de la Psicología,* 9, 230–238.

Treacher, A. (2004). Equal opportunities matter. *Group Analysis*, 37(1), 109–120.

Tuck, E., & Yang, K. W. (2012). Decolonization is not a metaphor. *Decolonization: Indigeneity, education & society*, 1(1), 1–40.

Turner, L (2011). Fanon and the bio-politics of torture: Contextualising psychological practices as tools of war. In N. C. Gibson (Ed.) *Living Fanon: Global perspectives* (pp. 117–130). New York: Palgrave.

Turshen, M. (2002). Algerian women in the liberation struggle and the civil war: From active participants to passive victims? *Social Research*, 69(3), 889–911.

Van Schoor, E. P. (2000). A sociohistorical view of group psychotherapy in the United States: The ideology of individualism and self-liberation. *International journal of group psychotherapy*, 50(4), 437–454.

Vergès, F. (1996). The heritage of Frantz Fanon. *The European Legacy*, 1(3), 994–998.

Vergès, F. (1997). Creole skin, Black mask: Fanon and disavowal. *Critical Inquiry*, 23(3), 578–596.

von Holdt, K. (2013). The violence of order, orders of violence: Between Fanon and Bourdieu. *Current Sociology*, 61(2), 112–131.

Walkerdine, V., & Lucey, H. (1989) *Democracy in the Kitchen*. London: Virago.

Wall, J. (2013). Childism: The challenge of childhood to ethics and the humanities. In *The children's table: Childhood studies and the humanities* (pp. 68–84). London: Routledge.

Walsh, S. (2010). *Kipling's Children's Literature: Language, identity and constructions of childhood*. Farnham, Surrey: Ashgate.

Wane, N. (2010). Reading Fanon differently: Black Canadian feminist perspectives. In G. S. Dei (Ed.) *Fanon and the Counterinsurgency of Education* (pp. 83–106). Rotterdam: Sense Publishers.

Warner, S. (2009). *Understanding the Effects of Child Sexual Abuse: Feminist revolutions in theory, practice and research*. London: Routledge.

Washick, B. and Wingrove, E. (2015). Ontologized agency and political critique. *Contemporary Political Theory*, 14(1), 63–79.

Watts, I. E., & Erevelles, N. (2004). These deadly times: Reconceptualizing school violence by using critical race theory and disability studies. *American Educational Research Journal*, 41(2), 271–299.

Weaver, M. (2016). Hate crime figures soar after EU referendum – Home Office figures confirm. www.theguardian.com/politics/2016/oct/13/hate-crimes-eu-referendum-home-office-figures-confirm

Wells, K. (2013). The melodrama of being a child: NGO representations of poverty. *Visual Communication*, 12(3), 277–293.

White, A. M. (2014). All the men are fighting for freedom, All the women are mourning their men, but some of us carried guns: A raced-gendered analysis of Fanon's psychological perspectives on war. *Signs*, 40(1), 857–884.

Widfeldt, A., & Brandenburg, H. (2017). What Kind of Party is UKIP?: The future of the extreme right in Britain or just another Tory party? Political studies. https://doi.org/10.1177/0032321717723509

Williams, D. C. (1976). Ressentiment and schooling. *Educational Theory*, 26(1), 72–80.

Winker, G., & Degele, N. (2011). Intersectionality as multi-level analysis: Dealing with social inequality. *European Journal of Women's Studies*, 18(1), 51–66.

Worsham, L. (1998). Going postal: Pedagogic violence and the schooling of emotion. *JAC*, 18(2), 213–245.

Wright, M. (2004). *Becoming Black: Creating identity in the African diaspora*. Durham, NC: Duke University Press.

Xala, W. (2017). Challenging Fanon: A Black radical feminist perspective on violence and the Fees Must Fall movement. *Agenda*, 31(304), 96–104.

Yacine, T. (2004). Pierre Bourdieu in Algeria at war: Notes on the birth of an engaged ethnosociology. *Ethnography*, 5(4), 487–509.

Yancy, G. (2012). *Look, a White! Philosophical essays on whiteness*. Pennsylvania: Temple University Press.

Yancy, G. (2015). Tarrying together. *Educational Philosophy and Theory*, 47(1), 26–35.

Yancy, G. (Ed.) (2017) *On Race: 34 conversations in a time of crisis*. New York: Oxford University Press.

Yancy, G., & del Guadalupe Davidson, M. (Eds). (2014). *Exploring Race in Predominantly White Classrooms: Scholars of color reflect*. New York: Routledge.

Young, R. J. (2005). *Colonial Desire: Hybridity in theory, culture and race*. London: Routledge.

Young-Bruehl, E. (2012). *Childism: Confronting prejudice against children*. New Haven and London: Yale University Press.

Yuval-Davis, N. (1997). *Gender & Nation*. London: Sage.

Zack, N. (2017). Interview. In G. Yancy (Ed.) *On Race: 34 conversations in a time of crisis* (pp. 179–184). New York: Oxford University Press.

Zarem, S. (2006) Homage to Helen Block Lewis, Shame Symposium, March. http://internationalpsychoanalysis.net/wp-content/uploads/2007/07/zarempaper.pdf

Zarzycka, M. (2016). Save the child: Photographed faces and affective transactions in NGO child sponsoring programs. *European Journal of Women's Studies*, 23(1), 28–42.

Zembylas, M. (2015a). Pedagogy of discomfort'and its ethical implications: The tensions of ethical violence in social justice education. *Ethics and Education*, 10(2), 163–174.

Zembylas, M. (2015b). Rethinking race and racism as technologies of affect: Theorizing the implications for anti-racist politics and practice in education. *Race, Ethnicity & Education*, 18(2), 145–162.

Žižek S. (1991). *For They Know Not What They Do. Enjoyment as a political factor*. London: Verso.

INDEX